The Shurangama Sutra

Volume Seven

The Shurangama Sutra

Volume Seven

with commentary by the

Venerable Master Hsuan Hua

A nine book series

Sutra Text and Supplements [first edition 2003]
Volume 1, 2, 3, 4, 5, 6, 7, 8 [second edition 2003]

English translation by the
Buddhist Text Translation Society
ISBN 0-88139-949-3

The Shurangama Sutra - Volume Seven

Published and translated by:

Buddhist Text Translation Society
1777 Murchison Drive, Burlingame, CA 94010-4504

© 2003   **Buddhist Text Translation Society**
Dharma Realm Buddhist University
Dharma Realm Buddhist Association

First edition 1977
Second edition 2003

12 11 10 09 08 07 06 05 04 03   10 9 8 7 6 5 4 3 2 1

ISBN 0-88139-947-7

Printed in Malaysia.

Addresses of the Dharma Realm Buddhist Association branches are listed at the back of this book.

Library of Congress Cataloging-in-Publication Data

Hsüan Hua, 1908-
The Shurangama sutra with commentary / by the Hsuan Hua ; English translation by the Buddhist Text Translation Society. - 2nd ed.
    p. cm.
    Sutra translated from Chinese originally written in Sanskrit.
    ISBN 0-88139-943-3 (set: alk. paper) -- ISBN 0-88139-941-8 (v. 1 : alk. paper)-
ISBN 0-88139-942-6 (v. 2 : alk. paper) - ISBN 0-88139-943-4 (v. 3 : alk. paper)-
ISBN 0-88139-944-2 (v. 4 : alk. paper) - ISBN 0-88139-945-0 (v. 5 : alk. paper)-
ISBN 0-88139-946-9 (v. 6 : alk. paper) - ISBN 0-88139-947-7 (v. 7 : alk. paper)-
ISBN 0-88139-948-5 (v. 8 : alk. paper)
    1. Tripiéaka. Sëtrapiéaka. SëraÛgamasëtra-Commentaries. I. Buddhist Text
Translation Society. II. Tripiéaka. Sëtrapiéaka. SëraÛgamasëtra. English. III. Title.
    BQ2127.H7813 2003
    294.3'85-dc21
                                                              2002151845

Contents

Introduction

This is Volume Seven of the *Shurangama Sutra* series, with commentaries by the Venerable Master Hsuan Hua.

In the previous volume, Ananda had asked what are the successive stages a cultivator of the Way will experience as one progresses forward. Here, the Buddha describes them in sequence and in detail.

In "The Three Gradual Stages," the Buddha describes the three initial stages of a cultivator. First, the cultivator must avoid eating the five pungent plants. Second, the cultivator must refrain from killing, stealing, lustful habits, and must control both physical and mental activity through the use of precepts. Third, the cultivator must counter and forbear their karmic manifestations as they gain their sagely positions.

As cultivators' emotional love and desires are extinguished, their residual habits will not arise anymore. Understanding that their minds are false, they proceed on to the next fifty-five stages, as described in "The Bodhisattva Stages": the ten faiths, the ten dwellings, the ten conducts, the ten tranferences, the four positions of additional practices, the ten positions of the ten grounds and finally, the position of equal and wonderful enlightenment. The Buddha, however, also reminds Ananda that the cultivator must not attach himself to any of these stages.

Upon hearing such wonderful explanations, Manjushri asks the Buddha for the name of the Sutra, and how it should be upheld. In "The Names of the Sutra," the Buddha declares the five names of the Sutra.

In "The Seven Destinies," Ananda, wishing to keep living beings from straying and lingering in the wheel of birth & death, asks about the painful destinies of rebirth. The Buddha then explains about the destinies of the hells, ghosts, animals, people, immortals, gods and asuras.

Although the seven destinies are ultimately false and unreal, the Buddha finally exhorts cultivators to rid themselves of the karmic habits of killing, stealing and lust (which exist in all seven destinies). Otherwise, one is destined to be with the retinue of demons.

User's Guide

to the Shurangama Sutra series

Because of the length of the *Shurangama Sutra*, and the need to provide aid to various readers, the sutra has been compiled into a series of 9 books: the "Sutra Text and Supplements," and the remaining volumes one to eight.

The "Sutra Text and Supplements" contains:

1. the entire sutra text, consisting of over 2700 paragraphs;
2. the entire outline, consisting of over 1670 entries; and
3. a master index for the eight commentarial volumes.

Volumes one to eight contain:

1. sutra text, with commentaries by Venerable Master Hua;
2. local outline entries; and
3. a local index.

Readers who wish to read, study or recite the sutra in its entirety will find the "Sutra Text and Supplements" very useful.

Those who wish to deeply delve into the sutra will find the commentaries in volumes one to eight indispensable.

Exhortation to Protect and Propagate

by Tripitaka Master Hsuan Hua

Within Buddhism, there are very many important sutras. However, the most important sutra is the *Shurangama Sutra*. If there are places which have the *Shurangama Sutra*, then the proper dharma dwells in the world. If there is no *Shurangama Sutra*, then the dharma ending age appears. Therefore, we Buddhist disciples, each and every one, must bring our strength, must bring our blood, and must bring our sweat to protect the *Shurangama Sutra*. In the *Sutra of the Ultimate Extinction of the Dharma*, it says very, very clearly that in the dharma ending age, the *Shurangama Sutra* is the first to disappear, and the rest of the sutras disappear after it. If the *Shurangama Sutra* does not disappear, then the proper dharma age is present. Because of that, we Buddhist disciples must use our lives to protect the *Shurangama Sutra*. We must use vows and resolution to protect the *Shurangama Sutra*, and cause the *Shurangama Sutra* to be known far and wide, reaching every nook and cranny, reaching into each and every dust-mote, reaching out to the exhaustion of empty space and of the dharma realm. If we can do that, then there will be a time of proper dharma radiating great light.

Why would the *Shurangama Sutra* be destroyed? It is because it is too true. The *Shurangama Sutra* is the Buddha's true body. The *Shurangama Sutra* is the Buddha's sharira. The *Shurangama Sutra* is the Buddha's true and actual stupa and shrine. Therefore, because the *Shurangama Sutra* is so true, all the demon kings use all kinds of methods to destroy the *Shurangama Sutra*. They begin by starting rumors, saying that the *Shurangama Sutra* is phony. Why do they say the *Shurangama Sutra* is phony? It is because the *Shurangama Sutra* speaks too truly, especially in the sections on the Four Decisive Deeds, the Twenty-five Sages Describing Perfect Penetration, and the States of the Fifty Skandha Demons. Those of off-center persuasions and externally-oriented ways, weird demons and strange freaks, are unable to stand it. Consequently, there are a good many senseless people who claim that the *Shurangama Sutra* is a forgery.

Now, the principles set forth in the *Shurangama Sutra* are on the one hand proper, and on the other in accord with principle, and the weird demons and strange freaks, those in various cults and sects, all cannot hide away their forms. Most senseless people, in particular the unwise scholars and garbage-collecting professors, "tread upon the holy writ." With their extremely scant and partial understanding, they are confused and unclear, lacking real erudition and true and actual wisdom. That is why they falsely criticize. We who study the Buddhadharma should very deeply be aware of these circumstances. Therefore, wherever we go, we should bring up the *Shurangama Sutra*. Wherever we go, we should propagate the *Shurangama Sutra*. Wherever we go, we should introduce the *Shurangama Sutra* to people. Why is that? It is because we wish to cause the proper dharma to dwell long in the world.

If the *Shurangama Sutra* is regarded as true, then there is no problem. To verify its truth, let me say that if the *Shurangama Sutra* were phony, then I would willingly fall into the hells forever through all eternity – for being unable to recognize the Buddhadharma – for mistaking the false for true. If the *Shurangama Sutra* is true, then life after life in every time I make the vow to propagate the great dharma of the Shurangama, that I shall in every time and every place propagate the true principles of the Shurangama.

Everyone should pay attention to the following point. How could the *Shurangama Sutra* not have been spoken by the Buddha?

No one else could have spoken the *Shurangama Sutra*. And so I hope that all those people who make senseless accusations will wake up fast and stop creating the causes for suffering in the Hell of Pulling Out Tongues. No matter who the scholar is, no matter what country students of the Buddhadharma are from, all should quickly mend their ways, admit their mistakes, and manage to change. There is no greater good than that. I can then say that all who look at the *Shurangama Sutra*, all who listen to the *Shurangama Sutra*, and all who investigate the *Shurangama Sutra*, will very quickly accomplish Buddhahood.

composed by,
Gold Mountain Shramana Tripitaka Master Hua

The Eight Guidelines

of the Buddhist Text Translation Society

1. A volunteer must free him/herself from the motives of personal fame and profit.
2. A volunteer must cultivate a respectful and sincere attitude free from arrogance and conceit.
3. A volunteer must refrain from aggrandizing his/her work and denigrating that of others.
4. A volunteer must not establish him/herself as the standard of correctness and suppress the work of others with his or her fault-finding.
5. A volunteer must take the Buddha-mind as his/her own mind.
6. A volunteer must use the wisdom of Dharma-selecting Vision to determine true principles.
7. A volunteer must request Virtuous Elders in the ten directions to certify his/her translations.
8. A volunteer must endeavour to propagate the teachings by printing Sutras, Shastra texts, and Vinaya texts when the translations are certified as being correct.

Outline

of the Shurangama Sutra

The outline for the *Shurangama Sutra,* compiled by Dharma Master Yuan Ying, categorizes the various parts of the sutra text of over 2,700 paragraphs to over 1,670 entries.

These entries are presented in the form of a tree-like structure which divides the various parts of the sutra text into sections and sub-sections.

Though the outline is not a prerequisite to reading the sutra text and the accompanying commentaries, it serves as a useful tool for students of the Way who wish to systematically study the sutra. Without this outline, students may find it difficult to refer to specific parts of the text.

Only outline entries which pertain to the sutra text contained within this volume is included.

For the outline of the entire sutra, please refer to the "Sutra Text and Supplements."

Outline of Shurangama Sutra – Volume Seven

Outline of Shurangama Sutra – Volume Seven

釋迦牟尼文佛

Namo Original Teacher Shakyamuni Buddha

Namo Original Teacher Shakyamuni Buddha

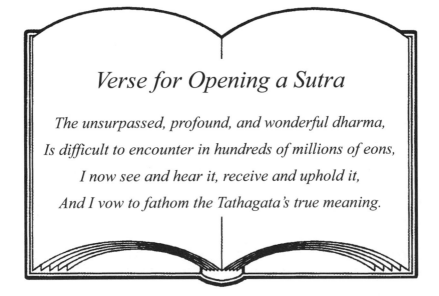

Verse for Opening a Sutra

The unsurpassed, profound, and wonderful dharma,
Is difficult to encounter in hundreds of millions of eons,
I now see and hear it, receive and uphold it,
And I vow to fathom the Tathagata's true meaning.

CHAPTER 1

The Three Gradual Stages

Sutra:

"Ananda, each of these categories of beings is replete with all twelve kinds of upside-down states, just as pressing on one's eye produces a variety of flower-like images.

Commentary:

Ananda, each of these twelve **categories of beings** which I have just described **is replete with all twelve kinds of upside-down states.** Not just the one kind of upside-down state that I mentioned is specific to each kind. Each category is influenced by all twelve kinds of upside-down states. The random thoughts and upside-down states arise from falseness, **just as pressing on one's eye produces a variety of flower-like images.** If you push your finger up against your eye and then look, you will see weird visions. If you release the pressure, the visions disappear. It's because you pursue the false thoughts and upside-down states that you cannot get out of rebirth and you keep revolving in the cycle of the twelve categories of living beings. If you do not follow after the false thoughts or pursue ignorance, but instead can return the light and illumine within – if you can return the hearing to hear the self nature – then you can break through ignorance, and all that exists disappears.

Sutra:

"With the inversion of wonderful perfection, the truly pure, bright mind becomes glutted with false and random thoughts.

Commentary:

From the falseness arises the state of being upside-down, which in turn creates false thoughts. In the nature of the treasury of the Thus Come One, ignorance arises. From the basis of truth, one gives rise to falseness. The "false and random thoughts" are those just described in detail. The originally pure and bright mind becomes filled with myriad thoughts that are totally false and unreal.

K2   Establishes that the position is the opposite of defilement.

Sutra:

"Now, as you cultivate towards certification to the samadhi of the Buddha, you will go through three gradual stages in order to get rid of the basic cause of these random thoughts.

Commentary:

Now, as you cultivate towards certification to the samadhi of the Buddha, you will go through three gradual stages. You must establish three gradual levels and cultivate little by little. Then you can put an end to false thinking and **get rid of the basic cause of these random thoughts.**

Sutra:

"They work in just the way that poisonous honey is removed from a pure vessel that is washed with hot water mixed with the ashes of incense. Afterwards it can be used to store sweet dew.

Commentary:

They work in just the way that poisonous honey is removed from a pure vessel that is washed with hot water mixed with the ashes. "Pure vessel" means that the jar was originally clean. It represents the nature of the treasury of the Thus Come One, inherent in us all, which is neither produced nor extinguished. The "poisonous honey" represents people's ignorance and afflictions. The "hot water" represents the Buddhadharma, which gradually washes us clean. "Washing" means to return the nature of the treasury of the Thus Come One to its original form. **Afterwards it can be used to store sweet dew.** It can store our genuine wisdom; it can hold the enlightenment to the Way. That's what "sweet dew" represents.

K3   Explains the establishment of the position.
L1   Asks for and lists their names.

Sutra:

"What are the three gradual stages? The first is to correct one's habits by getting rid of the aiding causes; the second is to truly cultivate to cut out the very essence of karmic offenses; the third is to increase one's vigor to prevent the manifestation of karma.

Commentary:

What are the three gradual stages? The first is to correct one's habits by getting rid of the aiding causes. That refers to causes which contribute to the creation of karma. **The second is to truly cultivate to cut out the very essence of karmic offenses.** That means to sweep clean the nature of karmic offenses that result from greed, hatred, stupidity, and so forth. **The third is to increase one's vigor to prevent the manifestation of karma.** One progresses in one's cultivation to counteract the creation of any new karma in the present. One does not follow along in the present with one's propensity to create karma.

M1   Caution in eating.
N1   Asks about and answers that they rely on eating and should stop eating pungent
      plants.

Sutra:

"What are aiding causes? Ananda, the twelve categories of living beings in this world are not complete in themselves, but depend on four kinds of eating; that is, eating by portions, eating by contact, eating by thought, and eating by consciousness. Therefore, the Buddha said that all living beings must eat to live.

Commentary:

What are aiding causes? Some causes aid in the creation of wholesome karma, and some contribute to the creation of unwholesome karma. Here, the Buddha is referring to causes which bring about bad karma. **Ananda, the twelve categories of living beings in this world,** just described, **are not complete in themselves, but depend on four kinds of eating.** They depend on eating to survive. **That is, eating by portions**: bite by bite, bit by bit, the way beings in the six desire heavens, the asuras, humans, and animals take their food. **Eating by contact**: the ghosts and spirits eat by contact, and some beings in the heavens also eat this way. **Eating by thought**: in the dhyana heavens of the form realm, beings don't have to actually ingest the food. They take the bliss of dhyana as food – they can eat by thinking. **Eating by consciousness**: this includes the beings of the formless realm up through those in the Heaven of Neither Thought Nor Non-thought. They eat by discriminations of consciousness. **Therefore, the Buddha said that all living beings must eat to live.** That was at the beginning of his teaching, when the Buddha wanted to break through the doctrines of externalists. When he said to them that all living beings must eat to live, the externalists laughed at him and said, "You call that 'dharma'? Do you think we had to wait for you to tell us that? Who doesn't know that beings have to eat to live? Even children understand that."

In reply the Buddha said, "Well, tell me, then, how many kinds of eating are there?"

At that point the externalists were speechless. They couldn't come up with the answer. Then the Buddha explained the four kinds of eating.

Sutra:

"Ananda, all living beings can live if they eat what is sweet, and they will die if they take poison. Beings who seek samadhi should refrain from eating five pungent plants of this world.

Commentary:

This passage discusses the first gradual stage, getting rid of the aiding causes. The five pungent plants aid in the creation of unwholesome karma, and so the first step is to eliminate them from one's diet. **Ananda, all living beings can live if they eat what is sweet, and they will die if they take poison.** "All living beings" refers to the twelve categories. "Sweet" here really means "edible"; the food is sweet in the sense that it is not poisonous, but is nourishing and palatable. "Poisonous" here does not necessarily mean lethal poison, but refers to such things as the five pungent plants, which in this context are considered poisonous. It refers to any food which has an unwholesome effect on beings, and contributes to an earlier death. It doesn't just mean eating something which is instantaneously fatal. **Beings who seek samadhi should refrain from eating five pungent plants of this world.** The first step is to get rid of contributing causes. The five pungent plants have been described already. They are onions, garlic, leeks, scallions, and shallots.

N2   Explains in depth the ill-effects of eating pungent plants.

Sutra:

"If these five are eaten cooked, they increase one's sexual desire; if they are eaten raw, they increase one's anger.

Commentary:

If these five are eaten cooked, they increase one's sexual desire. Meat has the same effect. That is one reason why people who cultivate the Way do not eat meat. The five pungent plants also increase desire, but not wholesome desire; rather, they are especially potent in increasing sexual desire, to the point that it is unbearable and one goes crazy with lust. **If they are eaten raw, they increase one's anger.** They make one more stupid. People with wisdom do not lose their tempers. Those who do lose their tempers, for the most part are people who cannot clearly distinguish either the principles or the specifics. Something happens and they can't see beyond it. It becomes an obstruction for them, and they do not know how to resolve it except by getting angry. But losing their temper doesn't actually help the situation one bit. Meat also increases one's afflictions and the propensity to get angry. And the more of these five pungent plants one eats, the bigger one's temper grows.

Sutra:

"Therefore, even if people in this world who eat pungent plants can expound the twelve divisions of the sutra canon, the gods and immortals of the ten directions will stay far away from them because they smell so bad. However, after they eat these things the hungry ghosts will hover around and kiss their lips. Being always in the presence of ghosts, their blessings and virtue dissolve as the days go by, and they experience no lasting benefit.

Commentary:

Therefore, even if people in this world who eat pungent plants can expound the twelve divisions of the sutra canon, the gods and immortals of the ten directions will stay far away from them because they smell so bad. This refers to people who eat the five pungent plants or drink wine or eat meat. On the other hand, the gods and immortals will protect someone who does not ingest these things. Body odors come largely from what one eats. People who enjoy eating beef, onions, and garlic have strong body odors. Their armpits often stink so badly that they can be smelled a long way off, and no one wants to get near them.

There are a number of people who are able to expound on the canon with all its twelve divisions:

> Repeating verses and predictions,
> Interjections and what was spoken
>   without request;
> Past events, analogies,
>   causes and conditions,
> This life, expansions,
>   and what never before existed;
> With discussion,
>   that is twelve all together,
> As in Great Wisdom Shastra's
>   thirty-third chapter.

Memorize the verse and you know the twelve divisions of the canon.

But if one's eating is not pure, one's sole listeners will be hungry ghosts. The gods and immortals will not listen. The hungry ghosts are creatures that don't have anything to eat. But after people who don't hold to pure eating **eat these things,** meaning the five pungent plants and the like, **the hungry ghosts will hover around and kiss their lips.** After people eat these strong-smelling foods, the odor lingers around them and attracts ghosts. The ghosts boldly go up and kiss those who partake of the five pungent plants, in an attempt to taste what they've eaten. Ghosts eat by contact, as we have learned, so those who eat these impure things are literally in the hands of ghosts who hang around and keep touching them. You may not be one who can see them, but they are really there doing just that. **Being always in the presence of ghosts, their blessings and virtue dissolve as the days go by, and they experience no lasting benefit.** Plain and simple, this passage says that people who eat the five pungent plants end up in the company of ghosts. Ghosts are their constant companions, even though the people themselves may be oblivious to the fact. Their blessings and virtue thereby decrease, and they end up with no advantages at all.

Sutra:

"People who eat pungent plants and also cultivate samadhi will not be protected by the bodhisattvas, gods, immortals, or good spirits of the ten directions; therefore, the tremendously powerful demon kings, able to do as they please, will appear in the body of a Buddha and speak dharma for them, denouncing the prohibitive precepts and praising lust, rage, and delusion.

Commentary:

People who eat pungent plants and also cultivate samadhi will not be protected by the bodhisattvas, gods, immortals, or good spirits of the ten directions. Who is referred to here? Whoever eats the five pungent plants. If you eat them, it's referring to you. If I eat them, it's referring to me. The text leaves the matter open. Why don't dharma protectors and good spirits guard such people? Because they smell too bad. Preferring purity, the protectors avoid the stench and do not come around to guard such people. However, protectors are essential in cultivation, for where the proper resides, the deviant does not, but where the proper is lacking, the deviant will win the advantage. The "proper" refers to the dharma protectors and good spirits who guard and aid cultivators of the Way. But in this case, where they do not come around, **the tremendously powerful demon kings, able to do as they please, will appear in the body of a Buddha and speak dharma for them.** Seeing an unprotected cultivator, the powerful demonic kings come on the scene and gather him into their retinue. They will enter when they catch you off guard. How great is their power? They can turn into Buddhas! I've advised you that if in the future you obtain the buddha eye, you may see Buddhas come or bodhisattvas come or gods and immortals come or spirits come. But if they are for real, they will have a light about them that is pure and cool, and when it shines on you, you will experience extreme comfort, such as you have never known. That, then, is a true sage.

If it's a demon, it puts out heat. However, it requires a lot of wisdom to make this distinction. If you lack sufficient wisdom, you will not notice the power of his heat. Of course, the heat is not hot like a fire, but it is the case that the light of a demon carries heat, while the light of a Buddha does not.

Another way you can tell the difference between a demon appearing as a Buddha and an actual Buddha appearing is to look at the teaching they propound. Demon kings will go about **denouncing the prohibitive precepts and praising lust, rage, and delusion.** They will say, "Don't hold the precepts, that's a Theravada practice. Those of the great vehicle kill, but it's not killing; steal, but it's not stealing; engage in lust, but it's not lust. So it's no problem. If you kill, you haven't broken any precept. The same goes for stealing and lust. Don't cling to such a small state. Don't hold to such fine distinctions in your conduct. Violations don't matter."

What you do before you receive the precepts does not count as a violation of them. But once you have taken a precept, for example, the precept against killing, it is then a violation of the precept if you commit the act of killing. Why? Because you clearly knew it was wrong but intentionally violated the prohibition. If you receive the precept against stealing and you go out and steal, you have violated that precept. You may have indulged in sexual misconduct before receiving the precept against it, but that doesn't count as an offense, because it's over and done. But if you conduct yourself in this way after taking the precept, then you violate it. Before you take the precept against lying, you are not in violation of the precept no matter what you say, but once you receive the precept you can't be irresponsible in what you say. Whatever it is, if you know, you know, and if you don't know, you don't know. You can't say you don't know when you really do; or say you know when you really don't. You can't beat around the bush when you speak. The straight mind is the bodhimanda.

Someone may think; well, then, if I don't take them, I won't commit any violations, right? But now you know that it is better to take them, and if you don't you are missing the opportunity. If you do not receive the precepts, you will not be able to make any progress, either in your personal life or with regard to the Buddha-dharma. You certainly should continue to make progress. Since we know it is a good thing to do, we should receive the precepts and then carefully uphold them.

But the demon kings do nothing but slander and tear down the precepts and encourage you not to receive them. They praise sexual desire. "It's great," they say. "The more sexual desire you have, the loftier the level of bodhisattvahood you will realize. Just take Ucchushma, who had to have two to three hundred women a day, but then later cultivated and became Fire-head Vajra. So what's the problem?" And so they go on. Actually, as soon as he begins praising sexual desire, you should know immediately that he is not a genuine Buddha. As to rage, he says, "Having a temper doesn't matter. The bigger your temper, the bigger your bodhi. After all, affliction is just bodhi, so it follows that the more affliction you have, the more bodhi you'll get. It doesn't matter. Lose your temper whenever you feel like it." The demon king praises rage in this way. "Delusion" just means being stupid and doing things that are upside-down. We discussed it earlier:

> Through a continual process of dullness and slowness,
> the upside-down state of stupidity occurs in this world. It
> unites with obstinacy to become eighty-four thousand kinds
> of random thoughts that are dry and attenuated.

And the beings without thought turn into earth, wood, metal, or stone. Of course, this doesn't happen to every stupid being. It does happen occasionally, however. But here the demon king praises delusion; he tells you that the stupider you are, the better it is, because if you are stupid it will be easier for him to get you to obey his instructions. You'll fall right in with him. You'll become one of the retinue of the demon kings.

Recently a book came out of India that specializes in praising the tantric practice of men and women cultivating together. This is a book written by demons. Demons praise sexual desire and do not instruct people to put a stop to it. They say that without cutting off sexual desire one can become a Buddha. But Buddhas are pure, whereas the filthiest thing, the most turbid emotion, is sexual desire.

In Chinese the word for marriage (婚 *hun*) contains a character which is a combination of the word for "woman" (女 *nu*) and the word for "confusion" (昏 *hun*), or "dark delusion." So the very word marriage itself says that as soon as one gets married, one loses wisdom. One's life is spent as if in perpetual night – in darkness and impurity. It is as if one were sleeping the days away, and when one is asleep, one is totally oblivious to everything. Just that is stupidity. Chinese characters often shed insight on the meanings they represent.

On the other hand, what I just said about marriage is not always the case. You have to be flexible when you view things. You can't be too rigid in your opinions. Although I said that marriage is confusion, you can try to gain understanding within that confusion. You can enter that confusion but not get muddled. Shakyamuni Buddha married, and yet he was the wisest of people.

When you just heard that people who eat the five pungent plants are kissed by ghosts, did it alarm you? If you weren't frightened, then you must see it as no problem. If it alarmed you, then stop eating the five pungent plants. If you don't eat them, the gods and immortals will protect you and the ghosts will leave you alone. If you can marry and stay alert, stay awake, then you won't sink into that confusion. If you enter into the situation, you must not be turned by it. Don't mistake what I said as meaning that I'm opposed to anyone getting married. I'm just exploring a principle.

Sutra:

"When their lives end, these people will join the retinue of demon kings. When they use up their blessings as demons, they will fall into the Relentless Hell.

Commentary:

When their lives end, these people will join the retinue of demon kings. This refers to people who eat the five pungent plants. Because they eat such things, the gods, immortals, bodhisattvas, and good spirits do not protect them. Therefore, the demon kings who possess great power can have their way with them. The demon king appears as a Buddha and says demonic things to them, praising sexual desire, anger, and stupidity. Having been confused by the demons, these people lose their proper knowledge and proper views and any real wisdom. Instead, they harbor deviant knowledge and deviant views. The demon king says sexual desire is good, and they believe it. "The Buddha told me so! He said it's no problem." That's called mistaking a thief for one's own son. One mistakes the demon king for the Buddha. Therefore, "When their lives end, these people will join the retinue of demon kings." When their worldly blessings are used up, they die and obediently go over to the retinue of the demon king. **When they use up their blessings as demons, they will fall into the Relentless Hell.** Demons also have their own kind of blessings.

Once there was a cultivator who recited the name of Amitabha Buddha. However, he was particularly greedy, especially for silver and gold. He did recite the Buddha's name, but that's because he had heard that the Land of Ultimate Bliss had ground made of gold, and he figured he could amass a pile of it when he got there. Then one day he saw Amitabha Buddha come. The Buddha said to him, "Today you should be reborn in the Happy Land, and you can take your gold and silver with you." So he put his four or five hundred ounces of gold on the lotus flower that Amitabha Buddha was holding. But before he had a chance to hop on the flower himself, it disappeared, as did the Buddha holding it. "Oh," thought the man, "Amitabha Buddha likes money, too. He's run off with all my gold!" At just about that time, in the household of the donor where he was living, a new-born donkey died. They noticed that the belly of the young donkey was hard and heavy, and when they cut it open, lo and behold, the old cultivator's gold and silver were tucked away inside!

At that point the old cultivator realized how heavy his greed was, and he rejoiced that he had not gone off with "Amitabha Buddha," for had he gone, he would have become that small donkey. And he knew that the "Amitabha Buddha" who had come was not a genuine state.

Someone wonders, is there really an Amitabha Buddha? Of course there is. But because people have deviant knowledge and deviant views, there are also demons who can appear in the likeness of Amitabha Buddha. Clearly, we should aim to be straight and proper. But how do you do that? Be extremely careful not to be greedy. Anybody who has the idea he can go to the Land of Ultimate Bliss and mine for gold had better wake up fast. Although the Pure Land may be paved with gold, you can't harbor thoughts of self-benefit and make plans to use it as you please. In cultivation, being off by just one thought can bring about demonic karma.

The text says that because people who eat the pungent plants have deviant knowledge and deviant views, they first become demons themselves, and after that they fall into the hells. When will they get out? Nobody knows.

N3   Concludes by calling this practice the foremost increase in vigor.

Sutra:

"Ananda, those who cultivate for bodhi should never eat the five pungent plants. This is the first of the gradual stages of cultivation.

Commentary:

Ananda, have you been listening? **Those who cultivate for bodhi** – anybody on the path to bodhi – **should never eat the five pungent plants.** You definitely must stop eating onions, garlic, leeks, scallions, and chives. If you eat these things, you can end up in the company of the demon kings. If you don't eat these things, you can join the Buddha's retinue. **This is the first of the gradual stages of cultivation.** This is the first step of progress for a cultivator of the Way. In cultivation, one must get rid of the causes which aid in the creation of bad karma. The five pungent plants are one cause which aids the demon kings. You should not regard them as unimportant. The five pungent plants make you turbid and confused. They make you impure, and your impurity puts you together with the retinue of demon kings, for the more impure one is, the better they like it.

M2   Revealing the proper nature.
N1   Asks about and answers that first one must cut off lust and killing.

Sutra:

"What is the essence of karmic offenses? Ananda, beings who want to enter samadhi must first firmly uphold the pure precepts.

Commentary:

The first gradual stage consists of getting rid of the aiding causes, which are eating meat and the like. The second gradual stage concerns the essence of karmic offenses. **What is the essence of karmic offenses? Ananda, beings who want to enter samadhi must first firmly uphold the pure precepts.** The "essence of karmic offenses" refers to the workings of the karmic consciousness. The karmic consciousness must be transformed, and that is done by holding the precepts. "Firmly uphold" means one is firm with oneself. One is not the least bit casual or sloppy. One relies on the precepts in cultivation.

Anything you did before receiving the precepts does not count as a violation of them, because you were in ignorance. If one doesn't know one is committing an offense, then one hasn't committed one. But once you receive the precepts, you can't perpetuate your offenses. Before you heard about the precepts, you may have enjoyed indulging in things which are not in accord with the rules. But once you learn about the precepts, you should receive them and then not indulge in such activities any more.

Sutra:

"They must sever thoughts of lust, not partake of wine or meat, and eat cooked rather than raw foods. Ananda, if

cultivators do not sever lust and killing, it will be impossible for them to transcend the triple realm.

Commentary:

They must sever thoughts of lust. "Lust" refers to love and desire, which are born of ignorance. Love which is not founded on ignorance, in the sense that it is loving regard for one's spouse and children, is not what is meant here. Or, if special causes and conditions arise where one wishes to help someone else, and one is not just selfishly seeking some ephemeral bliss, that too would not be considered a violation, because one's wish is to help someone else and one is basically doing something one would prefer not to do in order to help cross someone else over. It is a temporary expedient and is not a violation.

They must **not partake of wine or meat.** One should eat pure vegetarian food. What disadvantages are there in wine and meat? Wine and alcohol in general derange one's nature. Once you drink alcohol, you lose your concentration. And then you are likely to do just about anything. You'll be like the man in the story I told before who broke the one precept against intoxicants and subsequently violated all five. If one refrains from drinking, one's nature will not get scattered and one's actions will not be upside-down. Another reason is that the odor of wine and other alcoholic drinks, which may be considered fragrant by people and ghosts, upsets the bodhisattvas and good spirits. They do not like the smell. Bodhisattvas and arhats regard the smell of wine as we regard the smell of urine. To them it is rank and stinking. People don't like to be around toilets, cesspools, and sewers, but there are certain bugs – dung beetles – who spend their whole lives eating excrement in cesspools and sewers. They like it. Further, wine and meat are aphrodisiacs. So people who cultivate the Way should not consume these things.

They should **eat cooked rather than raw foods.** All foods should be cooked, even vegetables, before they are eaten, because almost all raw foods will increase one's anger. **Ananda, if cultivators do not sever lust and killing, it will be impossible for them to transcend the triple realm.** "Lust" refers to deviant, improper sexual desire. It is absolutely unprincipled to think that a lustful person could become a Buddha.

N2   And vigorously cultivate the other precepts.

Sutra:

"You should look upon lustful desire as upon a poisonous snake or a resentful bandit. First hold to the sound-hearer's four or eight parajikas in order to control your physical activity; then cultivate the bodhisattva's pure regulations in order to control your mental activity.

Commentary:

You should look upon lustful desire as upon a poisonous snake or a resentful bandit. Make this contemplation: lust is like a poisonous snake. If it bites you once, you may lose your life. If one regarded lust as being as poisonous as that, one would not be able to take delight in it. Even thoughts of lustful desire would not arise. Why? Just imagine that such a thought is as violent as a tiger or wolf. It's fine if you don't encounter such animals, but if you do, you're likely to lose your life. Or look upon such thoughts as upon a rebel or a thief who bears a grudge. His resentment pushes him to the point of murder.

First hold to the sound-hearer's four or eight parajikas. You must keep the shravaka precepts against killing, stealing, lust, and lying – these apply to both bhikshus and bhikshunis; in addition, the precepts against touching, the eight matters, covering, and not following apply to bhikshunis. Keep them **in order to control your physical activity.** You uphold these precepts to keep from creating these kinds of karma. **Then cultivate the bodhisattva's pure regulations in order to control your mental activity.** Then you cultivate the bodhisattva precepts. You receive the ten major and forty-eight minor precepts and pay special attention to regulations. Then your mind will not give rise to thoughts of lust. You won't have such deviant thoughts. This is the path that people who cultivate must walk.

N3   He explains the benefits in detail and concludes with the name.

Sutra:

"**When the prohibitive precepts are successfully upheld, one will not create karma that leads to trading places in rebirth and to killing one another in this world. If one does not steal, one will not be indebted, and one will not have to pay back past debts in this world.**

Commentary:

When the prohibitive precepts are successfully upheld. "Prohibitive" implies the practice of restraint. "Precepts" are defined as "stopping evil and counteracting wrongdoing." The precepts are divided into four aspects:

1) maintenance,
2) restraint,
3) exceptions,
4) violations.

Sometimes exceptions are made, so that you are not considered to have violated the precept even if you have acted against it. "Restraints," as already mentioned, refer to prohibitions. They are honored because to violate them would contribute to further violations, as in refraining from taking intoxicants one avoids breaking other precepts as well. "Maintenance" means upholding the precepts and cultivating in accord with them. "Violation" refers to breaking a precept.

The following event will illustrate the aspect of exceptions. Once when the Buddha Shakyamuni was in the world, there were two bhikshus cultivating in the mountains. One day, one of the bhikshus went down the mountain to get food and left the other one sleeping. In India at that time, the bhikshus simply wore their sashes wrapped around them; they did not wear clothing underneath. This bhikshu had shed his robe and was sleeping nude. He probably was a lazy person, and with no one on the mountain to watch after him, he'd decided to take a nap.

At that time a woman happened along, and seeing the bhikshu, she was aroused and took advantage of him. Just as she was running away from the scene, the other bhikshu returned from town and saw her in flight. Upon investigation he found out that the woman had taken advantage of the sleeping bhikshu, and he decided to pursue her, catch her, and take her before the Buddha in protest. He took out after her, and the woman became so reckless that she slipped off the road and tumbled down the mountain to her death. So one bhikshu had violated the precept against sexual activity and the other had broken the precept against killing. Although the bhikshu hadn't actually pushed her down the mountain, she wouldn't have fallen if he hadn't been pursuing her.

"What a mess!" concluded the two bhikshus. Messy as it was, they had to go before the Buddha and describe their offenses. The Buddha referred them to the Venerable Upali. But when Venerable Upali heard the details, his verdict was that, indeed, one had violated the precept against sexual activity and the other against killing, offenses which cannot be absolved. "You're both going to have to endure the hells in the future," he concluded.

Hearing this, the two bhikshus wept, and they went about everywhere trying to find someone who could help them. Eventually, they found the Great Upasaka Vimalakirti, who asked why they were crying. When they had related their tale, he pronounced his judgment that they had not violated the precepts. "If you can be repentant," he said, "then I can certify that you didn't break the precepts."

"How can that be?" they asked.

"The nature of offenses is basically empty," replied the upasaka. "You did not violate the precepts intentionally, and so it doesn't count. It is an exception."

Hearing this explanation by the great teacher Vimalakirti, the two bhikshus were enlightened on the spot and were certified as attaining the fruition. After that, they became arhats. So there are many explanations within the prohibitive precepts. But if people always look to the exceptions, they will simply not hold the precepts. They will beg the question. So the Buddha did not speak much about this aspect.

If one upholds the precepts, **one will not create karma that leads to trading places in rebirth and to killing one another in this world.** One is born and then kills, and the victim is reborn and kills the one who killed him. But now karmic offenses created in the cycle of mutual rebirth and mutual killing cease. **If one does not steal, one will not be indebted, and one will not have to pay back past debts in this world.** The offenses of stealing will also cease when one stops stealing. "I won't take your things, and you won't take mine. I won't eat your flesh, and you won't eat mine. I won't become indebted to you, and you won't become indebted to me. In that way we won't have to pay each other back." You won't have to pay back the debts for offenses committed in the past once you sever your relationship with animals by not eating meat. If you don't eat their flesh, then you don't have any connections with them.

Sutra:

"If people who are pure in this way cultivate samadhi, they will naturally be able to contemplate the extent of the worlds of the ten directions with the physical body given them by their parents; without need of the heavenly eye, they will see the Buddhas speaking dharma and receive in person the sagely instruction. Obtaining spiritual penetrations, they will roam through the ten directions, gain clarity regarding past lives, and will not encounter difficulties and dangers.

Commentary:

If people who are pure in this way, who do not eat the five pungent plants, do not drink intoxicants, and do not eat meat, and can firmly uphold the four or the eight parajikas – the precepts – if such people **cultivate samadhi, they will naturally be able to contemplate the extent of the worlds of the ten directions with the physical body given them by their parents; without need of**

the heavenly eye. They don't need to have the power of the heavenly eye in order to spontaneously see all around them. **They will see the Buddhas speaking dharma and receive in person the sagely instruction.** They will be able to encounter the Buddhas and hear the dharma. They will receive in person the Buddhas' compassionate guidance. **Obtaining spiritual penetrations, they will roam through the ten directions, gain clarity regarding past lives, and will not encounter difficulties and dangers.** Their spiritual powers will enable them to go through the ten directions while in this place. They will obtain the knowledge of past lives. They accomplish these things with their physical bodies. Although they haven't obtained the power of the heavenly eye, it is as if they had. The same is true for the power of the heavenly ear. They'll never get into difficult situations or find themselves in dangerous positions.

Sutra:

"This is the second of the gradual stages of cultivation.

Commentary:

What has been discussed is the need to cut out the essence of karmic offenses. One must rectify one's karma. Until now it has not been proper, and so one must work in order to change. One must guard and uphold the precepts and rules. Just that, the maintaining of precepts, **is the second of the gradual stages of cultivation.**

M3   Tells them they should counter the manifestations of their karma.
N1   He asks about and answers that based on the precepts one should cultivate samadhi.

Sutra:

"What is the manifestation of karma? Ananda, such people as these, who are pure and who uphold the prohibitive precepts, do not have thoughts of greed and lust, and so they do not become dissipated in the pursuit of the six external defiling sense-objects.

Commentary:

We first discussed the causes that aid in the creation of karma. Next we talked about rectifying the nature of the karmic consciousness which creates offenses. Now the discussion turns to the manifestation of karma. **What is the manifestation of karma?** It is the karma created in this very life. We must counteract it; oppose it. We should not allow ourselves to succumb to the creation of new karma. We should return; we should turn back from it. **Ananda, such people as these, who are pure and who uphold the prohibitive precepts, do not have thoughts of greed and lust.** This refers to the people we have been discussing, who at this stage are pure and keep the precepts. These people are not greedy for the false and illusory bliss of sexual desire, **and so they do not become dissipated in the pursuit of the six external defiling sense-objects.** They are not turned by the experience of the six sense-objects of forms, sounds, smells, tastes, touchables, and mental constructs. They return the light and come back home.

Sutra:

"Because they do not pursue them, they turn around to their own source. Without the conditions of the defiling objects, there is nothing for the sense-organs to match themselves with, and so they reverse their flow, become one unit, and no longer function in six ways.

Commentary:

Because they do not pursue them, they turn around to their own source. They are not turned by the six sense-objects, and so they go back to the origin. They return the light and illumine within, and turn back their hearing to hear their self-nature. They cultivate the perfect penetration of the ear. **Without the conditions of the defiling objects, there is nothing for the sense-organs to match themselves with.** They no longer have any connection with the six sense-objects. The relationship between them is severed when people stop pursuing them, and so the sense-organs no longer are matched with the sense-objects, **and so they reverse their flow.**

That refers to the cultivation of the perfect penetration of the ear, whereby one enters the flow and forgets the place of entry. They **become one unit**; the six organs are interpenetrated and function together. They **no longer function in six ways.** The six sense organs no longer are dissipated in their pursuit of the experiences of the six sense-objects.

N2   In conclusion he explains this is obtaining patience with the non-production of dharmas.

Sutra:

"All the lands of the ten directions are as brilliantly clear and pure as moonlight reflected in crystal.

Commentary:

At that time, **all the lands of the ten directions are as brilliantly clear and pure as moonlight reflected in crystal.** In other words, they are transparently clear and visible to all.

Sutra:

"Their bodies and minds are blissful as they experience the equality of wonderful perfection, and they attain great peace.

Commentary:

When the crystal captures the light of the full moon, there is both brilliance and transparency. It can be completely seen through. This analogy represents the state of cultivators who have reached the level where both their bodies and minds are pure. At that point, **Their bodies and minds are blissful as they experience the equality of wonderful perfection, and they attain great peace.** This sense of peace is something one experiences oneself, not something that is evident to others.

Sutra:

"The secret perfection and pure wonder of all the Thus Come Ones appear before them.

Commentary:

The secret perfection and pure wonder of all the Thus Come Ones refers to the Buddha's pure dharma nature. **At this point they appear before them.** A cultivator such as this can experience this state.

Sutra:

"These people then obtain patience with the non-existence of phenomena. They thereupon gradually cultivate according to their practices, until they reside securely in the sagely positions.

Commentary:

These people then obtain patience with the non-existence of phenomena. What is meant by patience with the non-existence of phenomena? One does not see the slightest phenomena arise, nor the slightest phenomena extinguished. Dharmas are neither produced nor destroyed. But it is not easy to obtain this state. **They thereupon gradually cultivate according to their practices, until they reside securely in the sagely positions.** From the point of attaining patience with the non-existence of phenomena, they gradually progress in their practice as they go through the sagely positions, without being shaken or moved.

N3   He concludes with the name: because of the gradual one can enter into the sudden.

Sutra:

"This is the third of the gradual stages of cultivation.

Commentary:

This is the third of the gradual stages of cultivation, that of preventing the manifestation of karma.

CHAPTER 2

The Bodhisattva Stages

J2   The single position of dry-wisdom.

Sutra:

"Ananda, these good people's emotional love and desire are withered and dry, the sense-organs and sense objects no longer match, and so the residual habits do not continue to arise.

Commentary:

Shakyamuni Buddha calls out: **Ananda, these good people's emotional love and desire are withered and dry.** The people referred to are the ones who have passed through the three gradual stages just discussed. "Withered and dry" means that they have no thoughts of emotional desire and love. **The sense-organs and sense objects no longer match.** The six sense organs no longer seek to match up with the six sense-objects. **And so the residual habits do not continue to arise.** "Residual habits" refers to the slight bit of ignorance that these people still harbor. Since the ignorance is so slight, it does not continue to increase.

Sutra:

"By means of their complete wisdom, they understand that attachments of the mind are false. The bright perfection of their

wisdom-nature shines throughout the ten directions, and this initial wisdom is called the 'stage of dry wisdom.'

Commentary:

The slight bit of ignorance that still remains does not grow and increase. The karmic obstacles are also very few, and so **by means of their complete wisdom, they understand that attachments of the mind are false.** Their minds become as clear as emptiness itself. Their own natures experience the perfection of wisdom. "Complete wisdom" means they don't have any other false thoughts. The thoughts in their mind are brought forth from wisdom. **The bright perfection of their wisdom-nature shines throughout the ten directions.** The nature of their wisdom is light and full. **And this initial wisdom is called the "stage of dry wisdom."** Since emotional love and desire are "dried up," all that's left is wisdom. This stage of dry wisdom is also called "the initial thought of vajra." "Vajra" means "indestructible." This stage is the first step towards the point of being like vajra.

What follows is a discussion of the fifty-five stages of a bodhisattva:

1. the ten faiths,
2. the ten dwellings,
3. the ten conducts,
4. the ten transferences,
5. the four levels of augmenting practice:
    a) heat,
    b) summit,
    c) patience,
    d) foremost in the world;
6. the ten grounds,
7. equal enlightenment.

Sutra:

"Although the habits of desire are initially dried up, they still have not merged with the Thus Come One's flow of dharma-water.

Commentary:

Although the habits of desire and emotional love **are initially dried up, they still have not merged with the Thus Come One's flow of dharma-water.** Here the "flow of dharma-water" does not refer to dharma which is spoken. It is the water of dharma that flows forth from the self-nature. But at this point in their development, they have not merged with the water of genuine wisdom.

The Ten Faiths

J3   The ten positions of the ten faiths.
K1   The mind that resides in faith.

Sutra:

"Then, with this mind centered on the middle, they enter the flow where wonderful perfection reveals itself. From the truth of that wonderful perfection there repeatedly arise wonders of truth. They always dwell in the wonder of faith, until all false thinking is completely eliminated and the Middle Way is totally true. This is called the Mind that Resides in Faith.

Commentary:

This begins the discussion on the ten faiths:

1. the mind that resides in faith,
2. the mind that resides in mindfulness,
3. the mind that resides in vigor,
4. the mind that resides in wisdom,
5. the mind that resides in samadhi,
6. the mind that resides in irreversibility,
7. the mind that resides in protecting the dharma,
8. the mind that resides in making transferences,
9. the mind that resides in the precepts,
10. the mind that resides in vows.

Then, with this mind centered on the middle, they enter the flow where wonderful perfection reveals itself. "This mind" refers to the mind at the level of dry wisdom, the initial vajra mind. They use this mind to enter the flow of the Buddhadharma, and they reach the state where "wonderful perfection reveals itself," where it opens out in abundance. One reaches the principle and substance of true suchness. **From the truth of that wonderful perfection there repeatedly arise wonders of truth.** In the wonderful perfection of the true suchness of the self-nature, truths within truths come forth. **They always dwell in the wonder of faith, until all false thinking is completely eliminated and the Middle Way is totally true.** Their belief becomes more and more subtle and wonderful. "Always dwell" means that they will not waver, they will not change their minds. Their faith is constant. At that point, all false thinking goes away, without exception. Even if they wanted to have false thoughts, the false thoughts just wouldn't arise. That is because false thoughts are helped out by ignorance. With false thoughts come love and desire. But now love and desire have been dried up and only a little ignorance remains, so that, quite naturally, they don't have false thoughts.

Why do you have false thinking? It is because you still have love and desire. There are things that you are greedy for. The desires compel you to think about this and that, so that your mind is always climbing on conditions. If people didn't have any greed, they wouldn't have any false thinking.

At this point in their cultivation, these people don't have false thinking. When that happens, one attains the nature of the principle of the Middle Way. It is "totally true," which means that there is no love and desire, no greedy false thoughts. **This is called the Mind that Resides in Faith.** This is the first of these ten positions. One brings forth genuine faith and dwells in it.

K2   The mind that resides in mindfulness.

Sutra:

"When true faith is clearly understood, then perfect penetration is total, and the three aspects of skandhas, places, and realms are no longer obstructions. Then all their habits throughout innumerable kalpas of past and future, during which they abandon bodies and receive bodies, appear to them now in the present moment. These good people can remember everything and forget nothing. This is called the Mind that Resides in Mindfulness.

Commentary:

Prior to this stage, when they were residing in the mind of faith, they cultivated the Middle Way – that wonderful perfection, the principle which one neither enters into nor departs from. Now, since they are replete with faith, **true faith is clearly understood.** Once one has true faith, one can gain true wisdom. "Clear understanding," then, refers to that true wisdom. **Then perfect penetration is total, and the three aspects of skandhas, places, and realms are no longer obstructions.** Not only do they accomplish the perfect penetration of the sense organs, but of everything else as well – the five skandhas of form, feeling, thought, activity, and consciousness; the twelve places of the eyes, ears, nose, tongue, body, and mind, together with forms, sounds, smells, tastes, tangible objects, and mental contructs; and the eighteen realms, which include the six sense-organs, the six sense-objects and the consciousnesses which connect them, that is, the eye-consciousness, the ear-consciousness, the nose-consciousness, the tongue-consciousness, the body-consciousness, and the mind-consciousness. Once you obtain perfect penetration, these things can no longer hinder you. **Then all their habits throughout innumerable kalpas of past and future, during which they abandon bodies and receive bodies, appear to them now in the present moment.** For time beyond calculation they have been undergoing rebirth and will continue to undergo rebirth – birth after birth, death upon death. And in each one of those lives, they have different habits. In one life they got into the habit of drinking wine. In another life they were in the habit of smoking. In another life, they were habitual gamblers. Another life found them with habits of lust. In another life they killed. Another life made them into thieves. In one life, they got into the habit of lying. In general, life after life, they developed habits that led them to do all kinds of bad things. That's looking at the bad habits. But there are also good habits. In one life, they got into the habit of bowing to the Buddhas. In another life, they habitually recited the Shurangama Mantra. In one life, they had the habit of listening to the explanation of the *Shurangama Sutra*. In another life, they habitually listened to the *Lotus Sutra*. In general, throughout all those lives in so many kalpas, they walked many paths. As a result, they had accumulated a tremendous number of habits. But now, just like a movie, all those habits appear before them. **These good people can remember everything and forget nothing.** These good people who are cultivating the Way can bring it all to mind. They can remember it all. When they attain that state, they never forget. That means they always have their mind on what's happening. They are always mindful of those causes and conditions. **This is called the Mind that Resides in Mindfulness,** the second of the ten faiths.

K3   The mind that resides in vigor.

Sutra:

"**When the wonderful perfection is completely true, that essential truth brings about a transformation. They go beyond the beginningless habits to reach the one essential brightness. Relying solely on this essential brightness, they progress toward true purity. This is called the Mind of Vigor.**

Commentary:

When the wonderful perfection is completely true, that essential truth brings about a transformation. They go beyond the beginningless habits to reach the one essential brightness, which is wisdom. **Relying solely on this essential brightness,**

they progress toward true purity. Their vigor takes them to a place of true purity which is devoid of any defilement. **This is called the Mind of Vigor,** the mind that resides in vigor.

K4   The mind that resides in wisdom.

Sutra:

"The essence of the mind reveals itself as total wisdom; this is called the Mind that Resides in Wisdom.

Commentary:

When one has progressed until the mind is truly pure, then **the essence of the mind reveals itself as total wisdom.** The mind is clear and understood, which means one has some genuine wisdom. "Total wisdom" means that there is not the least bit of random thinking remaining. The stupidity and false thoughts are all gone. Remember that this was described above, in the passage on the first dwelling of the mind, where it said that "all false thinking is completely eliminated." **This is called the Mind that Resides in Wisdom.** This is the dwelling of the mind of faith in wisdom.

K5   The mind that resides in samadhi.

Sutra:

"As the wisdom and brightness are held steadfast, a profound stillness pervades. The stage at which the majesty of this stillness becomes constant and solid is called the Mind that Resides in Samadhi.

Commentary:

As the wisdom and brightness are held steadfast, a profound stillness pervades. This means that you must hold onto the light of wisdom and not let it go slack. Then there is a profound stillness that extends throughout the dharma realm. **The stage at which the majesty of this stillness becomes constant and solid is called the Mind that Resides in Samadhi.** The "profound stillness" represents what is "tranquil and eternally illumining," and the "majesty of this stillness" represents what is "illumining and eternally tranquil." "Solid" here refers to the solidifying of the water of wisdom. It had been shallower before; now it deepens. "Solid" represents samadhi power. At this point, one will not be moved. One would not say, "That looks good," and run in that direction, and then say, "But that looks even better," and run to the next thing. One would not be always pursuing something better. If one had samadhi power, one would not run about hither and thither. A wind out of the east would not bend one westward; nor would a west wind blow one eastward. That just means that one would not be moved by the eight winds.

In order to tell about the eight winds, we must talk about the famous Song dynasty scholar and poet Su Dong Po. He was known as layman Dong Po and he carried on a dialogue with Dhyana Master Fo Yin. The former lived on the south bank of the Long River (Yang Tze) at Chen Chiang, and the latter on the north bank of the river.

The poet Su Dong Po meditated and cultivated, and one day in meditation he saw a state that moved him to write a verse. The verse went:

> I bow my head to the God among gods.
> And a ray of light illumines the great thousand worlds.
> The eight winds cannot move me,
> As I sit aloft a purple golden lotus.

The "God among gods" refers to the Buddha. The poet claimed that when he bowed to the Buddha, he emitted a light that went throughout the universe. The eight winds are: praise, ridicule, suffering, bliss, benefit, destruction, gain and loss.

"Praise" is someone's saying things like, "You are an excellent student. You really apply yourself. You have a fine personality and a good moral character." But you shouldn't look upon praise as something good, because if you are moved by it, you just prove that you don't have any samadhi power. The eight winds are difficult for cultivators to bear.

"Ridicule" means to chide or tease or use sarcasm. It's to use words in such a way as to break a person down. It may sound like praise but it's thick with sarcasm. This wind can cause one to lose one's temper. "How can you treat me like that!" is a typical reaction.

"Suffering" in all its manifold aspects is also one of the winds, as is "bliss." You may feel good, but you should not think that it's a great thing, because as soon as your mind moves to acknowledge the pleasure, a wind has moved you.

"Benefit" refers to something that will help you out. "Destruction" means something unbeneficial which is bad for you. "Gain" refers to getting something, "loss" to losing it. Getting something makes you happy; losing something upsets you. For instance, a person buys the latest model of a very fancy radio. He's so taken with it that he even dreams about it at night. Or maybe it's a camera or a telescope. In general, just imagine the thing that you are most fond of: buying it is what is meant by "gain." But once you have it, of course, other people find it attractive, too, and who would have guessed that someone would wait until you are a bit careless and steal it from you? At that point, your ignorance arises and you are afflicted by your loss. That's to be moved by the eight winds.

But Su Dong Po said that the eight winds did not move him as he sat aloft a purple golden lotus. He had his servant take the poem to Chan Master Fo Yin for his critique.

Chan Master Fo Yin scribbled two words across the poem. The two words were very meaningful, but Su Dong Po couldn't handle them. He exploded in a rage as soon as he glanced at them. What were the words? "Fart, fart."

Su Dong Po grabbed the poem, threw on his coat, and stormed across the river to confront Chan Master Fo Yin.

"What kind of bad-mouthed monk are you?" he demanded of the Chan master. "What right do you have to scold people like that?"

"But you said the eight winds would not move you," Chan Master Fo Yin replied calmly. "How is it that my two little farts have blown you all the way across the river?"

Thinking it over, Su Dong Po saw how right the Chan Master was, and so he hung his head and went back home.

K6   The mind that resides in irreversibility.

Sutra:

"The light of samadhi emits brightness. When the essence of the brightness enters deeply within, they only advance and never retreat. This is called the Mind of Irreversibility.

Commentary:

Once the mind resides in samadhi, **the light of samadhi emits brightness. When the essence of the brightness enters deeply within** these good people who are cultivating, **they only advance and never retreat.** Since they understand, their only intent is to progress, and they never turn around and go back. The reason they are irreversible is that they truly and genuinely understand. They have real wisdom. **This is called the Mind of Irreversibility,** the mind of faith that never retreats.

K7   The mind that resides in protecting the dharma.

Sutra:

"When the progress of their minds is secure, and they hold their minds and protect them without loss, they connect with the life-breath of the Thus Come Ones of the ten directions. This is called the Mind that Protects the Dharma.

Commentary:

When the progress of their minds is secure, they go ever forward; they never fly off the handle. They are firm and at peace, **and they hold their minds and protect them without loss,** so that their minds never retreat. Then **they connect with the life-breath of the Thus Come Ones of the ten directions.** When one reaches the point of irreversibility, the energy-force of the Buddhas unites with one's own. **This is called the Mind that Protects the Dharma.** This means that the Buddhas protect you, and you protect the Buddhadharma. With the Buddha's protection, you can accomplish your karma in the Way With your protection, the Buddhadharma can spread and grow. So this is the mind of faith that protects the dharma.

K8   The mind that resides in making transferences.

Sutra:

"**Protecting their light of enlightenment, they can use this wonderful force to return to the Buddha's light of compassion and to come back to stand firm with the Buddha. It is like two mirrors that are set facing one another, so that between them the exquisite images interreflect and enter into one another layer upon layer. This is called the Mind of Transference.**

Commentary:

Protecting their light of enlightenment, they can use this wonderful force. To join with the life-breath of the Buddha is a kind of enlightenment. When protected, this enlightenment is replete with wisdom and intelligence which is without loss. These people can **return to the Buddha's light of compassion and to come back to stand firm with the Buddha.** With this subtle wonderful power, you can unite with the Buddha's bright compassion. Your life-breath and light interact with the Buddha's life-breath and light, **like two mirrors that are set facing one another, so that between them the exquisite images interreflect and enter into one another layer upon layer.** When two mirrors are placed opposite one another, their images interreflect repeatedly. They display infinite layers of interreflection. **This is called the Mind of Transference,** the mind of faith that dwells in transference of merit.

K9   The mind that resides in precepts.

Sutra:

"**With this secret interplay of light, they obtain the Buddha's eternal solidity and unsurpassed wonderful purity.**

Dwelling in the unconditioned, they know no loss or dissipation. This is called the Mind that Resides in Precepts.

Commentary:

With this secret interplay of light, they obtain the Buddha's eternal solidity and unsurpassed wonderful purity. At this point, there is a hidden connection between the light of your mind and the light of the Buddha's mind; that is what is meant by the "secret interplay of light." The light of your heart reaches to the Buddha's light, and the Buddha's light reaches to your heart. After the light of the Buddha has entered your heart, it returns to the Buddha. After the light of your mind has entered the Buddha's mind, it returns to your own mind. This interplay of light goes full circle. One thus obtains a constant illumination from the Buddha. In fact, one simply becomes one with the Buddha. This purity is incomparable. Nothing surpasses it. **Dwelling in the unconditioned, they know no loss or dissipation.** One has obtained the unconditioned dharma, and no loss can occur. **This is called the Mind that Resides in Precepts.**

K10 The mind that resides in vows.

Sutra:

"Abiding in the precepts with self-mastery, they can roam throughout the ten directions, going anywhere they wish. This is called the Mind that Resides in Vows.

Commentary:

Abiding in the precepts – the unsurpassed Vajra Bright Jeweled Precepts – **with self-mastery** and spiritual penetrations, **they can roam throughout the ten directions, going anywhere they wish.** Such spiritual penetrations come with freedom and ease. There is no need for mental exertion, no need to set one's mind to it in order to be able to go anywhere in the ten directions. They can go anywhere they wish without any hindrance. **This is called the Mind that Resides in Vows.** Whatever wish or vow you make can be fulfilled.

The Ten Dwellings

J4 The ten positions of the ten dwellings.
K1 Dwelling of bringing forth the resolve.

Sutra:

"**Ananda, these good people use honest expedients to bring forth those ten minds. When the essence of these minds becomes dazzling, and the ten functions interconnect, then a single mind is perfectly accomplished. This is called the Dwelling of Bringing Forth the Resolve.**

Commentary:

This section of text discusses the ten dwellings, which are part of the bodhisattva stages. The ten dwellings are:

1) the dwelling of bringing forth the resolve,
2) the dwelling of the ground of regulation,
3) the dwelling of cultivation,
4) the dwelling of noble birth,
5) the dwelling of endowment with skill-in-means,
6) the dwelling of rectification of the mind,
7) the dwelling of irreversibility,
8) the dwelling of a pure youth,
9) the dwelling of a dharma prince,
10) the dwelling of anointing the crown of the head.

At this stage, the bodhisattva is about to reach the position of a Buddha, but isn't there yet. So the bodhisattva temporarily abides in these dwellings.

"Ananda," the Buddha calls out, **"These good people**, these bodhisattvas who are cultivating the Way, **use honest expedients to bring forth those ten minds."** The "ten minds" are the ten stages just discussed. **When the essence of these minds becomes dazzling, and the ten functions interconnect, then a single mind is perfectly accomplished.** The "ten functions" refer to the ways in which the ten minds are used. When they interconnect, they all come back to one single mind. **This is called the Dwelling of Bringing Forth the Resolve,** the first of the ten dwellings.

K2   Dwelling of the ground of regulation.

Sutra:

"From within this mind light comes forth like pure crystal, which reveals pure gold inside. Treading upon the previous wonderful mind as a ground is called the Dwelling of the Ground of Regulation.

Commentary:

From within this mind light comes forth like pure crystal. It is transparent and **which reveals pure gold inside. Treading upon the previous wonderful mind as a ground is called the Dwelling of the Ground of Regulation.** The "previous wonderful mind" is the "dwelling of bringing forth the resolve," where the functions of the earlier ten minds unite into a single mind. Then one walks upon this wonderful mind and turns it into a ground. This is the second dwelling, that of the "ground of regulation."

K3   Dwelling of cultivation.

Sutra:

"When the mind-ground connects with wisdom, both become bright and comprehensive. Traversing the ten directions then without obstruction is called the Dwelling of Cultivation.

Commentary:

This is the third dwelling, that of "cultivation." **When the mind-ground connects with wisdom, both become bright and comprehensive.** When the mind-ground you tread upon becomes level, it unites with wisdom, and both the mind and the wisdom are extremely clear and lucid. **Traversing the ten directions then without obstruction is called the Dwelling of Cultivation.** At this point you gain spiritual penetrations. Endowed with both wisdom and spiritual penetrations, you are not hindered from going anywhere at all in the ten directions. You can come and go as you please.

K4　Dwelling of noble birth.

Sutra:

"When their conduct is the same as the Buddhas' and they take on the demeanor of a Buddha, then, like the intermediate skandha body searching for a father and mother, they penetrate the darkness with a hidden trust and enter the lineage of the Thus Come One. This is called the Dwelling of Noble Birth.

Commentary:

This passage discusses the bodhisattvas of the fourth dwelling, the "dwelling of noble birth." It means being born in the household of the Dharma King, the home of the Buddha. The Buddha's family is the most honorable, and so this dwelling is called "noble birth."

When their conduct is the same as the Buddhas' and they take on the demeanor of a Buddha, they are at the stage of the fourth dwelling. Everything the bodhisattvas of the fourth dwelling do is like what a Buddha would do. Those bodhisattvas have taken on the demeanor of a Buddha. They have learned to be just like Buddhas. **Then** they are **like the intermediate skandha body searching for a father and mother.** We have discussed the meaning of "intermediate skandha body" before. It refers to our "soul," or efficacious nature, which transmigrates. The definition of the intermediate skandha body is that which exists,

Before a new set of five skandhas is taken on,
But after the old set of five skandhas is gone.

An intermediate skandha body – the body between the skandhas – lives in a world as black as ink. There is no light for it at all. Although the sun and moon are still there, the skandha body dares not look at them when they appear. And when they are not in evidence and the skandha body is conscious, there is total darkness wherever it looks. However, when its future parents engage in intercourse, then no matter how far away from them the intermediate skandha body may be, it perceives a bit of *yin* light, and it reaches the spot immediately in response to its thought. Its compulsion to reach that place is like that of iron filings toward a magnet. But in this case, the force, as it were, of the magnetic field extends for thousands of miles. Attracted in this way, the intermediate skandha body arrives, and rebirth immediately takes place: conception occurs.

Here the birth of the bodhisattva of the fourth dwelling into the household of the Buddha is likened to this process, but this is only an analogy, of course. It is used to describe the force of attraction that brings these bodhisattvas to birth in the household of the Dharma King. **They penetrate the darkness with a hidden trust.** No matter how many thousands of miles away it may be, it is as if there is a mutual connection based on faith. The bodhisattvas in this way **enter the lineage of the Thus Come One. This is called the Dwelling of Noble Birth.** They are born into an honorable and wealthy household, the Buddha's home.

"Oh?" you wonder. "The Buddha has a home? I thought the Buddha had left home." The home referred to here is just the home of leaving home. It is the place where the Buddha dwells. This is all just an analogy.

K5   Dwelling of endowment with skill-in-means.

Sutra:

"Since they ride in the womb of the Way and will themselves become enlightened heirs, their human features are in no way

deficient. This is called the Dwelling of Endowment with Skill-in-Means.

Commentary:

Since they ride in the womb of the Way: they roam in the household of the Buddha; they are carried, as it were, in the womb of the Way. **And** they **will themselves become enlightened heirs.** They have received the bequest of enlightenment. **Their human features are in no way deficient.** Their eyes, ears, nose, and other characteristics are perfect and full. Their appearance as Buddhas, as bodhisattvas, will also be without deficiency. **This is called the Dwelling of Endowment with Skill-in-Means.** This is the fifth dwelling.

K6   Dwelling of the rectification of the mind.

Sutra:

"With a physical appearance like that of a Buddha and a mind that is the same as well, they are said to be Dwelling in the Rectification of the Mind.

Commentary:

At this point the bodhisattvas of the sixth dwelling have **a physical appearance like that of a Buddha.** Their features are replete with the thirty-two hallmarks and eighty subtle characteristics. They also have **a mind that is the same** as the Buddhas'. Then **they are said to be Dwelling in the Rectification of the Mind,** the sixth dwelling.

K7   Dwelling of irreversibility.

Sutra:

"United in body and mind, they easily grow and mature day by day. This is called the Dwelling of Irreversibility.

Commentary:

Their body and mind are the same as the Buddhas'. They have **united** with the Buddhas and **easily grow and mature day by day.** Although they resemble the Buddhas, they are like children who have not yet grown up. This means that at this level the wisdom of these bodhisattvas is not yet as great as a Buddha's. They are like newborn children. But every day their wisdom grows, so they are not far from Buddhahood. They are courageous and vigorous, and so **this is called the Dwelling of Irreversibility.** At this point they do not turn back. They have reached the seventh dwelling and will not retreat hereafter.

K8   Dwelling of a pure youth.

Sutra:

"With the efficacious appearance of ten bodies, which are simultaneously perfected, they are said to be at the Dwelling of a Pure Youth.

Commentary:

At this stage, the bodhisattva can make ten bodies appear all at the same time. Each of these ten bodies can produce ten more bodies in turn, so that a hundred bodies come into being. Each of these hundred bodies brings forth yet another ten bodies, making a thousand bodies in all. This all happens simultaneously due to the magnitude of the bodhisattva's spiritual penetrations. This is called the "dwelling of a pure youth."

K9   Dwelling of a dharma prince.

Sutra:

"Completely developed, they leave the womb and become sons of the Buddha. This is called the Dwelling of a Dharma Prince.

Commentary:

The ninth is the "dwelling of a dharma prince." At the previous level, when the ten bodies efficaciously appeared, they were able to change and transform endlessly. However, the bodhisattvas have still not become genuine dharma princes. In the analogy, they have not yet left the womb. Now, **completely developed,** with the appearance of great heroes, **they leave the womb and become**

sons of the Buddha. The accomplishment of the body of a Buddha is likened in the analogy to birth from the womb. **This is called the Dwelling of a Dharma Prince.** They themselves are now sons of the Buddha. That describes the bodhisattva at the ninth dwelling.

K10 Dwelling of anointing the crown of the head.

Sutra:

"**Reaching the fullness of adulthood, they are like the chosen prince to whom the great king of a country turns over the affairs of state. When this Kshatriya king's eldest son is ceremoniously anointed on the crown of the head, he has reached what is called the Dwelling of Anointing the Crown of the Head.**

Commentary:

Reaching the fullness of adulthood, they are like the chosen prince to whom the great king of a country turns over the affairs of state. A "great king" refers to a wheel-turning sage king. When such a king is ready to relinquish the duties of the throne to his son, he performs a ritual in which he anoints the crown of the prince's head with the waters of the four seas. When this ceremony is completed, the prince is said to have inherited the throne. Here the passage refers to the bodhisattva who can become the son of the Buddha, who is the Dharma King. At this point the Buddha anoints the crown of the bodhisattva's head, making him a full-fledged bodhisattva. That's what's meant by the passage: **When this Kshatriya king's,** the Buddha's, **eldest son,** the bodhisattva of the tenth dwelling, **is ceremoniously anointed on the crown of the head, he has reached what is called the Dwelling of Anointing the Crown of the Head.**

The Ten Conducts

J5   The ten positions of the ten conducts.
K1   The conduct of happiness.

Sutra:

"Ananda, after these good people have become sons of the Buddha, they are replete with the limitlessly many wonderful virtues of the Thus Come Ones, and they comply and accord with beings throughout the ten directions. This is called the Conduct of Happiness.

Commentary:

These are called the ten conducts. They are the next step in the stages of a bodhisattva:

1) the conduct of happiness,
2) the conduct of benefiting,
3) the conduct of non-opposition,
4) the conduct of endlessness,
5) the conduct of freedom from deluded confusion,
6) the conduct of wholesome manifestation,
7) the conduct of non-attachment,
8) the conduct of veneration,
9) the conduct of wholesome dharma,
10) the conduct of true actuality.

Now we will discuss the first conduct, that of happiness. These ten conducts correspond to the ten perfections, the ten paramitas, so the first conduct relates to giving.

Shakyamuni Buddha called out: **Ananda, after these good people have become sons of the Buddha, they are replete with the limitlessly many wonderful virtues of the Thus Come Ones.** The crown of their heads are anointed, and they become sons of the Buddha. They are well on their way to possessing the virtuous conducts of a Buddha. They **comply and accord with beings throughout the ten directions. This is called the Conduct of Happiness.** To "comply and accord" means to practice giving. We have discussed giving many times and have mentioned that there are three kinds of giving:

1) the giving of wealth,
2) the giving of dharma,
3) the giving of fearlessness.

However, there are also two aspects to giving, which are not the same as the three kinds. The two aspects comprise another explanation entirely. Since it is called the "conduct of happiness," the first aspect is that one should practice giving with a happy heart. One should enjoy giving. It's not that one decides to give only under duress; it's not forced, such that on the one hand one wants to give, but on the other hand one doesn't want to. It's not that one is indecisive, thinking, "I'd like to make a gift, but it's my money..." It's said that giving up some money is like cutting off a piece of one's flesh. On the other hand, one knows that if one does not practice giving, one will not generate any merit. So it's a real dilemma: if one gives, one fears one will have no money left; if one doesn't give, one fears one will have no merit. So there one stands, not knowing whether to take a step forward or backward. That's certainly not called the "conduct of happiness." That's more like the "conduct of forcing it." Now you can't say that there wouldn't be any merit in this kind of giving, but the merit certainly would be depleted by the internal struggle. One is not doing it with a true mind.

Rather, one should be happy about the giving one does. Even if it means one must do without money oneself, one should be happy to give away to others whatever one has.

The second aspect of giving is that one should make living beings happy. When you practice giving, you should not act like someone tossing crumbs to a beggar. It shouldn't be that they have to come crawling to your door crying, "Old uncle, old auntie, can't you spare a little?" only to have you open the door a crack, throw out a dime or a quarter, and shout, "Take it and get out!" That can't even be called giving. There's no merit in that kind of act, and certainly the person on the receiving end will not be happy. In China there's the phrase: "One doesn't eat what is rudely offered." That's just what's been described above. People with any self-possession will not accept food or money that is offered in that way, even if they have to go hungry.

One should give sincerely and in good faith. But be careful not to give in such a way that one expects gratitude in response. If you avoid doing it in a way that makes people feel they must thank you, then you are giving in a way that causes people to be happy, which is the second aspect of giving. In the "conduct of happiness," both parties, oneself and the person one is giving to, are happy.

K2   Conduct of benefiting.

Sutra:

"Being well able to accommodate all living beings is called the Conduct of Benefiting.

Commentary:

Being well able to accommodate all living beings means to use precepts. It means getting beings to follow the precepts and in that way rescuing them. If everyone holds the precepts, the entire world is benefited. This **is called the Conduct of Benefiting** living beings. It is the second of these ten bodhisattva practices.

K3   Conduct of non-opposition.

Sutra:

"**Enlightening oneself and enlightening others without putting forth any resistance is called the Conduct of Non-Opposition.**

Commentary:

Enlightening oneself and enlightening others is something we all should do. Thus, it is not enough to study the Buddhadharma and come to understand it oneself. We must also enable all beings to come to understand it, to the extent that we should help bring all beings to the accomplishment of Buddhahood. We must benefit ourselves and benefit others. Don't be selfish and concerned about your own gains. Nor should you be jealous or obstructive of others. If someone understands the Buddhadharma better than you do, under no circumstances should you be jealous. If you are jealous of others, you will undergo the retribution of being stupid in the future. Do your utmost with regard to the dharma, but never, never become jealous of others. Don't have ideas of obstructing other people. It shouldn't be that if someone gets enlightened and you haven't, you have a fit, saying, "Really, the Buddhas are simply too unfair. How could they let *him* get enlightened instead of *me*?" With that, your ignorance arises. Or perhaps someone hears the dharma and grasps it immediately. He learns fast and masters the Shurangama Mantra within a couple of month's time. But someone else who hasn't mastered it by then goes into a jealous rage. "How did you get ahead of me? How did you learn it so fast?" Whatever you do, no matter what, under no circumstances should you be jealous of others. You should be happy at heart. "His mastering the mantra is just like my mastering it." "His enlightenment is like my own." You should give rise to thoughts of accordance with other beings, praising them and congratulating them. The most undesirable thing to have when you study the dharma is a jealous attitude.

I repeat, if you are jealous of others, you will be stupid in the future. So stupid will you be that you won't know how to do anything at all – even eat. What a mess you'll be in then! It happens, you know. There are living beings who are so dumb they don't even know how to feed themselves, and they end up starving to death. If someone is more accomplished than you, you should be happy for them.

The bodhisattvas reach the point of not **putting forth any resistance.** This method of non-resistance refers to patience, the third paramita. When something pleasant happens, one is happy; when something unpleasant happens, one is still happy. One doesn't put up any resistance; one doesn't oppose the opinions of others. That's patience. In all circumstances, one forebears. I've recited the poem by Maitreya Bodhisattva for you before:

> The Old Fool wears tattered clothes
> And fills his belly with bland food;
> Mends his clothes against the cold,
> And just puts up with whatever comes along.
> If someone scolds the Old Fool,
> He just says, "Fine."
> If someone strikes the Old Fool,
> He lays down to sleep.
> "Spit on my face? I'll just let it dry.
> I save the energy and you don't get upset."
> This kind of paramita
> Is the jewel within the wonderful.
> If you get this good news,
> What worry can there be
>   about not perfecting the Way?

The third conduct is the practice of patience; it **is called the Conduct of Non-Opposition.** No matter how you are treated, you don't get angry.

K4   Conduct of endlessness.

Sutra:

"To undergo birth in various forms continuously to the bounds of the future, equally throughout the three periods of

time and pervading the ten directions, is called the Conduct of Endlessness.

Commentary:

To undergo birth in various forms means to be able to appear by transformation within any of the twelve classes of living beings. One can send transformation bodies among all those kinds of beings, appearing in forms like theirs, **continuously to the bounds of the future, equally throughout the three periods of time** – past, present, and future. One can "pervade **the ten directions**" without end and has what **is called the Conduct of Endlessness,** the fourth conduct. It corresponds to the perfection of vigor.

K5   Conduct of freedom from deluded confusion.

Sutra:

"When everything is equally in accord, one never makes mistakes among the various dharma doors. This is called the Conduct of Freedom from Deluded Confusion.

Commentary:

This conduct corresponds with the perfection of dhyana samadhi, which aids those who are scattered and easily confused. **When everything is equally in accord, one never makes mistakes among the various dharma doors.** Within any dharma door spoken by the Buddha one naturally gains understanding and knows the function of any given dharma. **This is called the Conduct of Freedom from Deluded Confusion.**

K6   Conduct of wholesome manifestation.

Sutra:

"Then within what is identical, myriad differences appear; the characteristics of every difference are seen, one and all, in identity. This is called the Conduct of Wholesome Manifestation.

Commentary:

Then within what is identical, myriad differences appear. What is identical is the principle. What are different are the specifics. At the noumenal level there is identity; at the phenomenal level there are differences. **The characteristics of every difference are seen, one and all, in identity.** That is, the phenomena all tally with principle. There is:

1) the unobstructedness of principles in specifics;
2) the unobstructedness of specifics in principles;
3) the unobstructedness of specifics with specifics;
4) the unobstructedness of both principles and specifics.

Therefore, in identity appear differences; within differences identity is found. **This is called the Conduct of Wholesome Manifestation.** Identity and differences do not obstruct one another, and each appears within the other. This is the perfection of wisdom.

K7   Conduct of non-attachment.

Sutra:

"This continues until it includes all the dust motes that fill up empty space throughout the ten directions. In each and every mote of dust there appear the worlds of the ten directions. And yet the appearance of dust motes and the appearance of worlds do not interfere with one another. This is called the Conduct of Non-Attachment.

Commentary:

This continues until it includes all the dust motes that fill up empty space throughout the ten directions. Not only is it the case that within identity, differences can appear, and within differences, identity is evident, but within the few the many can appear, and within the many the few are evident. Within the small the great can appear; within the great the small are evident. "Empty space" is the manifestation of the great. "Dust motes" are the manifestation of the small. Within every dust mote, worlds appear, so that every world can fit within a mote of dust. But when a world appears in a dust mote, it's not the case that the world shrinks. Nor is it the case that the dust mote has to expand to contain the world. This is the great appearing in the small and the small manifesting the great without any hindrance.

In each and every mote of dust there appear the worlds of the ten directions. The worlds of the ten directions are tremendously large, while a fine mote of dust is minute; yet none of the worlds get smaller, nor does the mote of dust expand. **And yet the appearance of dust motes and the appearance of worlds do not interfere with one another.** They include one another without any obstruction. **This is called the Conduct of Non-Attachment.** Worlds are motes of dust; motes of dust are worlds. Little is big; big is little. To experience this is the "conduct of non-attachment." This is the seventh perfection, that of expedience.

K8   Conduct of veneration.

Sutra:

"**Everything that appears before one is the foremost paramita. This is called the Conduct of Veneration.**

Commentary:

The "conduct of veneration" is also the perfection of vows. It is brought to accomplishment through the power of vows. **Everything that appears before one is the foremost paramita.** All the states that manifest are the number one paramita, the dharma for reaching the other shore. **This is called the Conduct of Veneration.** This is the eighth conduct.

K9   Conduct of wholesome dharma.

Sutra:

"**With such perfect fusion, one can model oneself after all the Buddhas of the ten directions. This is called the Conduct of Wholesome Dharma.**

Commentary:

With such perfect fusion, when everything becomes the foremost paramita, **one can model oneself after all the Buddhas of the ten directions.** In one's cultivation one can be in accord with all the rules and regulations established by all the Buddhas of the ten directions. **This is called the Conduct of Wholesome Dharma.** It is the perfection of strength. One's own practice is strong. This is the ninth conduct.

K10   Conduct of true actuality.

Sutra:

"**To then be pure and without outflows in each and every way is the primary truth, which is unconditioned, the essence of the nature. This is called the Conduct of True Actuality.**

Commentary:

The tenth is called the "conduct of true actuality." **To then be pure and without outflows in each and every way is the primary truth, which is unconditioned, the essence of the nature.** "In each and every way" means that all the previous nine entries into conduct are conducted purely and without outflows. Then there is only one truth, that of the unconditioned. And that's the way the nature originally is. **This is called the Conduct of True Actuality.** This corresponds with the perfection of knowledge. These are the ten conducts of a bodhisattva.

The Ten Transferences

Sutra:

"**Ananda, when these good people replete with spiritual penetrations, have done the Buddhas' work, are totally pure and absolutely true, and remain distant from obstacles and calamities, then they take living beings across while casting aside the appearance of taking them across. They transform the unconditioned mind and go toward the path of nirvana. This is called the Transference of Saving and Protecting Living Beings, While Apart from the Appearance of Living Beings.**

Commentary:

Ananda, when these good people, these people who have cultivated the ten conducts, develop genuine wisdom to the point that their practice is said to be true and real, then they are **replete with spiritual penetrations,** and **have done the Buddhas' work.** Throughout the ten directions they perform a tremendous number of deeds on behalf of the Buddhas. And yet:

> The myriad practices they cultivate
>   are but flowers in space.
> The bodhimandas they sit in
>   are like the moon in water,

> And subduing the demonic armies
> mere reflections in a mirror.
> They do great deeds of the Buddhas
> while in the midst of a dream.

That represents their non-attachment. Everything is like an illusion, a transformation; nothing really exists. So don't be attached to anything. See through it all, put it down, and you can obtain self-mastery.

They **are totally pure and absolutely true**; they have accomplished that state, **and** they **remain distant from obstacles and calamities.** They are not hindered in any way. **Then they take living beings across while casting aside the appearance of taking them across.** They rescue those whom they should rescue without having any thought of having rescued them. The *Vajra Sutra* explains this as well; Shakyamuni Buddha says there:

> "I should take all beings across to extinction, and yet when all beings are thus taken across, there should not be any beings taken across to extinction."

Again, this means one must not be attached and think, "I did this, I did that." One builds a temple and then cannot get the thought out of one's mind that one was the builder and has accrued so much merit. That is to still have an appearance left.

They take living beings across while casting aside the appearance of taking them across. You don't look upon the deed as something you did, but rather as something you should have done. It was your responsibility in the first place; why would you need to let anyone know it had been done? If you brag about what you've done, it implies that it was something you didn't have to do. Conversely, some people say, "I didn't steal anything or kill anyone in this life. I've never done anything bad, so why aren't things better for me?" This implies that they were originally destined to steal and kill, but that they refrained from doing so and should be rewarded for that. This is a mistaken point of view.

They transform the unconditioned mind and go toward the path of nirvana. They turn the unconditioned mind of the lesser vehicle toward nirvana. **This is called the Transference of Saving and Protecting Living Beings, While Apart from the Appearance of Living Beings.** They see it as their responsibility to rescue living beings, and so they are apart from the appearance of having rescued them. They do not ponder the amount of merit and virtue involved in rescuing living beings. "It's my job. That's what I should be doing," should be how you think of it.

"But," you ask, "Isn't there merit and virtue involved in rescuing living beings?" Yes, there is. But don't dwell on it. What's past is past. What you've done, you've done. Don't hold on to the idea of having rescued living beings. This is not to say that you should not rescue beings; it's to say that you shouldn't harbor the appearance of having taken them across.

K2   Transference of indestructibility.

Sutra:

"To destroy what should be destroyed and to remain far removed from what should be left behind is called the Transference of Indestructibility.

Commentary:

To destroy what should be destroyed means to get rid of the things that one should not keep. What are they? No matter how much we talk it always comes back to the same things: karmic obstacles, ignorance, and afflictions. Get rid of these. Destroy them.

To remain far removed from what should be left behind means to get rid of your faults. For instance, people who cultivate the Way should not have any greed, anger, or stupidity. You should destroy them. All good things should be embraced. All bad things should be rejected. Get them far behind you. This **is called the Transference of Indestructibility.** What is indestructible? Your inherent good roots are indestructible. Your originally existent

enlightened nature is indestructible. With the transference of indestructibility you have to destroy what should be destroyed and keep
what is indestructible.

K3   Transference of sameness with all Buddhas.

Sutra:

**"Fundamental enlightenment is profound indeed, an
enlightenment equal to the Buddhas' enlightenment. This is
called the Transference of Sameness with All Buddhas.**

Commentary:

Fundamental enlightenment refers to the nature of the
treasury of the Thus Come One inherent in us all. It **is profound
indeed,** and pure. It is **an enlightenment equal to the Buddhas'
enlightenment.** The enlightenment of our minds is the same as the
enlightenment of the Buddhas. **This is called the Transference of
Sameness with All Buddhas.**

K4   Transference of reaching all places.

Sutra:

**"When absolute truth is discovered, one's level is the same
as the level of all Buddhas. This is called the Transference of
Reaching All Places.**

Commentary:

When the **absolute truth** of the previous transference **is
discovered, one's level is the same as the level of all Buddhas.**
This is a level which is a prelude to the Buddha's position. **This is
called the Transference of Reaching All Places.**

K5   Transference of the treasury of inexhaustible merit and virtue.

Sutra:

**"Worlds and Thus Come Ones include one another without
any obstruction. This is called the Transference of a Treasury of
Inexhaustible Merit and Virtue.**

Commentary:

Worlds and Thus Come Ones include one another without any obstruction. Worlds are the very body of the Thus Come One; the very body of the Thus Come One is itself the worlds. The wonderful function of spiritual penetrations enables them to contain one another. Nor is there any hindrance for either, nor anything contrived about it. **This is called the Transference of a Treasury of Inexhaustible Merit and Virtue.**

The Emperor Wu of Liang is a case in point of someone who was attached to the idea of creating merit. When he encountered the Patriarch Bodhidharma, he asked him, "I have built many grand temples. I have commissioned a tremendous number of people to enter the Sangha. I have made extensive vegetarian offerings. I've built bridges, improved highways, and much more. Tell me, how much merit have I accrued?"

Who would have guessed that the patriarch would scowl and retort, "None whatsoever."

The emperor was duly affronted and refused to have anything more to do with the patriarch. Actually, Patriarch Bodhidharma was intent upon saving the emperor. But because the emperor's karmic obstructions were so heavy he missed his chance, even though he was face to face with the first patriarch of China. It was like the saying, "Guan Shi Yin Bodhisattva was right before him and he didn't even recognize him." The "Mind from the West" was right before the Emperor Wu of Liang and he failed to see him.

Why did he need rescuing by Patriarch Bodhidharma? It's because the patriarch knew that the emperor had a disaster in store for him. He was hoping to wake him up so he would either leave the home life and cultivate or at least yield the throne to someone else, thereby avoiding having to starve to death. Basically the emperor was a devout believer in Buddhism, and during his reign Buddhism flourished because he used his imperial position to spread the Buddhadharma, building temples all about the land. The majority of the population was Buddhist during that reign period. But he had created some heavy karma in past lives. In a former life the emperor was a bhikshu who cultivated in the mountains. At one point he began to be visited every day by a monkey who stole the fruits and vegetables he had planted. Pretty soon there wasn't much left for him to eat. Because of that, he trapped the monkey in a cave and sealed the opening with a boulder. He had originally intended to leave it there for a few days to teach it a lesson and then let it go. The trouble was that he forgot about it, and the monkey starved to death in the cave.

In his life as an emperor, then, the monkey was reborn as a monkey-spirit who led an army and attacked Nan Jing. After conquering Nan Jing, the monkey-spirit locked the emperor in a tower, removed all food, and left him to starve. The bhikshu's retribution for having starved a monkey to death was that the monkey returned in a later life when the bhikshu was an emperor and starved him to death.

Patriarch Bodhidharma saw that the emperor had amassed a lot of merit and virtue, and he thought that the emperor might make use of the merit to lessen the offense. But in order for that to happen, the causes and conditions had to be right as well. That's why Patriarch Bodhidharma was so severe with him. But the emperor thought himself a mighty monarch to whom a penniless monk had no right to talk in such a way, so he shunned the patriarch. Although Patriarch Bodhidharma wanted to save him, there was nothing he could do but leave, since the emperor would have nothing to do with him and did not seek to be saved. In the end, the emperor starved to death at the hands of the monkey-spirit.

K6   Transference of the identity of all good roots.

Sutra:

"Since they are identical with the Buddha-ground, they create causes which are pure at each and every level. Brilliance emanates from them as they rely on these causes, and they go straight down the path to nirvana. This is called the

Transference of Following in Accord with the Identity of All Good Roots.

Commentary:

After the bodhisattvas have reached the accomplishment of the previous transference of a treasury of inexhaustible merit and virtue, then, **since they are identical with the Buddha-ground, they create causes which are pure at each and every level.** At each level along the way they give rise to causes which are clear and pure and undefiled. **Brilliance emanates from them as they rely on these causes, and they go straight down the path to nirvana.** They hold to the Way which is neither produced nor destroyed. **This is called the Transference of Following in Accord with the Identity of All Good Roots.**

K7   Transference of contemplating all living beings equally.

Sutra:

"When the true roots are set down, then all living beings in the ten directions are my own nature. Not a single being is lost as this nature is successfully perfected. This is called the Transference of Contemplating All Living Beings Equally.

Commentary:

When the true roots are set down, then all living beings in the ten directions are my own nature. They are one and the same as the bodhisattvas. That is why bodhisattvas want to rescue living beings without there being an appearance of living beings. Buddhas and Bodhisattvas see all living beings as their own substance. They are one with them. Therefore, for them to save living beings is not really to save other living beings; it's just to save themselves. **Not a single being is lost, as this nature is successfully perfected.** Since they are one with all beings, no being is neglected. **This is called the Transference of Contemplating All Living Beings Equally.**

To say that all beings are their own nature is to speak of living beings who exist outside themselves. But we can also speak of internal beings, because there are boundlessly many beings within the body of each of us. Science describes the white corpuscles and the red corpuscles and verifies that our bodies contain innumerable microscopic organisms. If you were to open your buddha eye and look into people's bodies, you would see an unknown number of beings there, uncountably many tiny forms of life, even to the point that when you exhale, you send a lot of beings out in your breath. At that point they are incarnated again as beings. By the same token, you ingest innumerable beings when you inhale. So it's pretty hard to draw a clear line between being a carnivore and not being one, if you get down to the subtler aspects of it. Here you are taking life with every breath, and that, too, is a form of killing if you do it with a murderous intent. Of course, we're getting down to details here.

The beings in your body are just ordinary creatures if you don't cultivate. If you do cultivate, they become the Buddha-nature. They can all return to the source. You return to the origin and they go right along with you – all those tiny forms of life that you harbor. If you cultivate to the point where you have some skill, then the beings external to you and the beings within you all become one with you. But as of right now, there are basically too many living beings.

K8   Transference of the appearance of true suchness.

Sutra:

"All phenomena are themselves apart from all appearances, and yet there is no attachment either to their existence or to separation from them. This is called the Transference of the Appearance of True Suchness.

Commentary:

All phenomena are themselves apart from all appearances. Right within phenomena one must be apart from all appearances. **And yet there is no attachment either to their existence or to separation from them. This is called the Transference of the Appearance of True Suchness.**

K9   Transference of liberation.

Sutra:

"That which is thus is truly obtained, and there is no obstruction throughout the ten directions. This is called the Transference of Unfettered Liberation.

Commentary:

One definition of true suchness is **that which is thus** being **truly obtained.** It is also described as "wisdom which is thus giving rise to principle which is thus." When that is obtained, **there is no obstruction throughout the ten directions.** You can roam throughout the Buddharealms of the ten directions without any hindrances. **This is called the Transference of Unfettered Liberation.** Nothing is tying you up. You are free.

K10 Transference of the limitlessness of the dharma realm.

Sutra:

"When the virtue of the nature is perfectly accomplished, the boundaries of the dharma realm are destroyed. This is called the Transference of the Limitlessness of the Dharma Realm.

Commentary:

Before the virtue of the nature is perfectly accomplished, before you have become one with the dharma realm, you do not even know the boundaries of the dharma realm. When the virtue of the nature has been perfectly accomplished and you become one with the dharma realm, then you know the boundaries of the dharma realm. But since it still has a boundary, you have not yet reached the ultimate accomplishment. Now, **when the virtue of the nature is perfectly accomplished, the boundaries of the dharma realm are destroyed.** Even the dharma realm is empty. **This is called the Transference of the Limitlessness of the Dharma Realm.**

The Four Positions of Additional Practices

J7 Four positions of additional practices.
K1 Concludes the former discussion and begins the next.

Sutra:

"Ananda, when these good people have completely purified these forty-one minds, they further accomplish four kinds of wonderfully perfect additional practices.

Commentary:

The bodhisattva, the person practicing, reaches a state of purity with regard to these forty-one minds. The "forty-one minds" are:

1)   the level of dry wisdom;
2-11)   the ten faiths;
12-21) the ten dwellings;
22-31) the ten conducts;
32-41) the ten transferences.

The level of dry wisdom, you'll remember, is also called "initial dry wisdom" and the "initial vajra mind."

Following these forty-one positions are four further levels. They are known as the wonderfully perfect additional practices; they are:

1) heat;
2) summit;

3) patience;

4) first in the world.

Sutra:

"When the enlightenment of a Buddha is just about to become a function of his own mind, it is on the verge of emerging but has not yet emerged, and so it can be compared to the point just before wood ignites when it is drilled to produce fire. Therefore it is called the Level of Heat.

Commentary:

This is the first of the four additional practices, the level of heat. The analogy is given of wood which is drilled to get fire; this level is compared to the point just before the wood ignites. **When the enlightenment of a Buddha is just about to become a function of his own mind** means that what the Buddhas are enlightened to and what he himself is enlightened to are the same thing. When **it is on the verge of emerging but has not yet emerged, and so it can be compared to the point just before wood ignites when it is drilled to produce fire.** The igniting of the wood being drilled is like enlightenment. The wood is right on the point of bursting into flame. With the enlightenment there is also heat, **therefore it is called the Level of Heat.** This is the forty-second position in the bodhisattva's progression.

L2   Level of the summit.

Sutra:

"He continues on with his mind, treading where the Buddhas tread, as if relying and yet not. It is as if he were climbing a lofty mountain, to the point where his body is in space but there remains a slight obstruction beneath him. Therefore it is called the Level of the Summit.

Commentary:

He continues on with his mind, treading where the Buddhas tread, as if relying and yet not. His own mind goes down the path the Buddhas take. He seems to be dependent and yet he is also independent. A different analogy is used here. **It is as if he were climbing a lofty mountain, to the point where his body is in space but there remains a slight obstruction beneath him.** He is like someone climbing a mountain, and when he gets to the top, it is as if he physically enters into empty space because he is so high up. But under his feet, as he stands on the mountain, there is still a slight hindrance. He still has not yet ascended into empty space. **Therefore it is called the Level of the Summit.**

L3   Level of patience.

Sutra:

"When the mind and the Buddha are two and yet the same, he has well obtained the Middle Way. He is like someone who endures something when it seems impossible to either hold it in or let it out. Therefore it is called the Level of Patience.

Commentary:

When the mind and the Buddha are two and yet the same, he has well obtained the Middle Way. The mind is the Buddha; the Buddha is the mind. Although they are said to be two, they come together as one. What is the mind is the Buddha. There is no Buddha outside the mind; there is no mind outside the Buddha. The mind and the Buddha are in a state of suchness. He has then genuinely obtained the principle and substance of the Middle Way. **He is like someone who endures something when it seems impossible to either hold it in or let it out.** It is as if a situation arises which a person must bear: he'd like to keep it contained, but that is impossible; at the same time, it's impossible for him to let it out. So at that point he bears with it. He'd like to keep it in his mind and he'd like to release it. He can't decide which would be the better thing to do. So he bears with it. He'd like to let it go, but he can't give it up. And yet he'd still like to let it go. At this time he must be patient. **Therefore it is called the Level of Patience.** It is the third of the additional practices.

L4   Level of being first in the world.

Sutra:

"**When numbers are destroyed, there are no such designations as the Middle Way or as confusion and enlightenment; this is called the Level of Being First in the World.**

Commentary:

When numbers are destroyed. At the tenth transference, the boundaries of the dharma realm are destroyed. Now all numbers and boundaries are destroyed. What is meant? It's the same as a zero. I've talked about zero before. It is the absence of numbers. At that point **there are no such designations as the Middle Way or as confusion and enlightenment.** Perfection is total and the light brilliant. There are no designations because it's a situation that's like zero. There's nothing that can be said about zero. Zero means the absence of everything. And yet everything outside the zero is contained within it. The zero is the mother of all things. But it is not designated as a mother, because there isn't anything there. To understand what I'm saying right now is enlightenment.

There isn't any confusion; there isn't any enlightenment. Why isn't there any confusion? Because he is not confused. Why isn't there any enlightenment? He's already enlightened; what further enlightenment could there be? For there to be no confusion and no enlightenment is zero. All the mountains, the rivers, the great earth, the plants, and all the myriad appearances come forth from it.

There is no designation for enlightenment and confusion, or for the Middle Way. Even though there's no name for this state, we still have to call it something, so we force the issue and call it **the Level of Being First in the World.** It's first in the world because there is no second. This is the last of the additional practices.

The Ten Positions of the Ten Grounds

J8   The ten positions of the ten grounds.
K1   Ground of happiness.

Sutra:

"Ananda, these good men have successfully penetrated through to great bodhi. Their enlightenment is entirely like the Thus Come One's. They have fathomed the state of Buddhahood. This is called the Ground of Happiness.

Commentary:

Ananda, these good men have successfully penetrated through to great bodhi. The "good men" are the bodhisattvas who have obtained the level of being first in the world. Although the text says he has successfully penetrated through to great bodhi, there really isn't anything that's been penetrated through to. **Their enlightenment is entirely like the Thus Come One's.** Their enlightenment is the Thus Come One; the Thus Come One is enlightenment. They have become enlightened to that which the Thus Come One has become enlightened to. They can be called a Thus Come One when they have enlightened to that zero. And yet the zero isn't anything at all, so don't get attached to it!

They have fathomed the state of Buddhahood. True emptiness is the state of being nothing at all. But when they fathom the state of a Buddha, then within true emptiness arises wonderful existence. That wonderful existence is happiness. "Oh, so originally it's just *that* way!" That's the arising of happiness. "I didn't understand before, but now I do." They are inexpressibly happy. **This is called the Ground of Happiness.** It's the first ground.

K2 Ground of leaving filth.

Sutra:

"**The differences enter into identity; the identity is destroyed. This is called the Ground of Leaving Filth.**

Commentary:

On the previous ground there was still happiness, and so an identity still existed, too. Although there were no designations, there was still an identity. That was when **the differences enter into identity** and become one. That is, although the phenomena and the noumenon are united, the noumenon still remains. Now when they reach the second ground, **the identity is destroyed.** The second ground is called the "ground of leaving filth," which means that they separate from ignorance. Basically there isn't much ignorance left by this time, for their enlightened natures are already like that of a Buddha. A slight bit of attachment, a little defilement remains for them. Now "identity is destroyed"; their likeness to the Buddha ceases to be. That's to return to the source, to go back to the nature of the treasury of the Thus Come One, which is a great storehouse of light. It has no name or appearance. **This is called the Ground of Leaving Filth.** Happiness is still a kind of defilement. If there is something you like, then you still have emotional reactions. At the second ground, all the defilements are left behind. Subtle ignorance is also lessened. But at this level the ignorance is still not completely cut off.

K3 Ground of emitting light.

Sutra:

"**At the point of ultimate purity, brightness comes forth. This is called the Ground of Emitting Light.**

Commentary:

A bodhisattva on the first ground does not know the state of a bodhisattva on the second ground. A bodhisattva on the second ground doesn't know the state of a bodhisattva on the third ground. **At the point of ultimate purity, brightness comes forth.** The previous ground was that of leaving filth. But as long as there is a necessity to "leave" it, there must still be defilement. Only when one has completely left the filth is one clean. Let's take sweeping as an example. We sweep in order to clean up the floor. We put the broom aside when the floor is clean. As long as we are still sweeping, it isn't clean yet.

When he reaches the ultimate purity, light comes forth. There is brightness. So the third ground **is called the Ground of Emitting Light.**

K4   Ground of blazing wisdom.

Sutra:

"When the brightness becomes ultimate, enlightenment is full. This is called the Ground of Blazing Wisdom.

Commentary:

When the brightness becomes ultimate, enlightenment is full. The light reaches its maximum and the enlightened nature is perfected. **This is called the Ground of Blazing Wisdom.** "Blazing" is descriptive of the wisdom that is bright like a torch.

K5   Ground of invincibility.

Sutra:

"No identity or difference can be attained. This is called the Ground of Invincibility.

Commentary:

No identity or difference can be attained. Not only are things that are the same identical at this stage; all things are identical. The bodhisattva cannot come to any distinction between sameness and difference. There is no way to represent them because basically there is no identity or difference. **This is called the Ground of Invincibility.** There isn't anything that can overcome this level of understanding. It transcends all the other previous grounds. This is the name given to the fifth level of these stages of the bodhisattvas' development.

Is it the case that one bodhisattva reaches the Ground of Invincibility? Yes, it is the case that one bodhisattva does. And yet this one bodhisattva is not just a single bodhisattva. There is only one, and yet there is not. Here is where the Buddhadharma is to be found. One bodhisattva comes up to this level. But millions of billions of other bodhisattvas also come up to this level. For instance, when someone earns a Ph.D. degree, is that one person alone in earning it? Certainly that one person has earned it, but someone else can also earn one. Everyone who has one has earned it. And so how many earn one? Millions. Not just one. The same principle applies here. Probably more bodhisattvas than there are sand grains in the Ganges River are certified as having attained each of these grounds.

K6 Ground of manifestation.

Sutra:

"With unconditioned true suchness, the nature is spotless, and brightness is revealed. This is called the Ground of Manifestation.

Commentary:

With unconditioned true suchness, the nature is spotless, and brightness is revealed. It is unconditioned, and yet there is nothing which is not conditioned. True suchness refers to the nature of the treasury of the Thus Come One. It is the one true dharma realm. With unconditioned true suchness everything is in a state of suchness, everything is true. There is nothing which is not true, nothing which is not in a state of suchness. The nature is extremely pure, and light shines forth. This is the sixth ground, **called the Ground of Manifestation.** That's because the bodhisattva's nature reveals itself.

K7   Ground of traveling far.

Sutra:

"Coming to the farthest limits of true suchness is called the Ground of Traveling Far.

Commentary:

True suchness has no limits and no farthest point, so how can this be? Again, it is descriptive. There really isn't any end to true suchness, because it really doesn't have any limits, so that's why the sutra says it this way: **Coming to the farthest limits of true suchness.** It's just like when we say that empty space is obliterated. But since empty space isn't even a substance to begin with, how can it be obliterated? This is the same kind of attempt to describe what is basically beyond comprehension.

True suchness doesn't have any limits. It includes the ten dharma realms with all their beings. How could it have a boundary? What's beyond the ten dharma realms? Nothing. And so it says "Coming to the farthest limits of true suchness." That is to travel far indeed! How far? Who knows? All we can say is that it's **called the Ground of Traveling Far.** Ordinary people could never get there. Only a bodhisattva at the seventh ground can go that far.

K8   Ground of immovability.

Sutra:

"The single mind of true suchness is called the Ground of Immovability.

Commentary:

The single mind of true suchness is the one true dharma realm. It was said above that the mind is the Buddha and the Buddha is the mind. Now true suchness is the mind and the mind is the Buddha. There is no distinction between true suchness and the mind. Since true suchness has no limits, the bodhisattva's mind has no limits. When his mind has no limits, where does he go? He doesn't go anywhere. Therefore, it is **called the Ground of Immovability.**

Unmoving in the bodhimanda, he pervades the dharma realm. This is the eighth ground.

K9   Ground of good wisdom.

Sutra:

"Bringing forth the function of true suchness is called the Ground of Good Wisdom.

Commentary:

At the eighth ground, true suchness and the mind become one, and this was called the ground of not moving. But to simply be unmoving and to never make a move would be useless. However, within true suchness, the function now comes forth. What is the function of true suchness? The function of true suchness is gigantic. If it were small, it would have only a single function. But this gigantic function can be used however one wishes. According with conditions, one is unmoving; unmoving, one accords with conditions. One constantly accords with conditions and yet is constantly unmoving; one is constantly unmoving and yet constantly accords with conditions. Such a functioning must be connected with wisdom. Therefore, **bringing forth the function of true suchness is called the Ground of Good Wisdom.** This is the ninth ground. This wisdom is totally true and real.

Sutra:

"Ananda, all bodhisattvas at this point and beyond have reached the effortless way in their cultivation. Their merit and virtue are perfected, and so all the previous positions are also called the Level of Cultivation.

Commentary:

Ananda, you should understand that **all bodhisattvas at this point and beyond have reached the effortless way in their cultivation.** From the beginning – the level of dry wisdom, also known as the initial vajra mind – to the culmination of the ninth ground, there are a total of fifty-four positions. When the bodhisattvas have passed through to this point, they've reached the effortless way. They have graduated. **Their merit and virtue are perfected.** In their study leading toward Buddhahood, they are just about to earn this degree; they're about to become Buddhas. **And so all the previous positions are also called the Level of Cultivation.**

K10 Ground of the dharma cloud.

Sutra:

"Then with a wonderful cloud of compassionate protection one covers the sea of nirvana. This is called the Ground of the Dharma Cloud.

Commentary:

"Wonder" and "compassion" are qualities. "Protection" and "covering" belong to the analogy of the cloud and represent a sheltering influence. **Then with a wonderful cloud of compassionate protection one covers the sea of nirvana.** One shelters all living beings. All Buddhas and Bodhisattvas emerge from the sea of nirvana, and so the tenth ground **is called the Ground of the Dharma Cloud.** At this level one shelters and protects all living beings.

The Position of Equal and Wonderful Enlightenment

J9   The position of equal enlightenment.
K1   Describing the position.

Sutra:

"The Thus Come Ones counter the flow as the bodhisattvas thus reach this point through compliance with practice. Their enlightenments intermingle; it is therefore called Equal Enlightenment.

Commentary:

The Thus Come Ones counter the flow. This means that the Thus Come Ones have already become Buddhas. But they counter the flow and appear in the world to rescue living beings. Thus from the Buddha-position, they come back along the bodhisattva path in order to greet the bodhisattva. That's what's meant by countering the flow. **The bodhisattvas thus reach this point through compliance with practice.** The bodhisattvas comply with the flow. This "flow" refers to going from an ordinary person to arhatship, through bodhisattvahood, and on to Buddhahood – which the bodhisattvas have not yet experienced at this point. So they are going along with the flow that leads to the Buddha's enlightened position. Now, they actually encounter the Buddhas. **Their enlightenments intermingle.** The enlightenment of the Buddhas and the enlightenment of the bodhisattvas merge at this point. **It is**

therefore called Equal Enlightenment. These bodhisattvas are equal to the Buddha. But theirs is still not wonderful enlightenment. It is still only similar to the Buddha's enlightenment, because at this level they still have left one bit of ignorance that seems to be that of production. They still must destroy that. So ignorance is difficult to leave behind. Once they smash it, however, they will be Buddhas.

When people claim to be Buddhas, I ask them, "From where did you come? What path did you take?" If they don't even know the name of the first position, have never seen the path that leads to the second position, and don't know how to get to the third position, then how can they have arrived at Buddhahood? They took a plane, perhaps? In that case a rocket would have been even faster. I suspect that such people will never reach the Buddha position. Why not? It is because they say they are there when in fact they are not. Do they speak the truth, or do they lie? They have not cultivated or done anything within the Buddhadharma, and yet they profess to be Buddhas. It just doesn't add up. How about those people who have practiced within the Buddhadharma for decades and still are not Buddhas? Maybe those people who say they are Buddhas have effected some scientific means to get themselves there so fast.

K2   Bringing out the wisdom obtained.

Sutra:

"Ananda, the enlightenment which encompasses the mind of dry wisdom through to the culmination of equal enlightenment is the initial attainment of the vajra mind. This constitutes the level of Initial Dry Wisdom.

Commentary:

Ananda, the enlightenment which encompasses the mind of dry wisdom, also called the initial vajra mind and the level of dry wisdom, **through to the culmination of equal enlightenment is the initial attainment of the vajra mind.** This refers to the latter vajra mind. **This constitutes the level of Initial Dry Wisdom** of the latter vajra mind. The previous level of dry wisdom referred to the drying up of emotional love and desire. At that point, he had not yet joined with the Thus Come One's dharma-water. Now, even though this latter level of dry wisdom is more encompassing, he still has not yet joined the sea of wonderful adornments of a Thus Come One, so it's also referred to as dry wisdom. However, it pertains to the latter vajra mind and is the final step.

J10   The position of wonderful enlightenment.

Sutra:

"Thus there are totals of twelve single and grouped levels. At last they reach wonderful enlightenment and accomplish the Unsurpassed Way.

Commentary:

Thus there are totals of twelve single and grouped levels. There are seven single levels:

1) initial dry wisdom;
2) heat;
3) summit;
4) patience;
5) first in the world;
6) equal enlightenment;
7) wonderful enlightenment.

There are five grouped levels:

1) the ten faiths;
2) the ten dwellings;
3) the ten conducts;
4) the ten transferences;
5) the ten grounds.

Because each of these levels includes ten positions, they are classed as groups. Together the seven single levels and the five groups make twelve. There are fifty-four positions from the initial dry wisdom to equal enlightenment. Some count the initial dry wisdom of the latter vajra mind as the fifty-fifth, but actually that level of dry wisdom is the same as equal enlightenment.

At last they reach Wonderful Enlightenment and accomplish the Unsurpassed Way. They come to the end of the path to wonderful enlightenment and accomplish the reward and the substance of wonderful enlightenment. They have accomplished Buddhahood.

I2   Conclusion: manifestation of pure dharmas.

Sutra:

"At all these levels they use vajra contemplation of the ten profound analogies for the ways in which things are like an illusion. In shamatha they use the Thus Come Ones' vipashyana to cultivate them purely, to be certified to them, and to gradually enter them more and more deeply.

Commentary:

At all these levels they use vajra contemplation of the ten profound analogies for the ways in which things are like an illusion. These levels are the ones just described, from the level of dry wisdom of the initial vajra mind through the ten faiths, the ten dwellings, the ten conducts, the ten transferences, the ten grounds, and the four additional practices. They use the vajra mind to cultivate with, to contemplate by. They contemplate how things are like an illusion. "Illusion" means that you say it is real, but it isn't; you say it's false, but it isn't. It's as I mentioned before:

> The myriad practices he cultivates
>   arc but flowers in space.
> The bodhimanda he sits in
>   is like the moon in water.
> And subduing the demonic armies,
>   mere reflections in a mirror.
> He does great deeds of the Buddhas
>   while in a dream.

The "ten profound analogies" are as follows:

1. All karma is like an illusion.

You should look upon karmic obstacles as illusory, not real.

2. All phenomena are like a mirage.

Sometimes in the spring you'll see what seems to be smoke rising, but when you approach the spot, you find there's really nothing there at all. It's just a mirage. You should look upon all phenomena in the same way.

3. All physical bodies are like the moon in water.
4. All wonderful forms are like flowers in space.
5. All wonderful sounds are like echoes in a valley.
6. All Buddhalands are like gandharva cities.

Basically the Buddhalands *are* real, but you should look upon them as if they were but the cities of gandharvas.

7. All deeds of the Buddha are like dreams.
8. The Buddha's body is like a reflection.
9. The reward body is like an image.
10. The dharma body is like a transformation.

You should not look upon any of these things as real. You should neither grasp nor reject these illusory states. That is because everything is empty; you should not regard anything as actually existent. What is the meaning behind these ten profound analogies? They tell you not to be attached to anything at all. You have to put everything down. If you see through it and put it all down, then you will obtain self-mastery.

In shamatha they use the Thus Come Ones' vipashyana to cultivate them purely, to be certified to them, and to gradually enter them more and more deeply. "Shamatha" means stopping and "vipashyana" means contemplating. We are to cultivate the dharma door of stopping and contemplating. "Vipashyana" also means "subtle, secret contemplation and illumination." Gradually, bit by bit, one progresses and enters into this purification and certification.

I3   He stresses the importance of vigor in the initial resolve.

Sutra:

"Ananda, because they put to use the three means of advancement throughout all of them, they are well able to accomplish the fifty-five stages of the true bodhi path.

Commentary:

The three means of advancement have already been explained. They are:

1) getting rid of aiding causes;
2) cleaning up the proper nature;
3) guarding against the manifestation of karma.

The fifty-five stages are:

1) the ten faiths;
2) the ten dwellings;
3) the ten conducts;
4) the ten transferences;
5) the four additional practices;
6) the ten grounds;
7) equal enlightenment.

I4   He decides the division of proper and deviant.

Sutra:

"This manner of contemplation is called 'proper contemplation.' Contemplation other than this is called 'deviant contemplation.'"

Commentary:

This manner of contemplation is called "proper contemplation." If you can look upon the triple world as upon flowers in space; if you can regard all deeds of the Buddha as if done in a dream; and if you rely on the three means of advancement in your cultivation, your contemplation is proper. If you can use the vajra mind in your contemplation to make a subtle, secret contemplation and illumination as you pass through the fifty-five stages, then you are practicing proper contemplation. This is proper cultivation of the dharma of neither production nor extinction. **Contemplation other than this is called "deviant contemplation."** If you don't cultivate this dharma-door; if you do not contemplate in this way; if you cultivate practices subject to production and extinction, your contemplation is deviant.

CHAPTER 3

The Names of the Sutra

E2   He explains the name of the entire sutra.
F1   Manjushri asks the sutra's name.

Sutra:

Then dharma prince Manjushri arose from his seat, and in the midst of the assembly he bowed at the Buddha's feet and said to the Buddha, "What is the name of this sutra and how should we and all living beings uphold it?"

Commentary:

At this point in the discussion, **dharma prince Manjushri arose from his seat, and in the midst of the assembly he bowed at the Buddha's feet and said to the Buddha** – Bodhisattva Manjushri now has a question to ask: **"What is the name of this sutra and how should we and all living beings uphold it?** World Honored One, what name do you give to this sutra? How should we in this assembly and living beings of the future uphold it? How should we cultivate it? How should we offer up our conduct with regard to this sutra?"

Sutra:

The Buddha told Manjushri, "This sutra is called 'The Summit, Syi Dan Dwo Bwo Da La, and Unsurpassed Precious Seal of the Seal of the Great Buddha, and the Pure, Clear, Ocean-Like Eye of the Thus Comes Ones of the Ten Directions.'

Commentary:

The Buddha told Manjushri, "This sutra is called 'The Summit, Syi Dan Dwo Bwo Da La, and Unsurpassed Precious Seal of the Seal of the Great Buddha.'" This refers to the invisible summit, the crown of the Buddha's head, which poured forth splendorous light. **Syi Dan Dwo Bwo Da La** is the great white canopy. There is nothing more revered or honored than the **Unsurpassed Precious Seal.** The "precious seal" is that of the Dharma King, the Buddha. This first name indicates how supreme the Shurangama Mantra is. If people recite the Shurangama Mantra, they are worthy of receiving the precious seal of the Dharma King. This sutra is also the **Pure, Clear, Ocean-Like Eye of the Thus Comes Ones of the Ten Directions.** This refers to pure wisdom. The "eye" represents wisdom.

Sutra:

"It is also called 'The Cause for Saving a Relative': to rescue Ananda and the bhikshuni Nature, who is now in this assembly, so that they obtain the bodhi mind and enter the sea of pervasive knowledge.

Commentary:

It is also called "The Cause for Saving a Relative": to rescue Ananda. The Buddha was related to Ananda; they were cousins. He wanted to save Ananda from the difficulty he got into with Matangi's daughter. He also rescued **the bhikshuni Nature, who is now in this assembly.** The bhikshuni Nature was Matangi's daughter. She was, by now, a fourth-stage arhat in the assembly. **They obtain the bodhi mind and enter the sea of pervasive knowledge.** These two people have attained levels of enlightenment. "Pervasive knowledge" is as in "One of Proper and Pervasive Knowledge," one of the titles of the Buddhas. "Proper knowledge" is knowing that the mind gives rise to the myriad things. "Pervasive knowledge" is knowing that the myriad things are only from the mind.

G3   Cultivation of the nature.

Sutra:

"It is also called 'The Tathagata's Secret Cause of Cultivation, His Certification to the Complete Meaning.'

Commentary:

It is also called "The Tathagata's Secret Cause." It has another name, which indicates that it is the most secret dharma door of the Thus Come One. It is the cause of his **Cultivation, His Certification to the Complete Meaning.** Through cultivation of it, one certifies to the fruition and fathoms the most fundamental principle. This is another name for this sutra.

G4   Wonderfully important.

Sutra:

"It is also called 'The Great Pervasive Method, the Wonderful Lotus Flower King, the Dharani Mantra which is the Mother of all Buddhas of the Ten Directions.'

Commentary:

It is also called "The Great Pervasive Method." This is a dharma. It is the greatest dharma; it pervades the ten directions and is boundlessly vast. **The Wonderful Lotus Flower King** is an analogy for the *Shurangama Sutra.* **The Dharani Mantra which is the Mother of all Buddhas of the Ten Directions** refers to the Shurangama Mantra. All the Buddhas of the ten directions are born from the Shurangama Mantra. "Dharani" is a Sanskrit word which means to "encompass and hold." It encompasses all aspects of the dharma; it holds limitless meanings. Another meaning is that it encompasses the three karmas of body, mouth, and mind so that no violations are made by them. With your body you do not kill, steal, or lust. With your mind you are not greedy, angry, or stupid. With your mouth you do not indulge in loose speech, harsh speech, lying, or gossip. You do not commit any of these ten evil deeds. And it holds the limitless dharma doors of all the Buddhas. That's another way to explain "dharani."

G5   Cause and effect.

Sutra:

"It is also called 'The Foremost Shurangama, Sections and Phrases for Anointing the Crown of the Head, and All Bodhisattvas' Myriad Practices.'

Commentary:

The Foremost Shurangama. This is the first and foremost of durable dharmas. It is a strong and firm dharma. **Sections and Phrases for Anointing the Crown of the Head** refers to the Shurangama Mantra. If you recite it, your karmic obstacles will very quickly be eradicated. Very soon you will obtain wisdom. Earlier, in his verse, Ananda said of it:

> The wonderfully deep dharani,
>   the unmoving honored one,
> The foremost Shurangama King
>   is seldom found in the world.
> It melts away my upside-down thoughts
>   gathered in a million kalpas.
> So I needn't endure asamkhyeya aeons
>   to obtain the dharma body.

The Shurangama Mantra can invisibly anoint you on the crown of the head and thereby eradicate your upside-down thoughts that have gone on for limitless aeons. There is no need to have to pass through three great asamkhyeya aeons before you obtain the dharma body.

And All Bodhisattvas' Myriad Practices are contained within this sutra.

G6   General answer.

Sutra:

"Thus should you respectfully uphold it."

Commentary:

Ananda, you should rely on this dharma in your cultivation. **Thus should you respectfully uphold it.**

D3   Those whose conditions are opportune obtain benefit.
E1   A description of those who hear.

Sutra:

After this was said, Ananda and all in the great assembly immediately received the Thus Come One's instruction in the secret seal, the meaning of Bwo Da La, and heard these names for the complete meaning of this sutra.

Commentary:

After this was said, after the Buddha finished explaining the names of this sutra, **Ananda and all in the great assembly immediately received the Thus Come One's instruction in the secret seal.** Everyone simultaneously took in the Thus Come One's teaching about the secret seal, **the meaning of Bwo Da La.** "Bwo Da La," again, is the great white canopy. They fathomed its wonderful meaning. **And** they **heard these names for the complete meaning of this sutra.** These names were the most comprehensive, the most ultimate, the most thoroughly meaningful titles.

E2   Their sudden enlightenment to dhyana.

Sutra:

They were suddenly enlightened to dhyana, advanced in their cultivation to the sagely position, and increased their

understanding of the wonderful principle. Their minds were focused and serene.

Commentary:

They were suddenly enlightened to dhyana. "Dhyana" is a Sanskrit word which means "cultivation of thought." "Suddenly enlightened" means that their awakening was immediate and swift. They **advanced in their cultivation to the sagely position.** The "sagely position" refers to the ultimate one – Buddhahood. They **increased their understanding of the wonderful principle.** This means that their wisdom increased. Each person's wisdom became further developed. **Their minds were focused and serene.** There was nothing cluttering their minds. They were clear and open. They were about to reach the fundamental substance of the nature of the treasury of the Thus Come One.

E3   Gradual certification to the second fruition.

Sutra:

Ananda cut off and cast aside six sections of subtle afflictions in his cultivation of the mind in the triple realm.

Commentary:

At this point, Ananda is certified to the second fruition of arhatship. **Ananda cut off and cast aside six sections of subtle afflictions in his cultivation of the mind in the triple realm.** He has already cut off the view-delusions, and now he severs the first six sections of the desire realm's thought-delusions. There are eighty-one thought-delusions in all, nine divisions with nine sections each. These afflictions are called "subtle" because it is not at all easy to detect them. It's hard to perceive them within one's self-nature, but now Ananda has been able to cut away some of this affliction.

CHAPTER 4

The Seven Destinies

C2   Aiding the path: specific explanation of the important dharma of protecting the samadhi.

DI   Discusses the seven destinies and urges separation from them in order to caution those of the future.

EI   Ananda requests.

FI   Expresses gratitude for prior teaching and traces benefit gained.

Sutra:

He arose from his seat, bowed at the Buddha's feet, placed his palms together respectfully, and said to the Buddha, "The great, awesome and virtuous World Honored One, whose compassionate sound knows no limit, has well instructed living beings as to their extremely subtle submersion in delusion and has caused me on this day to become blissful in body and mind and to obtain enormous benefit.

Commentary:

Then, Ananda **arose from his seat**. Because he had cut through some of his subtle afflictions upon hearing what the Buddha had to say, he got up at this point, **bowed at the Buddha's feet, placed his palms together respectfully, and said to the Buddha, "The great, awesome and virtuous World Honored One, whose compassionate sound knows no limit, has well instructed living beings."** "Great awesomeness" subdues living beings. Many living beings are stubborn and obstinate. They don't believe anything you tell them. They don't believe in cause and effect, they don't believe in the cycle of rebirth, they don't believe in retributions. So the Buddha, devising good and clever expedients, uses awesome virtue. With his awesomeness, which can be overwhelming, he subdues living beings. Virtue, on the other hand, gathers in living beings. So this phrase represents the two aspects of subduing and gathering in. He gathers in living beings who have faith and are receptive. His virtue is like a magnet that attracts iron filings, which represent the living beings he gathers in. The Buddha's compassionate voice has no limits. It is unhindered, reaching everywhere to rescue all. He **has well instructed living beings as to their extremely subtle submersion in delusion.** Originally living beings didn't even realize they were hindered by subtle delusions, so the Buddha pointed it out to them. **And** he **has caused me,** Ananda, **on this day to become blissful in body and mind.** I am experiencing physical and mental joy. I am unspeakably happy. **And** he has caused me **to obtain enormous benefit.** I've never known such tremendous benefit.

F2　He asks about the destinies.

Sutra:

"**World Honored One, if the wonderful brightness of this truly pure and wonderful mind is basically all-pervading, then everything on the great earth, including the grasses and trees, the wriggling worms and tiny forms of life are originally true suchness and are themselves the Thus Come One – the Buddha's true body.**

Commentary:

World Honored One, if the wonderful brightness, of this truly pure and wonderful mind is basically all-pervading – if, in fact, it pervades the dharma realm, then it is perfect without any excess or deficiency. **Then everything on the great earth, including the grasses and trees, the wriggling worms and tiny forms of life** are part of that. "Grasses and trees" are considered insentient beings. "Wriggling worms and tiny forms of life" are the smallest of the sentient realm. They don't have much awareness. They can move, but not far, and their perception is quite limited. Nonetheless, they **are originally true suchness and are themselves the Thus Come One – the Buddha's true body.** They are all replete with the true substance of a Buddha – the capacity to become a Buddha.

Sutra:

"Since the Buddha's body is true and real, how can there also be hells, hungry ghosts, animals, asuras, humans, gods, and other paths of rebirth? World Honored One, do these paths exist naturally of themselves, or are they created by living beings' falseness and habits?

Commentary:

Since the Buddha's body is true and real, how can there also be hells, hungry ghosts, animals, asuras, humans, gods, and other paths of rebirth? How do you explain the existence of these paths? **World Honored One, do these paths exist naturally of themselves, or are they created by living beings' falseness and habits?** Have the six paths of rebirth always been in existence or do living beings create them? I don't understand the principle here.

F3   Specifically asks about the hells.

Sutra:

"World Honored One, the bhikshuni Precious Lotus Fragrance, for example, received the bodhisattva precepts and then indulged in lustful desire, saying that sexual acts did not involve killing or stealing and that they carried no karmic retribution. But after saying this, her female organs caught fire, and then the raging blaze spread throughout all her joints as she fell into the Relentless Hell alive.

Commentary:

"Why do I say I don't understand the principle behind the six paths?" Ananda continues. **World Honored One, the bhikshuni**

Precious Lotus Fragrance, for example, received the bodhisattva precepts and then indulged in lustful desire, saying that sexual acts did not involve killing or stealing. This bhikshuni received the bodhisattva precepts, but she did not uphold them. She had sex on the sly. Having done this, what do you suppose she said? She had a pretty speech ready. She lied. She said that sex didn't involve killing or stealing. "It's not murder. It's not theft. You're not stealing anyone's things. It's just an enjoyment between men and women, a bliss that they share. What crime is there in that? Although the Buddha told us to refrain from it, I don't think that restraint is necessary in this case. It doesn't matter. It's no big sin. What could be wrong with men and women experiencing such a blissful encounter?" That was her general line of reasoning. She was really emphatic about it, too. She said of such sexual experiences **that they carried no karmic retribution.** "As to sex," she said, "have it as much as you want. The more the better. It doesn't matter." Thus it was that she actually advocated sexual desire. She was a bhikshuni and yet she was promoting sex.

But after saying this, her female organs caught fire, and then the raging blaze spread throughout all her joints. It doesn't matter, huh? In her female organs a fire sprang up. Terrible, wouldn't you say? I believe by then she was being burned so fiercely that she screamed and cried. She was no longer rationalizing that her conduct incurred no offense. Once her female organs were ablaze, the fire spread to all her limbs and joints. That's because during the sexual act men and women feel a sense of pleasure and contentment throughout their entire body. They take this as pleasure, not realizing that such abandonment is just the next thing to death. What's really happening is that they are going to die a little sooner, just die a little sooner. Plunging into such situations, they totally abandon themselves, to the point that they just want to die – both men and women. To die a little sooner is just fine, they feel. But actually they are drilling their way into the hells; they are burrowing into the hells. The bhikshuni's joints caught fire because sexual desire belongs to the element fire. At its peak there is a kind of fire involved. So we speak of the "fire of desire." The blaze was raging so that fire extinguishers and even the entire three-alarm crew would have been useless. Why is that? It's because the fire came from her own heavy sexual desire. No amount of water could quench it.

What happened to her then? There wasn't any other road to take at that point. **She fell into the Relentless Hell alive.** In the Relentless Hell, there are no lapses in time at all. There are no breaks. Also, its space is uninterrupted, in that one person fills it, and many people fill it. It's not roomy there, whether you're alone or in a crowd. Further, one knows not how many great aeons pass by while one continuously experiences bitter suffering there. There are no interruptions in time or in space. The extreme suffering is unintermittent. Birth and death are uninterrupted.

When this bhikshuni got to that hell, what do you suppose she found? There were iron-beaked birds and iron-mouthed worms that burrowed in and out of her limbs and joints. The place that received special attention was, of course, her female organs. These creatures would drill their way in and then drill their way back out. Each time they did this, their attack would kill her. But then a clever wind would blow – that wind is a special feature of the hells – and revive her. So in a single day and night she would experience tens of thousands of births and deaths. She would die and be revived, die and be revived, again and again, uncountably many times.

In addition, the hells are specially equipped for people who are fond of sexual desire. One of the implements is a copper pillar. It is red-hot because a fire blazes within it. However, when one who is fond of sexual desire looks at that hot pillar, one does not see it as such. When a man looks at the pillar, he sees a woman. When a woman looks at the pillar, it is a man. In fact, they see that pillar as their former boyfriend or girlfriend. So they race towards it and, unaware it is a copper pillar, they madly embrace it. The red-hot copper pillar then fries them to a crisp. As if that weren't enough, out of the corner of their eye they see a bed. Actually, it's an iron bed which is also red hot. But what the person sees is a former boyfriend or girlfriend on the bed. They run to the bed and get burned again. Why? Because their sexual karma is so heavy that every way they turn they must undergo this retribution. This is the kind of retribution the bhikshuni Precious Lotus Fragrance had to undergo. She experienced the hells while still alive. Could she have continued to state that the sexual act did not involve killing or stealing and that it incurred no retribution? Once she began experiencing the retribution, it was too late. She wasn't sorry soon enough. This happened at the time when the Buddha was in the world. There was a bhikshuni who was this lax. It's not just nowadays that bhikshunis are sometimes lax; it happened even during the Buddha's time.

Sutra:

"And there were the Mighty King Crystal and the bhikshu Good Stars. Crystal exterminated the Gautama clan and Good Stars lied and said he'd realized that all dharmas are empty. They both sank into the Relentless Hell alive.

Commentary:

And there were the Mighty King Crystal and the bhikshu Good Stars. Crystal exterminated the Gautama clan. King Crystal and the Buddha were supposedly relatives, though in fact they were not. King Crystal's father, also a king, wanted to marry into the Gautama clan. Since the Gautama clan was a more honorable one than the King's, the Gautama people did not like the idea. No one wanted to give a daughter to the King in marriage, but they didn't dare refuse outright, because the King was powerful. A refusal might have resulted in big trouble. Finally they decided among themselves to send one of their servant girls, a particularly beautiful one, and pretend she was of the Gautama clan. King Crystal was an offspring of that marriage.

Once, while that king was still a child, someone built a temple for the Buddha, complete with an elaborate dharma seat. When the seat was finished, but before the Buddha himself had ascended the platform to sit on it and speak dharma, the child who was to be King

Crystal climbed up and sat on it. The Buddha's disciples and the donors who saw him all scolded him, saying, "You're the son of a slave, how dare you sit in the Buddha's seat?" Hearing them call him that, he was outraged, and he said to his attendant, "Wait until I'm the King and then remind me of what was said here today, lest I forget it. People from the Gautama clan say I'm the son of a slave. Remind me of that. I intend to get even."

Later, when he was King, his attendant did remind him, and the King issued an edict that the entire Gautama clan was to be exterminated, including the Buddha himself. When Mahamaudgalyayana got wind of this, he went to the Buddha to report. "We have to think of a way to save them," he said. But the Buddha didn't say anything. So Maudgalyayana loosed his spiritual powers, put five hundred members of the Gautama clan into his precious bowl, and sent them to the heavens. He thought they'd be safe there. When the King had completed the extermination, Maudgalyayana told Shakyamuni Buddha, "I've got five hundred Gautamans in my bowl stashed away in the heavens, so the clan isn't totally gone after all. I'll bring them down now and let them go." But when he'd recalled them and took a look in his bowl, he found nothing there but blood. "Why was I unable to save them?" asked the puzzled Maudgalyayana. He wanted the Buddha to explain the causes and conditions.

"Ah, you don't know," said the Buddha. "On the causal ground, a long time ago, at a place where the weather was hot, there was a pool with schools of fish in it. The two leaders of the schools were named 'Bran' and 'Many Tongues.' The water in the pool evaporated in the intense heat, and since the people in the area didn't have anything else to eat, they ate the fish. In the end there was just a mud-hole, but even then they noticed a movement in the mud. Digging in, they found the two big fish-kings – Bran and Many Tongues. At that time, I, Shakyamuni Buddha, was a child among these people – who were later to become the Gautama clan. Seeing that the two fish were about to be devoured alive, I beat them over the head three times with a club to knock them out first."

That's why in his life as a Buddha, he had to endure a three-day headache as retribution. "Further, the fish, Bran, was the present King Crystal, and the fish, Many Tongues, was his attendant who reminded him of the words spoken by the Gautama clan to the King as a child. So it was fated that he would exterminate the Gautama clan." Even though Shakyamuni had become a Buddha, he could not rescue his people from the fixed karma they were destined to repay.

The bhikshu Good Stars was forever voicing his deviant knowledge and deviant views. When he spoke dharma, he did not speak in accord with what the Buddha taught. He made up his own. For instance, the Buddha instructed us to refrain from killing, but this bhikshu's instruction was, "It's not necessary. Why should we refrain from killing? Birth and death goes on and on for living beings, and some of them are especially intended for people to eat. If you don't eat them, what use will they be left alive? They don't have any sense." In this way he countered the Buddha's admonishment not to take life. This bhikshu had originally left home under the Buddha, but later he disagreed with the dharma the Buddha spoke. Whatever the Buddha said he found questionable, and he was able to influence a lot of the less intelligent bhikshus to go along with him. They began believing him. "Right!" they said. "What he says makes sense. What's the crime in killing?" It was much the same situation as with the bhikshuni Precious Lotus Fragrance. "We just take what we need; it's not that we steal. If we have something, then we don't need to take it. But if you don't take what you need, how can you get by in this life?" That's what he said about stealing. He thought of ways to counter the five most basic precepts established by the Buddha. **Good Stars lied and said he'd realized that all dharmas are empty.** His best line was, "Everything is empty. Killing is empty, and stealing is empty, since there isn't anything at all to begin with: There's no substance to karma. You talk about creating karma? Then bring out your 'karma' and show it to me. It doesn't exist!"

They both sank into the Relentless Hell alive. They didn't even wait until they died to fall into the hells. King Crystal, bhikshu Good Stars, and bhikshuni Precious Lotus Fragrance experienced hell in their physical bodies while still alive. So Ananda asks the Buddha about these causes and conditions.

Sutra:

"Are these hells fixed places, or do they arise spontaneously? Is it that each individual undergoes whatever kind of karma he or she creates? I only hope the Buddha will be compassionate and instruct those of us who do not understand this. May he cause all beings who uphold the precepts to positively and respectfully receive this determination upon hearing it and be careful and clear, free from any violations."

Commentary:

Are these hells fixed places, or do they arise spontaneously? Since bhikshuni Precious Lotus Fragrance, bhikshu Good Stars, and King Crystal all fell into the hells alive, Ananda brings them up as examples and then asks if the hells are in a fixed and certain place. **Is it that each individual undergoes whatever kind of karma he or she creates?** Each of these three people had to undergo retribution in accord with the kind of karma they created. What is the principle involved here? Are the hells prepared in advance for them, or do they make their own? Where do hells come from? How do they relate to the creation of karma and the undergoing of retribution? Are the hells public facilities like prisons, or are they private cells? **"I only hope the Buddha will be compassionate and instruct those of us who do not understand this.** I'm totally uninformed on this matter," says Ananda. "I'm as innocent as a child when it comes to this. **May he cause all beings who uphold the precepts to positively and respectfully receive this determination upon hearing it.** I hope they will all listen and obey the decisive instructions offered by the Buddha. I hope they will **be careful and clear, free from any violations.** May they cultivate with the utmost purity and be very cautious and clean, so that in no way do they transgress the pure precepts. Please, Buddha, explain this for us."

E2 The Thus Come One answers in detail.
FI Praises him and promises to speak.

Sutra:

The Buddha said to Ananda, "What a good question! You want to keep all living beings from entering into deviant views. You should listen attentively now and I will explain this matter for you.

Commentary:

When the Buddha heard Ananda ask how to help living beings of the future guard the precepts carefully, he was extremely happy. **The Buddha said to Ananda, "What a good question!** This is a most appropriate question. It's exactly the doctrine you should be asking about. **You want to keep all living beings from entering into deviant views.** This can keep them from falling into deviant knowledge and views and help them to obtain proper knowledge and views instead. **You should listen attentively now and I will explain this matter for you."**

F2 Clarifies the destinies.
G1 A general explanation of the basic principle of rising and falling according to emotion and reason.
H1 He enumerates the accumulated habits that divide emotion and thought.

Sutra:

"Actually, Ananda, all living beings are fundamentally true and pure, but because of their false views they give rise to the falseness of habits, which are divided into an internal aspect and an external aspect.

Commentary:

Actually, Ananda, all living beings are fundamentally true and pure, but based on the truth they give rise to falseness: they produce ignorance. From ignorance they give rise to false views. **Because of their false views they give rise to the falseness of**

habits. These false habits pertain to their internal physical being and to their external environment. They **are divided into an internal aspect and an external aspect.** There are false habits that occur outside the physical body and false habits that occur within it also.

H2　He specifically describes the rising or sinking at death.
I1　The internal aspect belongs to emotion and so causes one to fall.

Sutra:

"**Ananda, the internal aspect refers to what occurs inside living beings. Because of love and defilement, they produce the falseness of emotions. When these emotions accumulate without cease, they can create the fluids of love.**

Commentary:

Ananda, the internal aspect refers to what occurs inside living beings. This means within the physical body. What is within the physical body? **Because of love and defilement, they produce the falseness of emotions.** There is love and desire and various defilements. From the love and defilement, false emotions come up. **These emotions accumulate without cease.** The emotions pile up day by day, month after month. They become abundant and do not stop. The emotions of love are ever-present. **They can create the fluids of love.**

Sutra:

"**That is why living beings' mouths water when they think about delicious food. When they think about a deceased person, either with fondness or with anger, tears will flow from their eyes. When they are greedy for wealth and jewels, a current of lust will course through their hearts. When confronted with a smooth and supple body, their minds become attached to lustful conduct and from both male and female organs will come spontaneous secretions.**

Commentary:

That is why living beings' mouths water when they think about delicious food. Why is it said that once living beings have love and defilement they develop emotions which eventually, if not stopped, will produce fluids of love? Some examples will substantiate this. Just thinking about eating some delicacy makes people salivate. It happens because of their gluttonous thought. **When they think about a deceased person** – a friend or close relative, someone with whom they had the most affinities – **either with fondness or with anger, tears will flow from their eyes.** The person who has died was so close to them that they give rise to anger – resentment or even rage – and think, "He was so fine. Why did he have to die so soon? Things were so good between us. Why him?" Excessively fond regard or tremendous resentment both cause a person to cry. **When they are greedy for wealth and jewels, a current of lust will course through their hearts.** They dream about getting rich, and in their hearts a flow of lust is stirred. **When confronted with a smooth and supple body, their minds become attached to lustful conduct and from both male and female organs will come spontaneous secretions.** When they see a particularly attractive person they have thoughts of sexual desire. With that, their essence flows of itself. Strange, isn't it?

Sutra:

"**Ananda, although the kinds of love differ, their flow and oppression is the same. With this moisture, one cannot ascend, but will naturally fall. This is called the 'internal aspect.'**

Commentary:

Ananda, although the kinds of love differ – although there are various kinds of love – **their flow and oppression is the same.** Their currents and enticements are the same. **With this moisture, one cannot ascend, but will naturally fall.** Emotion sends one down. **This is called the "internal aspect."**

---

12   The external aspect belongs to thought and so one is able to ascend.

Sutra:

"**Ananda, the external aspect refers to what happens outside living beings. Because of longing and yearning, they invent the**

fallacy of discursive thought. When this reasoning accumulates without cease, it can create ascending vapors.

Commentary:

Ananda, the external aspect refers to what happens outside living beings. Because of longing and yearning, they invent the fallacy of discursive thought. The "longing and yearning" also refer to love. The "discursive thought" is in fact false thought, which accumulates. **When this reasoning accumulates without cease, it can create ascending vapors.** You think of it from all angles. You think about it today and you continue thinking about it tomorrow. You thought about it during your last life; you're thinking about it in this life. You thought about it in former kalpas and you think about it now in this kalpa. No one knows how long you've been thinking. And you never rest. However, from this continual thinking, a special response can occur, which is an "uplifting (ascending) motion of spirit."

Sutra:

"That is why when living beings uphold the prohibitive precepts in their minds, their bodies will be buoyant and feel light and clear. When they uphold mantra seals in their minds, they will command a heroic and resolute perspective. When they have the desire in their minds to be born in the heavens, in their dreams they will have thoughts of flying and ascending. When they cherish the Buddhalands in their minds, then the sagely realms will appear in a shimmering vision, and they will serve the good and wise advisors with little thought for their own lives.

Commentary:

That is why when living beings uphold the prohibitive precepts in their minds, their bodies will be buoyant and feel light and clear. This can happen to any living being. "Prohibitive" refers to things which one cannot do. These precepts keep people from doing bad things, from creating evil. Don't do the things you should not do, and then you are upholding the precepts in your mind. If your mind holds the precepts, then your body will experience a sensation of lightness. You feel almost like you're floating when you walk. And your mind will be extremely pure and clean.

When they uphold mantra seals in their minds, they will command a heroic and resolute perspective. If you specialize in holding the mantras in your mind – there are many mantras and this refers to any one of them – you will have a response. The "seal" refers to the mind-to-mind seal as it pertains to mantras. When you recite the mantra, a certain response occurs. If you are a specialist in mantras, you will have a heroic air about you when you gaze around. Your glance will be powerful and determined. You will know no fear.

When they have the desire in their minds to be born in the heavens, in their dreams they will have thoughts of flying and ascending. In your dreams you'll be able to fly and to soar into empty space. That's all because you want to go to the heavens.

When they cherish the Buddhalands in their minds, then the sagely realms will appear in a shimmering vision, and they will serve the good and wise advisors with little thought for their own lives. If you'd like to get born in the Land of Ultimate Bliss, or some other Buddhaland, then the Western Pure Land will secretly appear with its pools of seven jewels and waters of the eight meritorious virtues, with its white cranes, egrets, parrots, and kalavinka birds, and with a myriad other states. It won't be something others can see, but you will see it. Others will be unaware of it, but you will know. You will be able to see the Eastern Crystal World of Medicine Master Buddha as well. You will get to serve these good and wise advisors. You can draw near to them, respect them, and make offerings to them. And you will have total disregard for your former lifestyle. Your very life itself will seem unimportant when faced with this opportunity to serve and draw near those good and wise advisors. Nothing you might do will seem as important to you as serving these sages.

Sutra:

"Ananda, although the thought varies, the lightness and uplifting is the same. With flight and ascension, one will not sink, but will naturally become transcendent. This is called the 'external aspect.'

Commentary:

Ananda, although the thought varies, the lightness and uplifting is the same. Although the things one thinks about are different, the comfort and light ease that one attains, the feeling of floating, is the same. **With flight and ascension, one will not sink, but will naturally become transcendent.** With this upward movement one will not fall downward. "Transcendent" means rising above everything, surpassing all. **This is called the "external aspect."**

H3   He specifically describes the rising or sinking at death.
I1   The appearances that manifest at the time of death.

Sutra:

"Ananda, all beings in the world are caught up in the continuity of birth and death. Birth happens because of their habitual tendencies; death comes through flow and change. When they are on the verge of dying, but when the final warmth has not left their bodies, all the good and evil they have done in that life suddenly and simultaneously manifests. They experience the intermingling of two habits: an abhorrence of death and an attraction to life.

Commentary:

The Buddha calls again: **Ananda,** do you know that **all beings in the world are caught up in the continuity of birth and death?** They get born and die, die and get reborn, again and again in a never-ending cycle. They spin on the wheel of the six paths of rebirth. **Birth happens because of their habitual tendencies.** Birth is something living beings want. They tend toward it. **Death comes through flow and change.** When they die, they follow their karmic retribution to turn again in rebirth. According to the kind of karma they have created, they will revolve on the wheel.

When they are on the verge of dying, but when the final warmth has not left their bodies, all the good and evil they have done in that life suddenly and simultaneously manifests. "The final warmth has not left their bodies" means that the six consciousnesses and the seventh consciousness have passed out of the body, but the eighth consciousness still remains. Its passage will be marked by warmth, that is, the place on the body where the eighth consciousness leaves will be warm to the touch. For instance, if the eighth consciousness leaves through the soles of the feet, that spot will be warm. If it leaves from the legs, the legs will be warm. If it departs from the waist, the waist will be warm. If it goes out the top of the head, the top of the head will be warm. That's the "final warmth" that's mentioned here in the text. Before the eighth consciousness goes, it is referred to as the "present skandha body." Once it leaves the body it is the body between the skandhas, or "intermediate skandha body." So the text here refers to the present skandha body, before it has left the physical body. If one cultivates well, the skandha body is a Buddha. If one does not cultivate, it is a ghost. So when people ask, "Are there really ghosts?" they must first ask themselves if there are Buddhas. If they know there are Buddhas, then of course there are ghosts as well. If you are not sure that there are Buddhas or ghosts, ask yourself if there are people. If you acknowledge the fact that there are people, then you will know that there are also Buddhas and ghosts, because they are all different aspects of the same thing.

After one dies then, the eighth consciousness is called the intermediate skandha body. Before one dies it is called the present skandha body. It is also known as the "soul" and as the "Buddha-nature." When a person is on the verge of death, the good and evil he or she has done is revealed and a reckoning is at hand. Depending on what one did, one will have to undergo retribution or reward. If one did good, one can get rebirth in the heavens; if one did evil, one falls into the hells. If you did more in the way of good deeds and meritorious acts, then you can leave from your head. If you did more in the way of committing crimes and creating offenses, then you'll leave from your feet. Obviously then, to leave from the upper part of one's body means one will gain a higher rebirth, whereas to leave from the lower part means one is going to fall. One's kind of rebirth is evident at death. **They experience the intermingling of two habits: an abhorrence of death and an attraction to life.** They are repelled and attracted when confronted with death and birth.

I2   The scale of ascending and falling.
J1   Ascent with no fall.

Sutra:

"Endowed solely with thought, they will fly and can certainly be reborn in the heavens above. If they fly from the heart, and if they have blessings and wisdom, as well as pure vows, then their hearts will spontaneously open and they will see the Buddhas of the ten directions and all their pure lands and they will be reborn in whichever one they wish.

Commentary:

Endowed solely with thought, means that the person has no emotion, no *yin*, but has only reason, which belongs to *yang*. "Solely" means it is present to the exclusion of any other mental process. There is only thought, nothing else. It is a kind of true sincerity.

People's thoughts are such that they govern what happens. For instance, eating, drinking, and smoking all come about based on thought. First one thinks about it and then one does it. Conversely, if one decides not to do something, that thing won't be done. "If I want to eat something good, I go buy some good things to eat. If I want something nice to wear, I go buy it." The same is true for drinking. If one is thirsty, one goes out and gets some brandy, whiskey, rum, or beer. Just mentioning it is enough to make some people's mouths water. People who like to smoke are always mulling over the best brands of cigarettes. They've always got their mind on these things. Then they meet a good and wise advisor who tells them to stop smoking, stop eating meat, and stop drinking. Obediently they stop, but since heir minds habitually run to these things, they start having dreams about smoking cigarettes, drinking liquor, and eating meat. They don't actually do these things in their waking hours, but because the thought remains, they dream of indulging in them at night. When they awaken they regret their conduct in the dream. "I've already stopped doing that. Why would I resort to it in a dream?" they admonish themselves. As I've told you before, it's difficult to remain in control of yourself when you're sick and even more difficult to do so in a dream.

Endowed solely with thought, **they will fly and can certainly be reborn in the heavens above. If they fly from the heart, and if they have blessings and wisdom, as well as pure vows, then their hearts will spontaneously open.** However, if one's thought is of the heart and one does not wish to be reborn in the heavens, but instead keeps blessings and wisdom in mind at all times, then, even better than to be born in the heavens, one may have made pure vows to be reborn in a Buddhaland. The Buddha is known as the Doubly Complete One; that is, he is complete in both blessings and wisdom. Aware of this, one wants to cultivate blessings and wisdom oneself.

> But to cultivate blessings and not wisdom
>   is to be like an elephant wearing a necklace.
> And to cultivate wisdom and not blessings
>   is to be an arhat with an empty begging bowl.

The necklace is handsome and valuable, but it's all the elephant has; it doesn't have any thought-power, any wisdom. If you seek wisdom in your cultivation by studying the sutras and sitting in meditation, but fail to plant any blessings and are unable to practice giving, then you'll end up smart but hungry. To plant blessings means one should do meritorious and virtuous deeds, especially on the Buddhist holidays – the birthdays and anniversaries of the Buddhas and Bodhisattvas – or on your own birthday, or on the first and the fifteenth of the lunar month. If you practice giving and create merit before the Triple Jewel, then you will amass blessings. If you do not do meritorious and virtuous deeds, then you won't have any blessings. If you concentrate on wisdom and don't develop blessings, then no one will make offerings to you when you become an arhat. That's because on the cause ground you did not make offerings in your turn. So if you want people to make offerings to you when the time comes, you should make offerings to them now. It's as simple as the principle of

> Planting melons, you get melons.
> Planting beans, you get beans.

"Pure vows" means that before the Buddhas and Bodhisattvas you say:

> I vow to be born in the Western Pure Land
> With the nine grades of lotuses as my parents.
> When the flower opens I will see the Buddha
>   and awaken to non-production.
> Non-retreating bodhisattvas will be my companions.

Or you may wish to be reborn in the Eastern Land. Any such vow is a pure one. "Their hearts will spontaneously open" means they will awaken **and they will see the Buddhas of the ten directions and all their pure lands and they will be reborn in whichever one they wish.** If a person has blessings, wisdom, and vows, then at the end of his or her life he or she will see the Buddhas of the ten directions and be able to be reborn in whichever pure land he or she wants.

Sutra:

"When they have more thought than emotion, they are not quite as ethereal and so they become flying immortals, great mighty ghost kings, space traveling-yakshas, or earth-traveling rakshasas who roam the form heavens, going where they please without obstruction.

Commentary:

When they have more thought than emotion, they are not quite as ethereal. "Emotion" can be defined as sentience. It is said that,

> Those with sentience and those lacking sentience
> Have the sane potential for knowledge of all modes.

"Sentience," in turn, is defined as having thought and feeling. Insentient objects include grasses, trees, and so forth. It is said,

> People are not grass and trees,
> Who among them doesn't have emotion?

That's just a way of rationalizing. "Everybody's got emotion." True, everyone does. And when is it evident? In youth. That's why the character "emotion" (情 *qing*) is made up of the word for mind (心 *xin*) and the character for youth (青 *qing*). When we get right down to it, we're talking here about emotional love. Basically, the word for emotion is not limited to that meaning, but that's the use of it here.

Young men and women talk all the time about love and emotion. Why? Because they don't really know about it. They never finish talking about love and emotion. Day in and day out, month after month, year after year that's the entire topic of conversation. Young people become totally engrossed in emotion. It confuses them. It's said,

> Weighed down by karma and confused by emotion
> One is a common person.

Confusion is a kind of attachment, the inability to let go. Where does emotion come from? From your mind. Where does the mind come from? From your nature. That's why it's said,

> The nature flows out and becomes emotion.
> The emotion flows out into desire.

The "out" means "down." As when,

> The superior person's aims are lofty.
> The petty person's aims are base.

When a person goes down, down, down and reaches the level of desire, then the fire of desire consumes the body. One totally loses control. It happens to both men and women. They lose self-control.

"Thought" is persistent thought. This character also contains the character for "mind." It, too, comes from the mind. At first the mind has not moved, but with thought, something appears in the mind. So the character for thought (想 *xiang*) is the character for "appearance" (相 *xiang*) over the character for "mind" (心 *xin*). Whatever you think about appears. This character is quite descriptive. For instance, you think about drinking, and an image of wine appears in your mind. If you're thinking about eating meat, a piece of meat appears in your mind. It's the same for anything you think about from the affairs of state to your own private matters. The sutras talk about there being no appearance of self, no appearance of others, no appearance of people, and no appearance of a lifespan. But with thought, there are appearances. Is thought right then or wrong? Basically, it, too, is not right. But since people are attached to appearances, they end up with thought.

When the thought is more than the emotion, "they are not quite as ethereal." This can be explained in two ways. It can mean that they don't get far. Their flight is limited. But to hold strictly to that interpretation doesn't exactly fit the context here. A better way to explain it is that their flight is not very much less extensive than the kind of flight described in the previous section. "Not quite as ethereal" then, would mean that they can go quite far. How far? **They become flying immortals.** They are such that,

> In the morning they can roam
>   a hundred thousand miles,
> And in the evening
>   go to nine thousand altars.

Or they become **great mighty ghost kings,** or **space traveling-yakshas, or earth-traveling rakshasas.** These kinds of beings have already been described. They can **roam the form heavens, going where they please without obstruction.** Nothing hinders their travel. Nothing stops them.

Sutra:

"Among them may be some with good vows and good hearts who protect and uphold my dharma. Perhaps they protect the pure precepts by following and supporting those who hold precepts. Perhaps they protect spiritual mantras by following and supporting those who hold mantras. Perhaps they protect Chan samadhi by guarding and comforting those who are patient with dharmas. These beings are close at hand beneath the Thus Come One's seat.

Commentary:

Among them, among the great mighty ghost kings, space-travelling yakshas, and other such beings, **may be some with good vows and good hearts who protect and uphold my dharma.** By "my dharma" Shakyamuni Buddha is referring to the Buddha-dharma. **Perhaps they protect the pure precepts by following and supporting those who hold precepts.** Maybe they make the wholesome vow to guard and uphold the precepts spoken by the Buddhas. Then they will also follow and guard people who hold the precepts. They make sure that everything for these people who uphold the precepts is auspicious and in accord with their wishes. No difficulties or troubles will arise for them. **Perhaps they protect spiritual mantras by following and supporting those who hold mantras.** Maybe they protect the Shurangama Mantra, the Great Compassion Mantra, or any of the other various mantras. This is the kind of resolve they have. They follow along after the people who uphold mantras and protect them day and night. **Perhaps they protect Chan samadhi by guarding and comforting those who are patient with dharmas.** Maybe some of these beings make the good vow that in the future they will protect people who investigate Chan and sit in meditation, so that they obtain Chan samadhi. They help them obtain patience with phenomena so that they can endure anything whatsoever. **These beings are close at hand beneath the Thus Come One's seat.** These beings who have made good vows and are dharma protectors are always able to be beneath the Thus Come One's seat and to hear the dharma spoken.

J2   No ascent and no fall.

Sutra:

"When their thought and emotion are of equal proportions, they cannot fly and they do not fall, but are born in the human realm. If their thought is bright, their wits are keen. If their emotion is dark, their wits are dull.

Commentary:

With ninety-percent thought and ten percent emotion, one gains a higher rebirth. With ninety percent emotion and ten percent thought, it is certain that one will fall into the hells. Now **when their thought and emotion are of equal proportions, they cannot fly and they do not fall, but are born in the human realm.** With fifty percent thought and fifty percent emotion, there is a balance. They can't fly to the heavens to be a god or an immortal, and they can't fall into the hells to become a hungry ghost. Where do they end up? Right where you and I are now. To be born into the human realm does not mean one will remain forever in the human realm. The human realm is nothing more than a transit stop – a place to transfer to the next place. "From the human realm what will one transfer to?" you wonder. Well, in order to get to the human realm you had to have fifty percent thought and fifty percent emotion. All you have to do is take a look and see if you've got more emotion now or more thought. If you've got more emotion, your next transfer will be to the hells. If you've got more thought, your next transfer will be to the heavens. If you are devoid of emotion, you can transfer to the Buddhas' fruition, for then you are pure *yang*, without any *yin*. If you have ten percent emotion, you have *yin*. If you don't have any emotion, you are pure *yang* and can become a Buddha.

If their thought is bright, their wits are keen. If their emotion is dark, their wits are dull. This is the point of transfer. The more you think, the smarter you get and the more you understand. You attain wisdom if you cultivate and make progress day-by-day. In this way your light grows a little more day-by-day. It keeps increasing until it is the same as the light of the Buddhas. That's what's meant by "if their thoughts are bright, their wits are keen."

Emotion is said to be *yin*, because it is a private matter. Thought is very open and out front, very public and bright. To cultivate, investigate Chan, sit in meditation, study the Buddhadharma, and listen to the sutras are proper activities. From them you will gain keen intelligence. But love and emotion can't be discussed in a crowd. Rather, a man and woman must go to the park or the seashore or beneath a tree alone to speak in whispers. They must slowly talk things over in secret. This is what is meant by emotion being "dark." Things which others cannot see are dark. The darker they get, the less light there is for them to see by, and "their wits are dull." They go into the forest where they can't see the sky. Or they get into cars or on boats. They go to places where there are few people; is to be "dark." This belongs to *yin* and causes people to be stupid and dull-witted. They chat and chat and become stupider and stupider until eventually they fall into a bottomless pit. That's why emotion makes you fall. You talk together until you both slip and fall into the sea of suffering. Then it won't be easy to get out; you'll have to make a tremendous effort. Unless you're lucky enough to have a good and wise advisor who grabs you by the hand and shouts, "Get out!" getting out will be very difficult.

J3   Fall with no ascent.

Sutra:

"When they have more emotion than thought, they enter the animal realm. With heavier emotion, they become fur-bearing beasts; with lighter emotion, they become winged creatures.

Commentary:

When they have more emotion than thought, they enter the animal realm. With heavier emotion, they become fur-bearing beasts. People with heavy emotion end up getting born as cows, horses, sheep and the like. Do you see how dangerous it is? You'd better be careful! That's why I say the *Shurangama Sutra* is so important. This section shows exactly the point at which people and animals cross paths. One wrong step and you end up an animal. If you're off by just a little, then it gets you. **With lighter emotion, they become winged creatures.** This refers to a slight variation in the degree of emotion on the part of these animals. The creatures that fly still have a bit of thought about them. Did you ever wonder why birds are so colorful? It's because when they were human beings, they liked to wear colorful clothes. They would get all dressed up and then constantly admire themselves. The combination of excessive attention to clothing and a lot of emotion with a little thought caused them to fall into the realm of birds. Some birds are really exquisite. They must have been people who dressed especially well. Because of their emotion, they end up as animals, but the degree of their emotion is slightly less than that of beasts, and so they become birds.

Sutra:

"When they have seventy percent emotion and thirty percent thought, they fall beneath the wheel of water into the regions of fire, where they come into contact with steam which is itself like a terrible blaze. In the bodies of hungry ghosts, they are constantly burned by that fire. Even water harms them, and they have nothing to eat or drink for hundreds of thousands of kalpas.

Commentary:

With sixty percent emotion and forty percent thought, one falls into the animal realm. With sixty percent thought and forty percent emotion, one can gain a higher rebirth. Now, **when they have seventy percent emotion and thirty percent thought, they fall**

beneath the wheel of water into the regions of fire, where they come into contact with steam which is itself like a terrible blaze. Beneath the water cycle is fire. Volcanoes are a common example which proves that fire resides beneath the water level. **In the bodies of hungry ghosts, they are constantly burned by that fire.** At that time, they take on the bodies of hungry ghosts, and it would be too late for them if they decided they'd rather be birds or beasts. There are a myriad kinds of hungry ghosts. The worst kind there is to be is the one whose throat is as thin as a needle and whose stomach is as big as a drum. **Even water harms them, and they have nothing to eat or drink for hundreds of thousands of kalpas.** They don't even have a drop of water to drink. Why not? Because their karma is such that when they see water, it turns to a raging fire. Gods see water as crystal. Fish, shrimp, oysters, and things of the sea look upon water as their palace – their home. They live in it and therefore don't see it, in the same way that people live in air but aren't aware of it. If we people didn't have air, we would die. It's said that people must eat to live, but they also must have air to breathe. But do we see air? No. Fish see water as their home, and people see water as water, but ghosts see water as fire. Why don't we see it as fire? If you want to know the difference, you can try being a ghost and find out. But you protest that you'd like to know without having to be a ghost. All right, I can tell you. It's because of karmic obstacles. It's a result of the karma that they themselves created. If you make the karma that sends you into the body of a hungry ghost, then you will perceive water as fire. If you still don't believe it, you can try it out. But if you do, and really turn into a hungry ghost, it will be very difficult to get to be a person again. It won't be easy to return. So now I'm telling you, and the best would be to believe me, because I'm really not cheating you. Then you don't have to go try it out for yourself.

As a hungry ghost one is burned to death, but after a while one revives and then has to go through being burned to death again. In that way, one undergoes birth after birth and death after death as a ghost. Because they see water as fire, the ghosts have nothing to drink, and they can't eat, either. How long does this go on? It goes on for hundreds of thousands of kalpas.

Sutra:

"When they have ninety percent emotion and ten percent thought, they fall through the wheel of fire until their bodies enter wind and fire, in a region where the two interact. With lighter emotion they are born in the Intermittent Hell; with heavier emotion they are born in the Relentless Hell.

Commentary:

When they have ninety percent emotion and ten percent thought, they fall through the wheel of fire until their bodies enter wind and fire, in a region where the two interact. In this place there's not only fire but a wind that whips up the fire so that it burns even more fiercely. **With lighter emotion they are born in the Intermittent Hell; with heavier emotion they are born in the Relentless Hell.**

Sutra:

"When they are possessed entirely of emotion, they sink into the Avichi Hell. If the emotion has gone into their hearts so that they slander the great vehicle, defame the Buddha's pure precepts, speak crazy and false dharma, are greedy for offerings from the faithful, recklessly accept the respect of others, commit the five rebellious acts and the ten major offenses, then they are further reborn in Avichi Hells throughout the ten directions.

Commentary:

When they are possessed entirely of emotion – when they have no thought, only emotion – **they sink into the Avichi Hell. If the emotion has gone into their hearts** – if their minds are totally governed by emotion – **so that they slander the great vehicle**. They make judgments about things with their emotions and as a result they take right to be wrong and wrong to be right. They take black to be white and white to be black. They are totally unreasonable. They always oppose what others say. If you say, "Don't do things that are not good," they come back with, "What's there to be afraid of?" Their motto is "Eat meat, drink wine, and pass the time. The Buddha is only a figment of the imagination." They argue that "Your mind is the Buddha and the Buddha is your mind." That's the kind of deviant knowledge and deviant views they have.

Their views become so deviant that they **defame the Buddha's pure precepts.** "Don't take the precepts," they say. "What do you want to do that for? You end up with a bunch of precepts controlling you. If you don't take the precepts, see how free you'll be." In fact, if one does not take the precepts, it is very, very easy to end up in the hells. Do you call that freedom? But if you receive the precepts and then use them as a guide to govern yourself – if you receive the precepts and then govern yourself by the appearance, the dharma, and the substance of the precepts, it's not so likely that you'll fall into the hells. Even if you do fall into the hells, you'll get out much more quickly. But if you advocate not taking the precepts in order to be free, then when you fall into the hells there's no guarantee when you'll get out again. If you take the precepts, then a long term in the hells gets cut to a short term. It's as if you were a president's aide and broke some major law and were caught. Just a note from the president would suffice to effect your release. Without that help, it might be a long time before you were released. If you have the precepts for protection, then the suffering you have to endure for having committed major offenses will be lessened significantly. So don't outsmart yourself by deciding not to take the precepts. It's better to take the precepts. A living being who receives the Buddha's precepts enters into the position of a Buddha.

Don't slander the Buddha's precepts, and don't **speak crazy and false dharma.** Don't deny cause and effect. Don't say things like "There's no cause and no effect; people are just Buddhas, after all. There's no need to cultivate. Eat meat, drink, and be merry, because no matter what you do, you still can become a Buddha. It's really easy to become a Buddha."

Right, it is easy to become a Buddha, but the way to do it is to get rid of your faults. There aren't any Buddhas who have faults.

They are all pure and undefiled. They didn't become Buddhas by being filthy and full of karmic offenses. They didn't become Buddhas by drinking wine and eating meat. If that's the way it was, then the Buddha would not have had to speak the precepts.

Don't be **greedy for offerings from the faithful.** Don't scheme to get people to believe in you, to give you gifts, to make offerings to you. Don't think about how you'd have more money if you took more disciples. I never discuss money with my disciples. Usually when people take disciples it's made clear from the start that they should give at least fifty or sixty dollars just to take refuge. But I don't pay attention to that kind of thing.

These kinds of beings also **recklessly accept the respect of others.** Or they **commit the five rebellious acts,** which are killing one's father, killing one's mother, killing an arhat, shedding the Buddha's blood, and breaking up the harmony of the Sangha. Or they commit **the ten major offenses,** that is, they violate the ten major bodhisattva precepts. Having committed these grave offenses, **then they are further reborn in Avichi Hells throughout the ten directions.** After they have undergone suffering in the avichi hell of this world they go to avichi hells in every world in the ten directions. Can you imagine how long a time that would take? When this hell is finished, they are transported to another avichi hell. When that avichi hell is destroyed, they move on to the next avichi hell. It's endless. And so Devadatta, the one who tried to compete with the Buddha, fell into the hells alive. He's still suffering in the hells. From the time of Shakyamuni Buddha until now he's been undergoing hellish suffering, but in fact that's just the blink of an eye.

H4   He concludes that there are places where both individual and collective punishment are undergone.

Sutra:

"Although one receives one's due according to the evil karma one has created, a group can undergo an identical lot, and there are definite places where it occurs.

Commentary:

Although one receives one's due according to the evil karma one has created, by slandering the great vehicle dharma masters, by defaming the Buddha, the Dharma, and the Sangha, by committing the five rebellious acts and the ten major offenses, **a group can undergo an identical lot, and there are definite places where it occurs.** Although they fall into the hells because of what they themselves have done – they create the karma and undergo the retribution – still, a group can undergo similar retribution, and it can happen in a fixed and certain place. There are definite places where they create the karma, and there are definite places where they undergo the retribution.

Destiny of Hells

Sutra:

"Ananda, it all comes from the karmic responses which living beings themselves invoke. They create ten habitual causes and undergo six interacting retributions.

Commentary:

Ananda, it all comes from the karmic responses which living beings themselves invoke. They give rise to delusion, create karma, and undergo retribution. **They create ten habitual causes and undergo six interacting retributions.** The retributions are interconnected.

Sutra:

"What are the ten causes? Ananda, the first consists of **habits of lust and reciprocal interactions which give rise to mutual rubbing. When this rubbing continues without cease, it produces a tremendous raging fire within which movement occurs, just as warmth arises between a person's hands when he rubs them together.**

Commentary:

What are the ten causes? Ananda, I will now tell you in detail. **The first consists of habits of lust and reciprocal interactions.** The habits of lust bring men and women together, and their interactions **give rise to mutual rubbing. When this rubbing continues without cease, it produces a tremendous raging fire within which movement occurs.** The light of fire arises between them and has a movement of its own, **just as warmth arises between a person's hands when he rubs them together.**

Sutra:

"Because these two habits set each other ablaze, there come into being the iron bed, the copper pillar, and other such experiences.

Commentary:

Because these two habits. The "two habits" refer to one's past habits of lust which combine with one's present habits of lust. These two habits **set each other ablaze,** and so **there come into being the iron bed, the copper pillar, and other such experiences.** These are the names of specific hells. They are brought into being because people have sexual desire which is too heavy. They have created too much karma involving lust and so they must undergo this retribution.

Sutra:

"Therefore the Thus Come Ones of the ten directions look upon the practice of lust and name it the 'fire of desire.' Bodhisattvas avoid desire as they would a fiery pit.

Commentary:

Therefore the Thus Come Ones of the ten directions look upon the practice of lust and name it the "fire of desire." They tell you that the fire of desire burns up the body. **Bodhisattvas avoid desire as they would a fiery pit.** They see that staying away from lustful activity is as important as avoiding a fiery pit. You don't want to see the fiery pit and deliberately jump into it. If you do, it's for sure you'll burn to death. So bodhisattvas stay far away from lust and sexual desire. They do not give rise to thoughts of sexual desire.

J2   Habits of greed.

Sutra:

"**The second consists of habits of greed and intermingled scheming which give rise to a suction. When this suction becomes dominant and incessant, it produces intense cold and solid ice where freezing occurs, just as a sensation of cold is experienced when a person draws in a blast of wind through his mouth.**

Commentary:

The second consists of habits of greed and intermingled scheming which give rise to a suction. Greed is like a magnet which attracts things to it. **When this suction becomes dominant and incessant** – people who experience insatiable greed are always trying to figure out how to get things and make them their own. When greed reaches this extreme, **it produces intense cold and solid ice where freezing occurs.** These habits produce a sensation of freezing cold, **just as a sensation of cold is experienced when a person draws in a blast of wind through his mouth.**

Sutra:

"**Because these two habits clash together, there come into being chattering, whimpering and shuddering; blue, red, and white lotuses; cold and ice; and other such experiences.**

Therefore the Thus Come Ones of the ten directions look upon excessive seeking and name it 'the water of greed.' Bodhisattvas avoid greed as they would a sea of pestilence.

Commentary:

Because these two habits – one's past greed and one's present greed – **clash together** – the habits of grabbing and seizing feed on one another until **there come into being chattering, whimpering and shuddering.** "Chattering, whimpering, and suffering" is "*cha cha, bwo bwo, lwo lwo*" in Chinese, which indicate the sounds made by beings suffering in these freezing hells when undergoing the tortures of extreme cold. **Blue, red, and white lotuses** indicate the shapes the ice freezes into in these hells. The beings undergo **cold and ice; and other such experiences.**

J3   Habits of arrogance.

Sutra:

"**The third consists of habits of arrogance and resulting friction which give rise to mutual intimidation. When it accelerates without cease, it produces torrents and rapids which create restless waves of water, just as water is produced when a person continuously works his tongue in an effort to taste flavors.**

Commentary:

The third consists of habits of arrogance and resulting friction. "Arrogance" refers to self-satisfaction. One is arrogant when one thinks one is better than others. Such thoughts **give rise to mutual intimidation.** One looks down on others. **When it accelerates without cease, it produces torrents and rapids which create restless waves of water.** This refers to the hell of boiling oil, the hell of rapids, the hell of scalding soup, and so forth. It is **just as water is produced when a person continuously works his tongue in an effort to taste flavors.** Someone keeps trying to taste the flavor of his own mouth. The effort will produce saliva.

Sutra:

"**Because these two habits incite one another, there come into being the river of blood, the river of ashes, the burning sand, the poisonous sea, the molten copper which is poured over one or which must be swallowed, and other such experiences.**

Commentary:

Because these two habits incite one another – arrogant attitudes from the past combine with one's self-satisfaction in the present – **there come into being** many kinds of hells: The hell of the river of blood, the hell of the river of ashes, the hell of the burning sand, the hell of the poisonous sea, the hell of the molten copper which is poured over one, the hell where molten copper must be swallowed, and other such experiences.

Sutra:

"Therefore, the Thus Come Ones of the ten directions look upon self-satisfaction and name it 'drinking the water of stupidity.' Bodhisattvas avoid arrogance as they would a huge deluge.

Commentary:

It's as stinking as a place where a lot of people go to relieve themselves.

J4   Habits of hatred.

Sutra:

"The fourth consists of habits of hatred which give rise to mutual defiance. When this defiance binds one without cease, one's heart becomes so hot that it catches fire, and the molten vapor turns into metal.

"From it is produced the mountain of knives, the iron cudgel, the tree of swords, the wheel of swords, axes and halberds, and spears and saws. It is like the intent to kill surging forth when a person meets a mortal enemy, so that he is roused to action.

Commentary:

The fourth consists of habits of hatred which give rise to mutual defiance. "Defiance" means that you have wronged me and I have wronged you. When this defiance binds one without cease, one's heart becomes so hot that it catches fire, and the molten vapor turns into metal. Your heart feels hot and you give rise to the fire of ignorance. That kind of energy is so violent that it turns into metal. From it is produced the mountain of knives. Because the molten energy from one's anger forms into metal, the hell of the mountain of knives, the hell of the iron cudgel, the hell of the tree

of swords, the hell of **the wheel of swords,** the hell of **axes and halberds,** the hell of **spears and saws,** and the like all come into being. **It is like the intent to kill surging forth when a person meets a mortal enemy,** someone he bears a heavy grudge against, **so that he is roused to action.** His obsession to kill takes over.

Sutra:

"Because these two habits clash with one another, there come into being castration and hacking, beheading and mutilation, filing and sticking, flogging and beating, and other such experiences.

Commentary:

Because these two habits – past hatred and present hatred – **clash with one another, there come into being castration and hacking.** This is one kind of hell. **Beheading** – being killed; **mutilation** – having one's arms or legs chopped off or one's bones ground to powder; **filing and sticking** – being filed or being stuck with thorns; **flogging and beating; and other such experiences** are all further kinds of hells.

Sutra:

"Therefore, the Thus Come Ones of the ten directions look upon hatred and name it 'sharp knives and swords.' Bodhisattvas avoid hatred as they would their own execution.

Commentary:

Therefore, the Thus Come Ones of the ten directions look upon hatred and name it "sharp knives and swords." Anger is just like a keen knife or a sharp sword. **Bodhisattvas avoid hatred as they would their own execution.** Bodhisattvas regard anger and hatred as they would being killed by someone.

J5   Habits of deception.

Sutra:

"The fifth consists of habits of deception and misleading involvements which give rise to mutual guile. When such

maneuvering continues without cease, it produces the ropes and wood of a gallows for hanging, like the grass and trees that grow when water saturates a field.

Commentary:

The fifth consists of habits of deception and misleading involvements which give rise to mutual guile. "Deception" is a lack of honesty. "Misleading" means people getting involved in cheating and deceiving one another. You cheat me with some scheme and then I think up some trick to cheat you. **When such maneuvering continues without cease, it produces the ropes and wood of a gallows for hanging.** "Maneuvering" refers to the deceptive devices. The ropes and wood are used to construct a gallows to hang the person. This is a certain hell. It is **like the grass and trees that grow when water saturates a field.** Deception nourishes the hell of ropes and wood in the same way.

Sutra:

"Because the two habits perpetuate one another, there come into being handcuffs and fetters, cangues and locks, whips and clubs, sticks and cudgels, and other such experiences.

Commentary:

Because the two habits perpetuate one another, there come into being handcuffs and fetters. The habits of deception from the past combine with the habits of deception in the present to make a protracted pattern of deception. These "handcuffs and fetters" are implements of punishment, as are **cangues and locks.** When one is bound by this kind of thing, one cannot move about freely, much less escape. Or perhaps one is beaten with **whips and clubs, sticks and cudgels, and** there are many **other such experiences.** What is the origin of these experiences? How do they come into being? They come from deception.

Sutra:

"Therefore, the Thus Come Ones of the ten directions look upon deception and name it a 'treacherous crook.' Bodhisattvas fear deception as they would a savage wolf.

Commentary:

Being "treacherous" means that when one speaks, one doesn't tell the truth.

J6   Habits of lying.

Sutra:

"The sixth consists of habits of lying and combined fraudulence which give rise to mutual cheating. When false accusations continue without cease, one becomes adept at corruption.

"From this there come into being dust and dirt, excrement and urine, filth, stench, and impurities. It is like the obscuring of everyone's vision when the dust is stirred up by the wind.

Commentary:

The sixth consists of habits of lying and combined fraudulence which give rise to mutual cheating. "Lying" means not telling the truth, saying things that are false. "Combined fraudulence" means that people lie in order to cheat one another. "Mutual cheating" means that people are not straight with one another. What they say is not true. **When false accusations continue without cease, one becomes adept at corruption.** People end up accusing each other in ways which are not justified. If they continue in this vein, they end up being masters of deception. Everything they do is against the law. **From this there come into being** the hell of **dust and dirt,** and the hell of **excrement and urine.** These hells are full of **filth, stench, and impurities. It is like the obscuring of everyone's vision when the dust is stirred up by the wind.** That's what this particular karmic obstacle is like. The dust is so thick you can't even see it clearly, let alone anything else.

Sutra:

"Because these two habits augment one another, there come into being sinking and drowning, tossing and pitching, flying

and falling, floating and submerging, and other such experiences.

Commentary:

Because these two habits augment one another, there come into being sinking and drowning. The habits of lying from the past combine with the habits of lying in the present to bring about these various hells. **Tossing and pitching** means that one is tossed up high and then allowed to plummet down. **Flying and falling** is also a case of being rocketed off into space and then left to fall back down. **Floating and submerging** means one is left afloat at sea. These hells **and other such experiences** must be undergone.

Sutra:

"Therefore, the Thus Come Ones of the ten directions look upon lying and name it 'robbery and murder.' Bodhisattvas regard lying as they would treading on a venomous snake.

Commentary:

Therefore, the Thus Come Ones of the ten directions look upon lying and name it "robbery and murder." When they see people doing things to cheat others, they call it robbery and murder. **Bodhisattvas regard lying as they would treading on a venomous snake.** Lying, too, is undesirable.

J7   Habits of animosity.

Sutra:

"The seventh consists of habits of animosity and interconnected enmity which give rise to grievances. From this there come into being flying rocks, thrown stones, caskets and closets, cages on wheels, jars and containers, and bags and rods. It is like someone harming others secretly – he harbors, cherishes, and nurtures evil.

Commentary:

The seventh consists of habits of animosity and interconnected enmity which give rise to grievances. "Animosity" refers to resentment and can also mean the making of false accusations. False accusations cause suspicions to arise. In Chinese the word "grievances" (銜 *xian*) has a character which literally means to hold in the beak as a bird holds food. Here, someone harbors grievances and ill-will in his mouth and refuses to let it go. **From this there come into being flying rocks,** and the hell of **thrown stones,** in which one is struck with pieces of rubble. Or one is closed up in a **casket** or in a **closet,** or put in a **cage on wheels.** Or the person is put into a **jar** and a fire is lit under it, so that the ghost gets cooked, **bags and rods:** the ghost is put in a big bag and then beaten down. Inside he both suffocates and suffers the pain of beating. This kind of karma **is like someone harming others secretly – he harbors, cherishes, and nurtures evil.** He's always brewing evil thoughts in his mind.

Sutra:

"Because these two habits swallow one another up, there come into being tossing and pitching, seizing and apprehending, striking and shooting, casting away and pinching, and other such experiences.**

Commentary:

Because these two habits swallow one another up, there come into being tossing and pitching. The habit of animosity from the past combines with the habit of animosity in the present in such a way that they devour one another. That is, if the karmic power of one's habits from the past is stronger, one will undergo retribution for the past deeds. If the power of the karma in the present life is the stronger, one will undergo retribution for it in this very life. That's what's meant by swallowing each other up. The ghost is tossed about or thrown for a distance, so that when he lands he will undergo pain and suffering. **Seizing and apprehending**: after he's tossed away, he is seized and brought back. **Striking and shooting, casting away and pinching, and other such experiences** are all undergone as retribution.

Sutra:

"Therefore, the Thus Come Ones of the ten directions look upon animosity and name it a 'disobedient and harmful ghost.' Bodhisattvas regard animosity as they would drinking poisonous wine.

Commentary:

Therefore, the Thus Come Ones of the ten directions look upon animosity and name it a "disobedient and harmful ghost." They regard conduct governed by animosity, resentment, and revenge as a disobedient and harmful ghost. Such conduct goes against the wishes of the person who is the object of the resentment and ends up by killing the person. **Bodhisattvas regard animosity as they would drinking poisonous wine.** The Chinese language uses an adjective which is the name of a bird, *chen*, a deadly species of falcon. If a feather from this particular variety of falcon is soaked in wine, the wine will be poisoned so thoroughly that a sip of it would be lethal, for there is no antidote for it.

J8   Habits of views.

Sutra:

"The eighth consists of habits of views and the admixture of understandings, such as satkayadrishti, views, moral prohibitions, grasping, and deviant insight into various kinds of karma, which bring about opposition and produce mutual antagonism. From them there come into being court officials, deputies, certifiers, and registrars. They are like people traveling on a road, who meet each other coming and going.

Commentary:

The eighth consists of habits of views and the admixture of understandings, such as satkayadrishti. These are habits which we all have. If you make proper use of views, they are an aid to your mind and nature. But if you use them incorrectly, if you have biases, then you can create bad karma. *Satkayadrishti* is a Sanskrit word which means "view of having a body." There are five kinds of views:

1. the view of having a body,
2. one-sided views,
3. the view of prohibitive morality,
4. views that grasp at views,
5. deviant views.

These have been explained in detail before. With the first view, people become attached to the view that their bodies are themselves and attached to the things around them as being their own. One-sided views are not in accord with the Middle Way. They fall into either the view of annihilationism or the view of externalism. With the former, one believes that death is like the extinguishment of a lamp – there is nothing that follows it. One doesn't believe in a soul or in rebirth. With the latter, one believes that if one is a person this life, one will be a person in every life. They think it is impossible for a person to undergo rebirth as an animal.

The third is an attachment to extremes of morality, like that found in some sects in India such as those that would follow the behavior of cows or dogs. The fourth, to have the view that grasps views, means being fraught with attachments. People with this view have very decided opinions and an overbearing view of self. There are also deviant views. Satkayadrishti, **views, moral prohibitions, grasping, and deviant insight into various kinds of karma** refer to these five views. One may have a bit of intelligence, but the principles one grasps at are deviant. Because they are not proper views, one creates karma, **which bring about opposition and produce mutual antagonism.** With this kind of karma, one is always opposing other people and disagreeing with them. **From them there come into being court officials, deputies, certifiers, and registrars.** They ask for certification and proof in writing; they insist upon records and the like. These views **are like people traveling on a road, who meet each other coming and going.**

Sutra:

"Because these two habits influence one another, there come into being official inquiries, baited questions, examinations, interrogations, public investigations, exposure, the youths who record good and evil, carrying the record books of the offenders' arguments and rationalizations, and other such experiences.

Commentary:

Because these two habits influence one another, there come into being official inquiries. The two habits again refer to the habits involving the five views that one built up in former lives, coupled with the habits involving the five views which one continues to grasp hold of in this life. "Official inquiries" means one is thoroughly questioned. **Baited questions** are raised when an examiner uses expedients to get you to admit your wrongdoings. This kind of thing happens in courts and also happens in the hells. **Examinations** means that after you've stated your case, the officials set about to examine its accuracy, step-by-step. They send people out to verify everything you've said. **Interrogations** bring everything out in the open, just as if it were to appear in a mirror. **Public investigations** and **exposure** do the same. **The youths who record good and evil, carrying the record books of the offenders' arguments and rationalizations.** These youths are young employees of the hells who keep records on good and evil done in the world. When your turn comes, they read out your record. If you try to argue or rationalize, they just find the page and place and read it out just as it actually happened. They have unquestionable proof, and your protestations are useless. These **and other such experiences** are the lot of those with deep-seated views.

Sutra:

"Therefore, the Thus Come Ones of the ten directions look upon evil views and name them the 'pit of views.' Bodhisattvas regard having false and one-sided views as they would standing on the edge of a steep ravine full of poison.

Commentary:

Therefore, the Thus Come Ones of the ten directions look upon evil views and name them the "pit of views." To them, the habits of evil views are like a deep abyss. It's fine if you don't fall in it, but if you do, it's not at all easy to climb back out. **Bodhisattvas regard having false and one-sided views as they would standing on the edge of a steep ravine full of poison.** They are extremely dangerous, and it is very easy to slip and fall into them, so bodhisattvas stay far away from them.

J9   Habits of injustice.

Sutra:

"The ninth consists of the habits of injustice and their inter-connected support of one another; they result in instigating false charges and libeling. From them are produced crushing between mountains, crushing between rocks, stone rollers, stone grinders, plowing, and pulverizing. It is like a slanderous villain who engages in persecuting good people unjustly.

Commentary:

The ninth consists of the habits of injustice and their inter-connected support of one another; they result in instigating false charges and libeling. "Injustice" means to accuse someone without cause – to frame him. The person in question is in fact innocent, but the government brings a case against him, or else some private individual sues him. It is biased and unfair. Included here are both the habits of being unjustly accused and of having done injustice to others. If you have unjustly accused others in the past, then those karmic obstacles will bind together with what goes on in this life. If you've never been unjustly accused, then perhaps the karma of it is being newly created in this lifetime. If you know that the person you are accusing did not actually commit the crime, and you are fully aware that you are bearing false witness, then you are being unjust. **From them are produced crushing between mountains, crushing between rocks.** This is the Hell of Squeezing Mountains, in which mountains on all four sides close in and crush the offender. The same kind of experience is undergone in the Hell of Crushing Rocks. You are squeezed into a meat patty. **Stone rollers** is another hell, as are **stone grinders, plowing, and pulverizing.** If a person is a constant liar and bears false witness – if his speech is totally unreliable – then in this hell his tongue is cut out. Or it is grappled with an iron hook and pulled out, and then oxen drag plows back and forth across it. With "pulverizing" the offender is put into a grinder and ground to bits. **It is like a slanderous villain who engages in persecuting good people unjustly.** "Slanderous" refers to any kind of unreliable speech or accusation.

Sutra:

"Because these two habits join ranks, there come into being pressing and pushing, bludgeons and compulsion, squeezing and straining, weighing and measuring, and other such experiences.

Commentary:

The karmic obstacles from former lives combine with the karma from one's conduct in the last life to cause one to be pressed or pushed down or to be beaten with bludgeons or to be forcefully controlled. Sometimes the ghost is put into a bag and then the blood is squeezed out of it, just the way apple sauce is made. Or one's injustices are weighed and measured with precise accuracy. These are the kinds of experiences one has to undergo.

Sutra:

"Therefore, the Thus Come Ones of the ten directions look upon harmful accusations and name them 'a treacherous tiger.' Bodhisattvas regard injustice as they would a bolt of lightning.

Commentary:

Therefore, the Thus Come Ones of the ten directions look upon harmful accusations and name them "a treacherous tiger," even more vicious than an ordinary tiger. **Bodhisattvas regard injustice as they would a bolt of lightning.** Bodhisattvas who cultivate the Way don't want to make any mistakes in cause and effect, and so they see that the habit of acting in unjust ways is as dangerous as encountering a bolt from the blue. It's just as frightening a situation and in the same way can strike people down dead on the spot.

J10 The habits of litigation.

Sutra:

"The tenth consists of the habits of litigation and the mutual disputations which give rise to covering. From them there are produced a look in the mirror and illumination by the lamp. It is like being in direct sunlight: there is no way one can hide one's shadow.

Commentary:

The tenth consists of the habits of litigation and the mutual disputations which give rise to covering. "Litigation" means taking someone to court. It involves attorneys for the plaintiff and the defense. The offense involved is one of covering. That means that the evidence brought out in court by either side is not the whole truth. Each person claims to be right. In divorce cases, for example, the husband says he is in the right and the wife claims she is in the right. Actually, neither one is in the right, for if even one of them were right, they would not be getting a divorce. The one in the right would simply forgive and forget if the other were being unreasonable, and no problems would arise. It's only when both parties refuse to yield that they have to get lawyers and go to court. Probably they feel sorry for the lawyers and are afraid they will starve to death if they don't give them some business. And of course the lawyer advises them to go to court because it's his livelihood. His fee can range from hundreds of dollars to thousands of dollars; it depends on the kind of case involved. He names his own price. "Disputations" refers to the arguments that ensue. Each side claims to be sane and reasonable. Why do they go to court? Because they are not open and frank with one another. They put on masks and cover up the truth. They are actually wrong, but they cover up their mistakes and bring up the points where they appear to be in accord with principle. They talk about all the things they did that were legal and avoid mentioning the things they did which were not. That's covering.

From them there are produced a look in the mirror and illumination by the lamp. If you liked to get involved in litigations and to commit crimes when you were alive, then when you get to the hells, your crimes will be revealed in a mirror on a stand there. As you look into the mirror, every mistake you ever made in your entire life will appear in it. It's just like a movie: every frame shows up your actions quite vividly. With the "illumination by the lamp" you are left with no place to hide. Everything is clearly revealed. **It is like being in direct sunlight: there is no way one can hide one's shadow.**

Sutra:

"Because these two habits bicker back and forth, there come into being evil companions, the mirror of karma, the fiery pearl, exposure of past karma, inquests, and other such experiences.

Commentary:

Because these two habits bicker back and forth, there come into being evil companions. Not only companions, but relatives are included here. One's whole family may be bad. **The mirror of karma** is like the crime-revealing mirror mentioned above. **The fiery pearl** illuminates past offenses. **Exposure of past karma** reveals all the crimes you ever committed in whatever former life. **Inquests** happen when you don't admit what you've done. Then the evidence is brought out against you. It's proved for you to see.

Sutra:

"Therefore, all the Thus Come Ones of the ten directions look upon covering and name it a 'hidden villain.' Bodhisattvas regard covering as they would having to carry a mountain atop their heads while walking upon the sea.

Commentary:

Therefore, all the Thus Come Ones of the ten directions look upon covering and name it a "hidden villain." Because of what's just been described, Thus Come Ones look upon the practice of covering and call it a "hidden" thief. **Bodhisattvas regard covering** – litigation – **as they would having to carry a mountain atop their heads while walking upon the sea.** How could they ever stay up? It wouldn't be possible. So bodhisattvas don't go to court.

I3   Explains the six retributions.
J1   A general introduction.

Sutra:

"What are the six retributions? Ananda, living beings create karma with their six consciousnesses. The evil retributions they call down upon themselves come from the six sense organs.

Commentary:

What are the six retributions? Ananda, living beings create karma with their six consciousnesses – the consciousnesses of the eyes, ears, nose, tongue, body, and mind. **The evil retributions they call down upon themselves** when they create the evil karma **come from the six sense organs.** They arise out of the eyes, ears, nose, tongue, body, and mind.

J2   Detailed explanation.
K1   Retribution of seeing.
L1   At the end of one's life, one sees one's own fall.

Sutra:

"What are the evil retributions that arise from the six sense organs? The first is the retribution of seeing, which beckons one and leads one to evil ends. The karma of seeing intermingles, so that at the time of death one first sees a raging conflagration which fills the ten directions. The deceased one's spiritual consciousness takes flight, but then falls. Riding on a wisp of smoke, it enters the Relentless Hell.

Commentary:

Above were discussed the ten habitual causes which lead to six interconnected retributions. They are called "interconnected" because although one of the six may have been the predominant factor in an offense, the others are all involved to some extent. They act as accomplices. For instance, the eyes commit some offense with regard to objects they see. So the eyes are the major offender; however, the ears, nose, tongue, body, and mind also play their parts in the crime. The major offender is the first to commit the offense, while the others help it along in their turn.

But you will remember that earlier the Buddhas of the ten directions spoke directly and simultaneously to Ananda, saying that it is from the six sense organs that Buddhas are accomplished and it is from the six sense organs that one falls into the hells. So now that we have come to the six interconnected retributions, you should remember that originally these six are capable of accomplishing Buddhahood. It's just that people don't know how to use them properly, and so within the nature of the treasury of the Thus Come One they give rise to the false from within the true. The falseness that arises goes from the three subtle appearances to the six coarse appearances to limitless boundless appearances. That's why it is said that there are eighty-four thousand kinds of karmic obstacles.

Why do we create so many karmic offenses? It's because we are not able to gain control. We can't keep ourselves from being turned by the experiences of the six sense objects. We are unable to return the hearing and listen to the self nature so that the nature can accomplish the Unsurpassed Way. Just because we don't return the hearing, we race out through the six sense organs to get at the six sense objects.

What are the evil retributions that arise from the six sense organs? The first is the retribution of seeing, which beckons one and leads one to evil ends. Because the perceiving nature of the eye sees a form, one is influenced by that object of form. But in this process there are a lot of involvements and ramifications. From these appearances a lot of karmic offenses are created. A lot of karmic offenses result in a lot of evil retributions. **The karma of seeing intermingles, so that at the time of death one first sees a raging conflagration which fills the ten directions.** The "karma" referred to here is offense-karma. With what does it intermingle? With the other five sense organs. They exchange opinions, and their karma gets mixed up together. Being influenced by the objects of sight in this way, one chases after sounds and pursues forms.

For example, a man sees a beautiful woman and gives rise to greed and desire. Then he listens for her gentle voice. Once the eyes have seen the beautiful form, the ears want to follow and hear a beautiful sound. The nose wants a whiff of her powder and perfumes. If the eyes hadn't seen her, the ears wouldn't have been eager to hear her voice and the nose wouldn't have been enticed to smell the feminine fragrances. After that the tongue starts having ruinous false thoughts – maybe something like, "She's such a fine woman that I bet it wouldn't be bad to kiss her." In his heart this kind of ignorance arises. Then the body wants to come in contact with her and the mind relents. The mind is agreeable and goes along with the rest. At that point he goes ahead and creates the karma of lust. The result in the future will be an evil retribution such as hugging the copper pillar or sleeping on the iron bed. Or the male and female organs are infested with iron-beaked creatures. How did it come about? It all started with the first offender – the seeing. Seeing by itself is just seeing: what he should not have done was to pursue what he saw. Rather,

When the eyes see forms, inside there is nothing.

Do you have that kind of skill? If so, then it doesn't matter if you look every day. The more you see, the less you will be moved. But if you don't have that skill, then you had better be a little bit more careful. With a little more care, you won't have to hug the copper pillar or fall into some other hell.

The text says, "at the time of death." Everyone will die. There isn't anyone who can say he or she will live forever, unless one cultivates and becomes a sage or an immortal, in which case one can live if one wants and die if one wants. Or, if you are a bodhisattva or an arhat, you have freedom over birth and death. If you're not at that level, then you too will have a "time of death." When death comes for this offender, he will first see a "raging conflagration." That's because of his "fire of desire" – his sexual desire. And the conflagration is not limited to one place. To the ends of empty space and throughout the dharma realm – everywhere is ablaze. At that time **the deceased one's spiritual consciousness takes flight, but then falls.** The "spiritual consciousness" refers to the eighth consciousness. It is also the soul, which has the potential to become a Buddha or a ghost. It is called the "intermediate skandha body," because at this stage the five skandhas have been severed from the former body and have not yet entered a new body. What happens to this offender's intermediate skandha body? It first flies up, but then falls. The spiritual consciousness has the power to fly through space, but in this case its spiritual penetrations are not very great, and so once it gets a little way into space, it falls. **Riding on a wisp of smoke, it enters the Relentless Hell,** a place which is no playground. I think that even jet-setters would not want to take in those sights. So everybody should avoid planting the causes which lead to the hells. It would be infinitely better to go to the Buddha-fruition than to go to the hells. Don't follow this poor soul.

L2　Two fundamental appearances.

Sutra:

"There, it is aware of two appearances. One is a perception of brightness in which can be seen all sorts of evil things, and it gives rise to boundless fear. The other is a perception of darkness in which there is total stillness and no sight, and it experiences boundless terror."

Commentary:

The person who has committed karmic offenses by pursuing defiling objects of form falls into the Relentless Hell. **There, it** – his intermediate skandha body – **is aware of two appearances. One is**

a perception of brightness in which can be seen all sorts of evil things. With this perception of brightness, it can see absolutely everything. What is there to be seen? Evil things; every kind of terrible thing that you can possibly imagine. There are things like wolves and tigers and creatures with human bodies and ox heads or horse faces. The ghost of impermanence in his tall hat is also very much in evidence. There are also cruel and horrifying beasts. All he sees are these evil creatures, and so his skandha body **gives rise to boundless fear.** One experiences tremendous terror. **The other is a perception of darkness in which there is total stillness and no sight.** It can't see anything at all, because there is not the least bit of light from the sun or moon or from stars or lamps. "Total stillness and no sight" means there is not a creature, not a thing, not a sound, and no visual perception. But it is not a quieting experience; rather, **it experiences boundless terror.** He experiences nothing but fear and terror. If he saw a beautiful woman then, I wonder if he'd be able to muster up any sexual desire. The only way to know for sure would be to ask him. He has to undergo fear and terror in this hell because he created the karma of lust.

L3   A detailed explanation of the intermingled retributions.

Sutra:

"When the fire that comes from seeing burns the sense of hearing, it becomes cauldrons of boiling water and molten copper. When it burns the breath, it becomes black smoke and purple fumes. When it burns the sense of taste, it becomes scorching hot pellets and molten iron gruel. When it burns the sense of touch, it becomes white-hot embers and glowing coals. When it burns the mind, it becomes stars of fire that shower everywhere and whip up and inflame the entire realm of space.

Commentary:

Now the six interconnecting aspects are described. **When the fire that comes from seeing burns the sense of hearing, it becomes cauldrons of boiling water and molten copper.** When the fire reaches the ears and the hearing, it turns into the hell of cauldrons of boiling water and the hell of molten copper. The water is brought to a boil and the ghost is plunged into the pot. The "ghost" is just the spiritual consciousness of the deceased one. Do you remember what he did so that he now ends up in a pot of boiling water? His ears aided and abetted his seeing. When his eyes saw the beautiful form, his ears should have had sense enough to warn him not to listen to her voice. But instead his ears got right in there and enticed him to listen. He was all ears. And what he heard pleased him to no end. So now he's in the cauldron of boiling water and molten copper. **When it burns the breath, it becomes black smoke and purple fumes.** When the fire reaches the nose, he has to breathe black smoke and purple soot. This happens because he got caught up in smelling nice fragrances. But I believe that the black smoke is not as much fun to inhale. In fact, the stench of it is appalling. But that is the retribution he must undergo.

When it burns the sense of taste, it becomes scorching hot pellets and molten iron gruel. The "pellets" are little iron tablets, but when you put them in your mouth they burn your tongue to a crisp. He liked the "taste of women" – he liked to kiss them – and so now he gets hot iron gruel for breakfast every day. **When it burns the sense of touch, it becomes white-hot embers and glowing coals.** When the fire from seeing burns through to the sense of touch, it becomes ashes, but the ashes aren't dead and cold; they still have fire in them.

When it burns the mind – that is, thoughts– **it becomes stars of fire that shower everywhere and whip up and inflame the entire realm of space.** The fire that scatters to burn you is as plentiful as the stars in the sky. It creates a wall of heat that builds up and fills all of empty space.

K2   Retribution of hearing.
L1   At the end of one's life one sees one's own fall.

Sutra:

"The second is the retribution of hearing, which beckons one and leads one to evil ends. The karma of hearing intermin-

gles, and thus at the time of death one first sees gigantic waves that drown heaven and earth. The deceased one's spiritual consciousness falls into the water and rides the current into the Relentless Hell.

Commentary:

The second of the six interconnected retributions is the retribution of hearing. Originally, if one had returned the hearing to hear the self-nature, the hearing-nature could have accomplished the Unsurpassed Way. Instead, the person in question turned all his attention outside and listened to defiling sounds. He listened to sounds that gave him enjoyment. Perhaps he liked to listen to women sing. Perhaps he enjoyed listening to women talk. The same applies for men as for women. Women like to listen to men. It's not a one-way street. The sutra is talking about both sexes. You shouldn't think that if the sutra uses the masculine form, it just means that men are bad, while women are not included. The offenses the two sexes commit are the same. They are those which beckons one and leads one to evil ends.

This person's retribution beckons him just as if it were calling to him, "Come here! Come here!" in very persuasive tones. It entices him. The karma of hearing intermingles, and thus at the time of death one first sees gigantic waves that drown heaven and earth. The "intermingling" refers to the way in which the six organs are interconnected in their retribution. The ear gets involved with all the other five sense organs. The ghost – the intermediate skandha body – sees the entire universe filled up with billowing waves; but is it really that way? No. It is a manifestation which appears because of his karmic retribution. The same is true when we people see mountains, rivers, the earth, vegetation, buildings, San Francisco, New York, Japan, China, and everything else – it's all a manifestation due to the power of our karma. Without that power of karma, it is all empty space. If your karma is ended and your emotion is empty, then everything throughout the dharma realm is void. It is all emptiness. There isn't anything at all. But because of attachment to appearances, you see all kinds of colors, shapes, and forms.

This ghost sees the entirety of heaven and earth as submerged in a vast expanse of billowing waves. **The deceased one's spiritual consciousness falls into the water and rides the current into the Relentless Hell.** He flows along with the stream and ends up at his brother's house. Where's that? The Relentless Hell. Who's his brother? His seeing. The six brothers race right after one another.

L2   Two fundamental appearances.

Sutra:

"There, it is aware of two sensations. One is open hearing, in which it hears all sorts of noise and its essential spirit becomes confused. The other is closed hearing, in which there is total stillness and no hearing, and its soul sinks into oblivion.

Commentary:

Such a graphic and sobering explanation, and yet people still willingly go ahead and create offenses. You talk about how fine it is to become a Buddha, but people aren't interested in becoming Buddhas. You tell about the horrors of the hells, and they decide to try them out. Becoming a Buddha is so fine, but they don't even give it a try. "We'll talk about it later," they procrastinate. They've been told that listening to defiling sounds creates karmic offenses, but as soon as they find themselves in such a situation they are compelled to listen. They think, "I hear about that in the sutra, but I'm not convinced it's right." So they try it out.

There, when the intermediate skandha body gets to the Relentless Hell, **it is aware of two sensations. One is open hearing, in which it hears all sorts of noise and its essential spirit becomes confused.** All pandemonium breaks loose. "Confused" means that it cannot remember anything any more. **The other is closed hearing, in which there is total stillness and no hearing, and its soul sinks into oblivion.** It experiences total deafness. Then its soul goes one knows not where. It sinks into oblivion.

L3   A detailed explanation of the intermingled retributions.

Sutra:

"When the waves from hearing flow into the hearing, they become scolding and interrogation. When they flow into the seeing, they become thunder and roaring and evil poisonous vapors. When they flow into the breath, they become rain and fog that is permeated with poisonous organisms that entirely fill up the body. When they flow into the sense of taste, they become pus and blood and every kind of filth. When they flow into the sense of touch, they become animals and ghosts, and excrement and urine. When they flow into the mind, they become lightning and hail which ravage the heart and soul.

Commentary:

When the waves from hearing flow into the hearing – the organ of the ear – **they become scolding and interrogation. When they flow into the seeing, they become thunder and roaring and evil poisonous vapors.** There is a hell of thunder and roaring. One is saturated in poisonous vapors. **When they flow into the breath, they become rain and fog that is permeated with poisonous organisms that entirely fill up the body.** There's a hell where there's eternal rain and fog. The rain is polluted with poisonous organisms, and when they strike the skin, they bite into every pore and work their way in. Pretty soon one's whole body is covered with poisonous organisms. **When they flow into the sense of taste, they become pus and blood and every kind of filth.** It is utter muck and scum. **When they flow into the sense of touch, they become animals and ghosts, and excrement and urine.** He undergoes his punishment in the hell of excrement and urine. **When they flow into the mind, they become lightning and hail which ravage the heart and soul.** In the Hell of Lightning and Hail, there is an eternal storm, and one is struck by lightning and hailstones.

It's a painful retribution. The ghost's very heart and soul are ripped to smithereens.

K3   Retribution of smelling.
L1   At the end of one's life one sees one's own fall.

Sutra:

"The third is the retribution of smelling, which beckons one and leads one to evil ends. The karma of smelling intermingles, and thus at the time of death one first sees a poisonous smoke that permeates the atmosphere near and far. The deceased one's spiritual consciousness wells up out of the earth and enters the Relentless Hell.

Commentary:

"The nose doesn't do anything but smell," you protest. "What karma can it create?" However, smelling can also create karma. That's because there is greed involved in the smelling. Because of its greed for fragrances, the nose sometimes ends up doing improper things, like pursuing the fragrances of women. With this kind of deviant view, all kinds of evil karma can be created. Then there are various kinds of interconnected evil retributions which must be borne. Therefore, **the third is the retribution of smelling, which beckons one and leads one to evil ends. The karma of smelling intermingles, and thus at the time of death one first sees a poisonous smoke that permeates the atmosphere near and far.** When the person was alive he liked to smell fragrances, but now everything has turned into a poisonous vapor. You should realize that the fragrant things of this world, when inhaled to the ultimate, become poisonous vapors. **The deceased one's spiritual consciousness wells up out of the earth and enters the Relentless Hell.** When it sees that everything is permeated with poison, it tries to leap out of it – to bound up above the earth and escape it. Little does it realize that with that single bound it will end up in the Relentless Hell.

L2   The fundamental appearances.

Sutra:

"There, it is aware of two sensations. One is unobstructed smelling, in which it is thoroughly infused with the evil vapors and its mind becomes distressed. The other is obstructed smelling, in which its breath is cut off and there is no passage, and it lies stifled and suffocating on the ground.

Commentary:

There, it – the intermediate skandha body – **is aware of two sensations. One is unobstructed smelling, in which it is thoroughly infused with the evil vapors and its mind becomes distressed.** His mind is in total chaos and turmoil. **The other is obstructed smelling, in which its breath is cut off and there is no passage.** He can't breathe. **It lies stifled and suffocating on the ground.** He's in total despair and on the verge of death.

L3   A detailed explanation of the intermingled retributions.

Sutra:

"When the vapor of smelling invades the breath, it becomes cross-examination and bearing witness. When it invades the seeing, it becomes fire and torches. When it invades the hearing, it becomes sinking and drowning, oceans, and bubbling cauldrons. When it invades the sense of taste, it becomes putrid or rancid foods. When it invades the sense of touch, it becomes ripping apart and beating to a pulp. It also becomes a huge mountain of flesh which has a hundred thousand eyes and which is sucked and fed upon by numberless worms. When it invades the mind, it becomes ashes, pestilent airs, and flying sand and gravel which cut the body to ribbons.

Commentary:

When the vapor of smelling invades the breath, it becomes cross-examination and bearing witness. One undergoes constant questioning. Or one is obligated to do certain things. **When it invades the seeing, it becomes fire and torches.** This is the Hell of Fire and Torches. **When it invades the hearing, it becomes sinking and drowning.** There is a Hell of Sinking and Drowning which contains blood and urine. Or **it becomes oceans, and bubbling cauldrons.** These are other hells. **When it invades the sense of taste, it becomes putrid or rancid foods.** "Putrid" describes rotten fish-flesh. "Rancid" describes spoiled candy. In general it means having to eat food that's gone bad. **When it invades the sense of touch, it becomes ripping apart and beating to a pulp. It also becomes a huge mountain of flesh which has a hundred thousand eyes and which is sucked and fed upon by numberless worms.** They devour one's flesh and blood. **When it invades the mind, it becomes ashes, pestilent airs, and flying sand and gravel which cut the body to ribbons.** When the vapors of the smelling invade the mind, one is saturated with foul air – with ashes and vapors carrying disease-ridden organisms. Or stones and clods of earth come hurtling at one unexpectedly and totally riddle one's body.

K4   Retribution of tasting.
L1   At the end of one's life one sees one's own fall.

Sutra:

"The fourth is the retribution of tasting, which beckons one and leads one to evil ends. This karma of tasting intermingles, and thus at the time of death one first sees an iron net ablaze with a raging fire that covers over the entire world. The deceased one's spiritual consciousness passes down through this hanging net, and suspended upside-down it enters the Relentless Hell.

Commentary:

When people nourish their own bodies with animal flesh, they become greedy for meat and investigate flavors. They are always investigating ways to come up with new and different combinations to make superb delicacies. Because of this, they end up creating a lot of bad karma. How do they make bad karma? In the study of flavors, Chinese people have decided that the most nourishment lies in living flesh. They have taken to eating live creatures – the "freshest" meat. Westerners put their meat in refrigerators for a while before they eat it. But Chinese people feel that cooling the meat robs it of its nutrients. They prefer to cut the flesh off living animals and eat that. For instance, there's one technique in which the cook sets a hog to running and forces it to run for a couple of hours by beating it. Eventually its heart is racing, and its circulation increases to the point that its flesh swells. At the strategic moment the cook slices off a big piece of flesh from the pig's hindquarters and roasts it. This is considered to be the tastiest meat.

The Chinese have another ingenious method: first they cut a hole in the center of the table and stick the monkey's head up through the hole – the monkey is still alive at this point. Then they smash the skull with a club and the people sit around and eat the monkey's brains. They say this is a most nutritious food. These are examples of creating karmic offenses because of the sense of taste. Because of a greed for fine flavors, people will go to all kinds of extremes and invent various strange methods of creating karmic offenses.

The fourth is the retribution of tasting, which beckons one and leads one to evil ends. This karma of tasting intermingles, and thus at the time of death one first sees an iron net ablaze with a raging fire that covers over the entire world. The karma of tasting intermingles with the experiences of the other five sense organs. When the person is about to die, he sees a conflagration in an iron net that extends over the whole world. **The deceased one's spiritual consciousness passes down through this hanging net, and suspended upside-down it enters the Relentless Hell.** His soul falls and gets hung up in the net. Head-first, upside-down, he enters the unspaced hell.

L2   Two fundamental appearances.

Sutra:

"There, it is aware of two sensations. One is a sucking air which congeals into ice so that it freezes the flesh of his body.

The other is a spitting blast of air which spews out a raging fire that roasts his bones and marrow to a pulp.

Commentary:

There, it is aware of two sensations. One is a sucking air which congeals into ice so that it freezes the flesh of his body. The sucking is an intake of breath, and it is cold. It becomes ice – bitter cold. It freezes the flesh of the body. **The other is a spitting blast of air which spews out a raging fire that roasts his bones and marrow to a pulp.** This is the exhalation. It's a spitting fire which burns up his bones and marrow.

L3   A detailed explanation of the intermingled retributions.

Sutra:

"When the tasting of flavors passes through the sense of taste, it becomes what must be acknowledged and what must be endured. When it passes through the seeing, it becomes burning metal and stones. When it passes through the hearing, it becomes sharp weapons and knives. When it passes through the sense of smell, it becomes a vast iron cage that encloses the entire land. When it passes through the sense of touch, it becomes bows and arrows, crossbows, and darts. When it passes through the mind, it becomes flying pieces of molten iron that rain down from out of space."

Commentary:

When the tasting of flavors and the evil karma it creates **passes through the sense of taste, it becomes what must be acknowledged and what must be endured.** "What must be acknowledged" means that, however unwilling, you are forced to admit to the evil karma you have created. "What must be endured" means that you must undergo what is basically unendurable. You can't evade your responsibility. **When it passes through the seeing, it becomes burning metal and stones.** There's a hell where the fire gets so hot that it melts the metal and rocks. **When it passes through the hearing, it becomes sharp weapons and**

knives. In this hell a lot of keen weapons pierce your body. **When it passes through the sense of smell, it becomes a vast iron cage that encloses the entire land.** It extends over an area as large as an entire country. **When it passes through the sense of touch, it becomes bows and arrows, crossbows, and darts.** Arrows and darts pierce the offender's body. **When it passes through the mind, it becomes flying pieces of molten iron that rain down from out of space.** These red-hot bits of metal fall out of the sky and burn the body.

K5   Retribution of touching.
L1   At the end of one's life one sees one's own fall.

Sutra:

"The fifth is the retribution of touching, which beckons one and leads one to evil ends. The karma of touching intermingles, and thus at the time of death one first sees huge mountains closing in on one from four sides, leaving no path of escape. The deceased one's spiritual consciousness then sees a vast iron city. Fiery snakes and fiery dogs, wolves, lions, ox-headed jail keepers, and horse-headed rakshasas brandishing spears and lances drive it into the iron city toward the Relentless Hell."

Commentary:

The fifth is the retribution of touching, which beckons one and leads one to evil ends. If one is greedy for objects of touch, one gets drawn into an evil retribution. **The karma of touching intermingles, and thus at the time of death one first sees huge mountains closing in on one from four sides, leaving no path of escape.** The karma created from the sensation of touch combines with the karma of the other five sense organs. A person with this kind of karma will experience the karmic response of seeing gigantic mountains surrounding him and pushing in on him to crush him. There is no way for him to escape the position he's in. No road is open to him. **The deceased one's spiritual consciousness then sees a vast iron city.** At that point, when he's caught in the midst of these mountains that are moving in on him, he spies a big iron city.

Fiery snakes and fiery dogs, wolves, lions, ox-headed jail keepers, and horse-headed rakshasas brandishing spears and lances drive it into the iron city toward the Relentless Hell. These beasts are alive, but they are composed of fire. The ox-headed jail keepers are responsible for looking after the iron city. The horse-headed rakshasa ghosts and the jailers are heavily armed with various sorts of spears and other terrifying weapons. This vicious entourage compels the offender to enter the vast iron city. As soon as he gets inside the city, he falls into the Relentless Hells.

L2   Two fundamental appearances.

Sutra:

"**There, it is aware of two sensations. One is touch that involves coming together, in which mountains come together to squeeze its body until its flesh, bones, and blood are totally dispersed. The other is touch that involves separation, in which knives and swords attack the body, ripping the heart and liver to shreds.**

Commentary:

There, it is aware of two sensations. One is touch that involves coming together, in which mountains come together to squeeze its body until its flesh, bones, and blood are totally dispersed. From four sides, huge mountains close in to press one's body. Every part of the body is smashed to smithereens. The mountains squeeze one into a meat patty. At that point one dies, of course, but then the "clever wind" revives one. Replete with a new body, one has to go through the same experience again. In this way one gets squeezed to death and revived, again and again, birth after birth and death after death. This is touch that involves contact.

The other is touch that involves separation, in which knives and swords attack the body, ripping the heart and liver to shreds. Knives, swords, lances and the like assault the body, and the internal organs are completely destroyed.

L3   A detailed explanation of the intermingled retributions.

Sutra:

"When this touching passes through the sensation of touch, it becomes striking, binding, stabbing, and piercing. When it passes through the seeing, it becomes burning and scorching. When it passes through the hearing, it becomes questioning, investigating, court examinations, and interrogation. When it passes through the sense of smell, it becomes enclosures, bags, beating, and binding up. When it passes through the sense of taste, it becomes plowing, pinching, chopping, and severing. When it passes through the mind, it becomes falling, flying, frying, and broiling.

Commentary:

When this touching passes through the sensation of touch, it becomes striking, binding, stabbing, and piercing. The text actually reads "questioning, investigating, court examinations, and interrogation" but these are more appropriate to the retribution for hearing, whereas "striking, binding, stabbing, and piercing," which appear in the text under hearing, are more appropriate to the sense of touch. "Striking" occurs when two things are hit together, "binding" is being tied up. "Stabbing" is being cut by knives, and "piercing" is what happens when arrows are shot at one. **When it passes through the seeing, it becomes burning and scorching.** When the sense of touch is influenced by seeing, then the retribution is burning and intense heat, like the hell of fiery soup and charcoals and the like. **When it passes through the hearing, it becomes questioning, investigating, court examinations, and interrogation.** "Questioning" means being brought before the courts of hell. "Investigating" means being examined by officials before passing through the gates. "Court examinations" are designed to cross-examine you about the offenses you have created. **When it passes through the sense of smell, it becomes enclosures, bags, beating, and binding up.** "Enclosures" means one is put inside something and contained. "Bags" refers to being tied in a bag. "Beating" means that besides being contained, you are beaten up. "Binding" up means that you are tied down and restricted. **When it passes through the sense of taste, it becomes plowing, pinching, chopping, and severing.** "Plowing" refers to having one's tongue plowed through. First it is hooked and pulled out, and then it is plowed through. "Pinching" means that the tongue is seized with pincers and pulled out. "Cutting" refers to having the tongue cut through. "Severing" means chopping the tongue clear off. **When it passes through the mind, it becomes falling, flying, frying, and broiling.** "Falling" is when one is tossed into space and left to drop as one will. "Flying" also refers to being hurtled into space and then allowed to crash down to earth. "Frying" means the application of intense heat to burn one to a crisp, as if one were an oil cake. "Broiling" is another way one's body is burned.

K6   Retribution of thinking.
L1   At the end of one's life one sees one's own fall.

Sutra:

"The sixth is the retribution of thinking, which beckons one and leads one to evil ends. The karma of thinking intermingles, and thus at the time of death one first sees a foul wind which devastates the land. The deceased one's spiritual consciousness is blown up into space, and then, spiraling downward, it rides that wind straight into the Relentless Hell.

Commentary:

The sixth is the retribution of thinking, which beckons one and leads one to evil ends. The bad retribution which thinking can create is extremely severe, and the evil karma it calls up is enormous. **The karma of thinking intermingles, and thus at the time of death one first sees a foul wind which devastates the land.** The karma of thinking intermingles with the karma of the other sense organs. It accumulates so that at the time of death all one sees is a horrendous wind which is blowing everything in the world to bits. **The deceased one's spiritual consciousness is**

blown up into space, and then, spiraling downward, it rides that wind straight into the Relentless Hell. The dead person's soul is blown up into empty space, but then it takes a dive and spins into the unspaced hell.

L2   Two fundamental appearances.

Sutra:

"**There, it is aware of two sensations. One is extreme confusion, which causes it to be frantic and to race about ceaselessly. The other is not confusion, but rather an acute awareness which causes it to suffer from endless roasting and burning, the extreme pain of which is difficult to bear.**

Commentary:

There, it is aware of two sensations. One is extreme confusion, which causes it to be frantic and to race about ceaselessly. The first is a lack of awareness. One doesn't understand anything at all at that time. One is sunk into a stupor, like an idiot. In that deep confusion, one becomes incoherent and races about senselessly. One never stops to rest. Wouldn't you say that is a lot of suffering? **The other is not confusion, but rather an acute awareness which causes it to suffer from endless roasting and burning, the extreme pain of which is difficult to bear.** The other alternative is not to be confused, but to be clearly aware of what is going on. But this awareness allows one to experience intense suffering. Although one is not confused, everything one experiences is suffering. The suffering comes from the raging blaze that burns one. The pain is the worst one could know. It's like when our bodies itch; pretty soon we can't bear the itch, so we have to scratch. It's that way here, but what is felt is pain – ultimately intense and ceaseless pain.

L3   A detailed explanation of the intermingled retributions.

Sutra:

"**When this deviant thought combines with thinking, it becomes locations and places. When it combines with seeing, it** becomes inspection and testimonies. When it combines with hearing, it becomes huge crushing rocks, ice and frost, dirt and fog. When it combines with smelling, it becomes a great fiery car, a fiery boat, and a fiery jail. When it combines with tasting, it becomes loud calling, wailing, and regretful crying. When it combines with touch, it becomes sensations of large and small, where ten thousand births and ten thousands deaths are endured every day, and of lying with one's face to the ground.

Commentary:

When this deviant thought combines with thinking, it becomes locations and places. "Deviant thought" means that the things one thinks about are improper, and one indulges in fantasies – that is, one's thoughts dwell on strange and weird things. When the deviant thought receives a retribution directed at itself, it turns into evil places of inquisition and interrogation. When it combines with seeing, it becomes inspection and testimonies. "Inspection" refers to the offense-spotting mirror in the hells. When you arrive, you have to go before the mirror and watch all the offenses you created in your life appear there, just as if they were frames of a movie. They are all in vivid detail, and there's no way you can back out of them. You can't avoid owning up to them. If you refuse to admit them, you have to endure "testimonies," in which people prove what you did. When it combines with hearing, it becomes huge crushing rocks. They close in on the four sides surrounding you and crush you between them. And it's cold with ice and frost, and there is dirt and fog. This hell is polluted – a yellow haze defiles the atmosphere so that you can't see anything and you get dizzy and disoriented.

When it combines with smelling, it becomes a great fiery car. This does not refer to trains that take us on vacations here in the world, but rather to a car red-hot with fire that one is forced to sit in. A fiery boat means that the entire boat is ablaze and you must climb aboard. A fiery jail is a prison full of fire that you must enter. When it combines with tasting, it becomes loud calling, wailing,

and regretful crying. The noise in this hell is tremendous. One experiences regret in this hell and one moans and weeps.

When it combines with touch, It becomes sensations of large and small – big hells and little hells – **where ten thousand births and ten thousands deaths are endured every day.** In the course of one single day, one dies a myriad times and is born a myriad times. And it becomes **lying with one's face to the ground.** Whether lying down, crawling, or standing up, one undergoes punishment. In general, this is not a pleasant place to be. It's not a likely spot to want to go, for the pain and suffering is tremendous.

I4   General conclusion: they are empty and false.
J1   Concludes that they are falsely created.

Sutra:

"Ananda, these are called the ten causes and six retributions of the hells, which are all created by the confusion and falseness of living beings.

Commentary:

Ananda, these are called the ten causes and six retributions of the hells. Many different hells have just been named, and all come from the ten habitual causes, which are these:

1. lust
2. greed
3. arrogance
4. hatred
5. deception
6. lying
7. animosity
8. views
9. injustice
10. litigation

They result in the six intermingling retributions that involve the eyes, ears, nose, tongue, body, and mind as they react to forms, sounds, smells, tastes, objects of touch, and mental constructs. These hells **are all created by the confusion and falseness of living beings.** They come from giving rise to falseness within the one truth. Once ignorance arises, various karmic manifestations result from it. From the karma, various offenses are created. But if one returns the hearing to hear the self-nature and cultivates this path to enlightenment, then all this karma becomes empty. It disappears.

J2   Distinguishes the comparative weight of the offenses.

Sutra:

"If living beings create this evil karma simultaneously, they enter the Avichi Hell and endure limitless suffering, passing through limitless kalpas.

Commentary:

If living beings create this evil karma simultaneously, they enter the Avichi Hell. If they indulge in behavior that includes all ten causes and all six intermingling retributions, they go to the Avichi Hell. It is a relentless hell, but it is the most severe one, so here it is named specifically. Basically all the relentless hells can be called avichi, but here the most severe one is specifically given that name. In that hell, they **endure limitless suffering, passing through limitless kalpas.**

Sutra:

"If each of the six sense organs creates them and if what is done includes each state and each sense organ, then the person will enter the eight relentless hells.

Commentary:

If each of the six sense organs creates them: if the eyes, ears, nose, tongue, body, and mind each create these offenses – the ten habitual causes – but not all at the same time as in the previous passage, **and if what is done includes each state and each sense organ, then the person will enter the eight relentless hells.** What's done means what the sense organs do in reaction to the states of the sense objects – the kind of karma they create. "Each state" refers to the sense objects and "each sense organ" to the eyes, ears, nose, tongue, body, and mind individually. "What is done" is the offenses which are created from the habitual causes. Here, all the sense organs create all the habitual causes, but they do not do it simultaneously. A person who follows his six sense organs and six sense objects to create such offenses will undergo the retributions of the eight relentless hells. There are eight hot and eight cold hells, and this refers to the eight cold hells.

Sutra:

"If the three karmas of body, mouth, and mind commit acts of killing, stealing, and lust, the person will enter the eighteen hells.

Commentary:

If the three karmas of body, mouth, and mind commit acts of killing, stealing, and lust – there are three evils of the body.

1. killing
2. stealing
3. lust

There are four evils of the mouth.

1. loose speech
2. false speech
3. harsh speech
4. backbiting

There are three evils of the mind.

1. greed
2. hatred
3. stupidity

If the karmas of the body, mouth, and mind are not pure, then one creates these ten evils. **The person will enter the eighteen hells.** There are terrible punishments in these eighteen consecutive hells.

Sutra:

"If the three karmas are not all involved, and there is perhaps just one act of killing and/or of stealing, then the person must enter the thirty-six hells.

Commentary:

In the situation described above, the karma created was heavy. Now, the three karmas are not all involved in making offenses. **If the three karmas are not all involved, and there is perhaps just one act of killing and/or of stealing**: maybe the person commits one murder or one theft, or he commits murder and a theft, or he commits a murder and an act of lust or a theft. In short, he doesn't do them all, but some partial combination of them. The offense-karma of a person in that situation is a bit lighter. **Then the person must enter the thirty-six hells.** Although he has to undergo more hells, the offenses are lighter and the suffering in these hells is not as severe.

Sutra:

"If the sense organ of sight alone commits just one karmic offense, then the person must enter the one hundred and eight hells.

Commentary:

The sense organ of sight is the source of all offenses. It is said:

> If the eyes didn't see it, the mouth
>   would not be gluttonous for it.
> If the ears didn't hear it, the mind
>   would not make transgressions concerning it.

If you didn't see something good to eat, your mouth would not commit the offense of gluttony. If the ears did not hear lovely sounds, the mind would not give rise to thoughts of desire. Seeing them is the beginning of evil and the source of offenses. Therefore, the text says: **If** the sense organ of sight **alone commits just one karmic offense** – perhaps it commits only one of the three karmas of the body: killing, or stealing, or lust. **Then the person must enter the one hundred and eight hells.**

J3   Even the heavy offenses are clearly an arisal of falseness.

Sutra:

"Because of this, living beings who do certain things create certain karma, and so in the world they enter collective hells, which arise from false thinking and which originally are not there at all."

Commentary:

Because of this, because of the various circumstances described above, **living beings who do certain things create certain karma.** They do individual things, they create their own special offenses, and then they have to undergo a retribution. **And so in the world they enter collective hells.** All the people who create a particular kind of karma enter that collective hell. Each category of offense has its retribution, and all who create that offense collectively undergo the retribution in the hells, **which arise from false thinking and which originally are not there at all.** These hells arise from offenses. Offenses are created because of ignorance. They arise from false thinking. Originally, though, they don't exist at all. Originally there is purity and no defilement – there isn't anything at all. But,

> Just because you make one false move,
> You blow the whole chess game.

As it is said:

> If one is off by a hair in the beginning,
> One will miss it by a thousand miles.

Destiny of Ghosts

H2   Destiny of ghosts.
I1   Concludes prior discussion and begins this.

Sutra:

"And then, Ananda, after the living beings who have slandered and destroyed rules and deportment, violated the bodhisattva precepts, slandered the Buddha's nirvana, and created various other kinds of karma, pass through many kalpas of being burned in the inferno, they finally finish paying for their offenses and are reborn as ghosts.

Commentary:

Since the explanation of the ten habitual causes and the six intermingling retributions is not yet finished, Shakyamuni Buddha says: **And then, Ananda,** let me tell you some more about this principle. **After the living beings** who have created karmic offenses, **who have slandered and destroyed rules and deportment** – they said things like, "Those precepts and rules in your Buddhism are not necessary. People should be free to do as they please, especially in America. This is a democratic country, and everyone is free and independent. So there shouldn't be prohibitions in Buddhism, either." They denounce the idea of the Buddha's precepts. They say that one can be a left-home person, a member of the Sangha, whether one has taken precepts or not. They claim that the precepts and rules are unnecessary and that there is no need to abide by the three thousand modes of deportment and the eighty thousand subtle aspects of conduct. They **violated the bodhisattva precepts.** They don't uphold the ten major and forty-eight minor bodhisattva precepts. They violate them. They **slandered the Buddha's nirvana.** They say that the principle of nirvana is also incorrect. These kinds of people are steeped in offenses. They have **and created various other kinds of karma** as well – a lot of bad karma. After creating offenses such as these, they **pass through many kalpas** – a tremendously long time – **of being burned in the inferno** before **they finally finish paying for their offenses.** Eventually their offenses are gone and they no longer have to dwell in the hells undergoing bitter retributions. When their offenses are paid back, they **are reborn as ghosts.** True enough, they've finished being punished for their offenses, but then they get reborn as ghosts.

People who call themselves disciples of the Buddha and yet don't believe in ghosts should pay attention to the mention of ghosts in the *Shurangama Sutra.* There are many kinds of ghosts, not just one kind. In fact, I'll tell you something: the Shurangama Mantra for the most part consists of the names of ghosts. *La She Pwo Ye, Ju La Bwo Ye* are names of ghosts. The reason we recite the mantra is to call out the names of the ghost kings. When we recite names of the big ghosts, all the lesser ones don't dare make trouble, either. Mantras are the names of ghosts and spirits.

The beings discussed here are reborn as ghosts. What kind of ghosts? Ten kinds of ghosts are now discussed in connection with the karma created from the ten habitual causes. But, in fact, there are many kinds of ghosts, not just ten. These are just representative.

J1   Strange ghosts result from the habit of greed and take form when they encounter material objects.

Sutra:

"If greed for material objects was the original cause that made the person commit offenses, then, after he has finished

paying for his crimes, he takes shape when he encounters material objects, and he is called a strange ghost.

Commentary:

If greed for material objects was the original cause on his causal ground **that made the person commit offenses, then, after he has finished paying for his crimes, he takes shape when he encounters material objects.** What kind of objects was he greedy for? The greatest desire is the desire for sex. If he sought such things when he was on the causal ground, and if he committed crimes while doing so, then he has to fall into the hells. After his term in hell is finished, he takes shape when he encounters material objects. What kind of objects? Any kind; whatever kind it is, he can attach himself to it and take his form from it. He's **called a strange ghost.**

J2   Drought ghosts result from the habit of lust and take form when they encounter wind.

Sutra:

"If it was greed for lust that made the person commit offenses, then, after he has finished paying for his crimes, he takes shape when he encounters the wind, and he is called a drought-ghost.

Commentary:

If it was greed for lust that made the person commit offenses, then, after he has finished paying for his crimes, he takes shape when he encounters the wind. In China, someone who is lustful is said to be greedy for "the wind and the current." People who are like this end up as drought-ghosts. What are drought-ghosts like? Wherever they go, it doesn't rain, and this is due to the "tricks of desert and of drought-ghosts." If you encounter a place where the rain does not fall, where the sprouts in the fields dry up and die, you know now that such a place is inhabited by a drought-ghost. This is true! By listening to the *Shurangama Sutra*, you can unravel all the mysteries of the world. All the questions of physical science are clarified in this sutra. If you hadn't heard this sutra, you wouldn't understand the reason behind droughts and deserts. Basically, these are due to the tricks of the drought-ghost.

This kind of person was greedy for "the wind and the current," and so now when his ghost encounters the wind it takes its shape and **is called a drought-ghost.** He causes drought wherever he goes. Pretty talented, huh?

J3   Mei ghosts result from the habit of lying and take form when they encounter animals.

Sutra:

"If it was greed to lie that made the person commit offenses, then, after he has finished paying for his crimes, he takes shape when he encounters an animal, and he is called a mei ghost.

Commentary:

This kind of ghost takes its shape when it encounters an animal – perhaps a fox spirit or a yellow wolf, or even a cat or a dog. It's possible for animals to have these weird essences attached to them. I've seen a cat that was possessed by a ghost. It could perform some great stunts. It could jump more than ten feet in the air and land on the top of the house. Then it would leap off the house and land on the ground; it would go through this routine over and over. It also howled and wailed. A fox that is possessed in this way can in turn possess a person. Although it's an animal, it can send out its soul and enter a person, and talk through him or her. A yellow wolf can also do this. It sends out its efficacious spirit and possesses someone. Then it can speak through the person it has possessed. There are a lot of these strange manifestations. This is called the *mei* ghost. When it possesses a person, the person's mind becomes totally confused by it, and he loses his sense of awareness. It's as if he were asleep.

J4   Poisonous ghosts result from the habit of hatred and take form when they encounter worms.

Sutra:

"If it was greed for hatred that made the person commit offenses, then, after he has finished paying for his crimes, he

takes shape when he encounters worms, and he is called a ku poison ghost.

Commentary:

If it was greed for hatred that made the person commit offenses, then, after he has finished paying for his crimes, he takes shape when he encounters worms. All ten of these ghosts are described by means of their greed. Ultimately, it is greed that creates their forms as ghosts. This one was greedy for hatred. Full of hatred, he would attack people without reason, and so he committed offense-karma involving hatred. That caused him to fall into the Relentless Hell. When he finishes working out his punishments in the hells, he becomes a ghost, and he takes shape when he encounters worms.

He is called a ku poison ghost. This *ku* poison is found in Canton province in China. People use it to put hexes on other people. They take the *ku* poison from these worms and make it into a medicine. If they slip a pill of this medicine into your tea, then ever after that you must obey their every instruction. If you don't, you'll die. That's to contract *ku* poisoning. In the southeast Asian countries like Singapore, Thailand, Vietnam, and so forth, *ku* poisoning is common. There is a ghost behind this kind of poisoning – it is his specialty. His potions are extremely potent.

The only way to undo such a hex is for the person who put it on you to recite a mantra designed to release you from it. But if he won't do that, then you're in real trouble. You are forever in his control. One amusing use of it is by the southern women who hex the northern men from Canton province whom they take a fancy to. After they marry, the wife puts a hex on her northern husband so that if he ever gets the idea in his head to leave her, he will die. So those northern men are very faithful to their southern wives. A lot of people have this trick played on them. But you should be clear that this is a deviant trick.

J5   Pestilence ghosts result from the habit of resentment and take form when they encounter degeneration.

Sutra:

"If it was greed for animosity that made the person commit offenses, then, after he has finished paying for his crimes, he takes shape when he encounters degeneration, and he is called a pestilence ghost.

Commentary:

If it was greed for animosity that made the person commit offenses, then, after he has finished paying for his crimes, he takes shape when he encounters degeneration. "Animosity" means that he's always thinking about things that happened in the past and remembering them with resentment. Because he's always wanting to get even, he commits offenses. From these crimes, he is forced to fall into the Relentless Hells. After the offenses are paid for and disappear, the criminal is free. But his freedom is such that when he encounters degeneration he takes shape. It may be a debilitated person or any kind of animal that is feeble and old. He borrows the physical forms of such beings and becomes **a pestilence ghost.** Sometimes, rather than taking over a person who is debilitated, he possesses a person who then becomes debilitated. This kind of ghost is terrible and fierce. It can wipe out a human life as easily as it can pull something out of its pocket.

J6   Hungry ghosts result from the habit of arrogance and take form when they encounter gases.

Sutra:

"If it was greed to be arrogant that made the person commit offenses, then after he has finished paying for his crimes, he takes shape when he encounters gases, and he is called a hungry ghost.

Commentary:

If it was greed to be arrogant that made the person commit offenses, then after he has finished paying for his crimes, he

takes shape when he encounters gases. He was a really haughty individual. Therefore, people should not look down on others. People should not be haughty and self-satisfied, or be totally lacking in courtesy toward others. A person like this doesn't even acknowledge others when he encounters them – he's downright rude.

During the Three Kingdoms period in China, there was a pedant named Ze Ce who went to see General Cao Cao. Cao Cao prepared everyone in advance of the visit, saying that when the pedant walked in, no one should look at him. When the pedant arrived for his appointment with Cao Cao, none of the several dozen attendants who surrounded the general stood up. It was just as if they hadn't even noticed that he had come in. So what do you suppose Ze Ce did? He started to cry. Cao Cao asked, "What are you crying about?"

He replied, "How could you expect me not to weep when I encounter a whole group of dead people? They are all dead, aren't they? That's why they can't speak or move, isn't it?"

After that scolding, Cao Cao was at a loss. This happened at the time when Cao Cao was in his greatest days of power. That's why he was rude to Ze Ce. And what he displayed was the kind of arrogance being discussed here.

A person who is arrogant will commit offenses, and after his term in the unspaced hells, he will take shape when he encounters gases. The kind of gas doesn't matter – any kind will do for him to use to make his appearance. This kind of ghost **is called a hungry ghost.** "Hungry ghosts" are just what their name implies – ghosts that don't have anything to eat. Their necks are as skinny as needles, and their bellies are as big as barrels. Since their throats are so thin, they can't swallow any food. If you were to see such a ghost, wouldn't you consider it to be ugly?

J7　Paralysis ghosts result from the habit of injustice and form when they encounter darkness.

Sutra:

"If it was greed to be unjust to others that made the person commit offenses, then after he has finished paying for his

crimes, he takes shape when he encounters darkness, and he is called a paralysis ghost.

Commentary:

If it was greed to be unjust to others – to hurt other people – **that made the person commit offenses, then after he has finished paying for his crimes, he takes shape when he encounters darkness.** Being greedy to oppress and prone to being unfair, one creates offenses. These offenses will cause one to fall into the unspaced hells. After hundreds of thousands of millions of kalpas, one's karmic offenses are wiped away and one is free to go, but one's left-over habits still remain and have not been changed, and so one is still unjust and greedy to oppress others. The habits persist. So he takes his form when he encounters darkness. He appears in dingy, shadowy places, **and he is called a paralysis ghost.** Do you remember the kumbhanda ghost that was discussed before? This is he. One of my disciples tells me that he has met this type of ghost dozens of times. He fought them off each time and didn't lose his life, however.

It's dangerous business to get mixed up with them, though, because it's possible for a paralysis ghost to kill you with his techniques. But now that this disciple believes in the Buddha, I believe that this type of ghost won't have the audacity to bother him anymore.

J8   Wang-liang ghosts result from the habit of views and take form when they encounter essential energy.

Sutra:

"If it was greed for views that made the person commit offenses, then, after he has finished paying for his crimes, he takes shape when he encounters essential energy, and he is called a wang-liang ghost.

Commentary:

"Views" refers to opinions – to one's own viewpoint. With the habit of views, one considers oneself to be extremely intelligent. In actual fact, such a person as this is thoroughly confused in what he does. He may be smart, but he ends up outsmarting himself. He clearly knows that murder is not a good thing to do, but he goes out and kills people. He knows that one should not steal but he commits robbery. Sure, he's smart, all right, and he's an effective speaker, but his own actions are a total mess. Someone like this has **greed for views** – he's intelligent, but his conduct is disreputable, and he **commit offenses.** Because of the offenses, he falls into the Relentless Hells and there passes through hundreds of thousands of millions of aeons. After his term is served, he's free, but when he gets out of the hells, what do you suppose happens to him? Well, he doesn't change his old habits. He's still endowed with worldly intelligence that goes awry and so **he takes shape when he encounters essential energy, and he is called a wang-liang ghost.** If he encounters a person who is robust and full of energy, or if he encounters some weird essence, he will make his appearance. What do *wang liang* ghosts look like? Sometimes they will turn into a child. But whereas most children have two legs, this ghost will have one. Sometimes it will appear as an adult, but whereas people's heads are between their shoulders, its head will grow out from between its legs. Have you ever seen anything like that? If you do, you'll know that it's what's called a *wang liang* ghost. It's always just a little off in its appearance – weird looking.

It also acts as an "accomplice for tigers." How does it do that? Say, for example, that a certain mountain region is infested with tigers, so that no one dares to traverse that area for fear of being attacked and eaten. What this ghost does in such a place is to transform himself into the appearance of a person and go walking along the road there. When an actual person sees that there appears to be a person on the road ahead of him, he is not afraid, and he follows along into the dangerous area. Who would have guessed that the *wang liang* would lead the person right to the tiger's den? That's his game, to help tigers get their meals. He cheats animals this way just as he does people; he turns into one of their kind and leads them to their doom. Those who profess not to believe that there are ghosts should pay attention to these descriptions.

J9   Servant ghosts result from the habit of deceit and take form when they encounter brightness.

Sutra:

"If it was greed for deception that made the person commit offenses, then, after he has finished paying for his crimes, he takes shape when he encounters brightness, and he is called a servant ghost.

Commentary:

If it was greed for deception that made the person commit offenses, then, after he has finished paying for his crimes, he takes shape when he encounters brightness. This refers to the habit of deception. Since he wants accomplishments, he gets them by deceiving other people, acting in underhanded ways. By doing this, he commits many offenses and falls into the Relentless Hells. After passing through hundreds of thousands of aeons, he finally gets free, but he still hasn't gotten rid of his left-over habits, and so he still wants to cheat people. Therefore, he takes his shape when he meets brightness. "Brightness" refers to people with wisdom who know how to recite mantras. Or you could say it refers to a "bright teacher." When this ghost meets with that kind of a wise person, it makes its appearance. What does it do? It attends upon such people so **is called a servant ghost.** It helps such people do the things they want to do.

In China there was a man named Ji Xiao Tang who had five servant ghosts that helped him out. One went about gathering news – keeping up on the latest goings-on. Another ghost helped Ji Xiao Tang listen to things. Since ghosts have five penetrations, they could see things that the ordinary eyes cannot see. Ghosts lack the penetration of the extinction of outflows, but they can possess the other five.

1. the penetration of the heavenly eye
2. the penetration of the heavenly ear

3. the penetration of others' thought
4. the penetration of past lives
5. the penetration of the complete spirit

These kinds of ghosts have a little cultivation, some practice the Way, and so they are endowed with these spiritual penetrations. The ghosts that attended on Ji Xiao Tang could know what people were talking about and could see what was happening at great distances to find out what was happening round and about, and then he would use that information to go and rescue people from difficulty. For example, he would find out that at such and such a place there were some weird creatures out to harm people, and he would immediately go to that place and subdue the weird beings and exorcise the strange creatures. These five servant ghosts helped him in that way. They got to be servant ghosts because in the past they were greedy to deceive others.

J10   Messenger ghosts result from the habit of litigiousness and take form when they encounter people.

Sutra:

"If it was greed to be litigious that made the person commit offenses, then, after he has finished paying for his crimes, he takes shape when he encounters people, and he is called a messenger ghost.

Commentary:

If it was greed to be litigious that made the person commit offenses, then, after he has finished paying for his crimes, he takes shape when he encounters people. "Litigious" refers to getting involved in court cases. Sometimes when people go to court, they get together a party or faction to support their case. These people offer testimony on the instigator's behalf, but they tell stories and invent evidence. What really isn't true, they say is true; what is actually not so, they say is so. They argue their case when there is really no principle behind it. Often they are lawyers and the like. They challenge the people who are not of their faction, and they win their cases.

A person who does this kind of thing commits offenses. When he has finished paying for his wrongdoing, he takes his shape when he encounters a person, **and he is called a messenger ghost.** This kind of ghost possesses a person and speaks through him, saying such things as, "I am such and such a Buddha," or "I am such and such a Bodhisattva," or "I am God. I am also Jesus." A person who is so possessed will be restless and have a lot of nervous mannerisms. He's called a "messenger" because he can predict lucky and unlucky events. He may say, "There's going to be an earthquake at such and such a place, and it will kill more than ten thousand people." When the time comes, his prediction is completely accurate. He can foretell the future.

Someone doubts that such predictions are really accurate. But in fact they are often extremely accurate. It's right at this place that you need to know how to distinguish between the proper and the deviant. The proper is recognized as having come from cultivation of the Way. It's not that you rely on a ghost or spirit or a bodhisattva or a Buddha to tell you such things. Be sure to recognize this clearly. In China, such people who are possessed by a ghost are called mediums or shamans. They are able to heal people. But it is not the person who does the healing. What does it is the ghost or the spirit which is possessing the person. It's like those people I described earlier who can stick knives into their skulls and swords into their shoulders. They are examples of possession by messenger ghosts.

---

13   Probes the source and shows it to be non-existent.

Sutra:

"Ananda, such a person's fall is due to his totally emotional level of functioning. When his karmic fire has burned out, he will rise up to be reborn as a ghost. This is occasioned by his own karma of false thinking. If he awakens to bodhi, then in the wonderful perfect brightness there isn't anything at all.

Commentary:

The Buddha calls out again: **Ananda,** do you understand? **Such a person's fall is due to his totally emotional level of functioning.** It's because this person is totally immersed in emotion. Whatever he does is based on emotional desire. Because he's totally emotional, without any power of reason, without any discursive thought, he acts out of emotion, he functions out of desire, and that causes him to fall. Emotion belongs to *yin*, and discursive thought belongs to *yang*. After he falls and his **karmic fire has burned out** – after he goes to the hells and burns until there is nothing left to burn, he can come out, but **he will** then **rise up to be reborn as a ghost.** He's released, but he still cannot become a person. Where does he "rise up" from? The evil hells. He gets out and comes to the world. But although he's out of the hells, his residual habits are still not cut off. Although the offenses from his karma have been eradicated, he still has the same old habits of thinking. He's not completely pure. So he has to become a ghost.

His predicament **is occasioned by his own karma of false thinking.** In the one truth, he himself gave rise to falseness and produced ignorance. This ignorance arises in the nature of the treasury of the Thus Come One, and with it comes false thinking. It is false thinking that creates these kinds of karma. Because of it, the person in question must undergo this bitter retribution. He gave rise to delusion, created karma, and underwent retribution. **If he awakens to bodhi, then in the wonderful perfect brightness there isn't anything at all.** If he could fathom the wonderful path to enlightenment, then there would be nothing at all in the mind, which is perfect and bright in the nature of the treasury of the Thus Come One. There's none of this trouble. There are no such problems; there isn't any of this pain and suffering. There is no distress.

Destiny of Animals

Sutra:

"Moreover, Ananda, when his karma as a ghost is ended, the problem of emotion as opposed to discursive thought is resolved. At that point he must pay back in kind what he borrowed from others to resolve those grievances. He is born into the body of an animal to repay his debts from past lives.

Commentary:

Moreover, Ananda, let me continue to explain this principle lest you fail to understand it completely. **When his karma as a ghost is ended, the problem of emotion as opposed to discursive thought is resolved.** He's wiped the slate clean of emotion and thought. **At that point he must pay back in kind what he borrowed from others to resolve those grievances.** He has to pay back what he owes others. If he ate the flesh of other animals in the past, he will now be eaten by others. If he took others' lives in the past, then in this life he will be killed. **He is born into the body of an animal to repay his debts from past lives.** He will pay back the debts amassed for limitless kalpas in the past. They have to be paid back in kind. If you killed and harmed others, then the same thing will happen to you as repayment. If you owe someone a pig, then you become his pig to repay him. If you owe someone a dog, then you become his dog to repay him. If you owe someone a cow, you repay by being his cow. If you owe someone a horse, you become his horse to repay him. If you owe someone a chicken, then you go lay eggs for him. You lay a few eggs every day and in that way you gradually repay your debt. So it's not easy to act in this world's play. If you make a mistake, a lot of trouble results. If you do it correctly, then everything is clear and pure.

I2   Specifically lists ten categories.
J1   Owl category.

Sutra:

"The retribution of the strange ghost of material objects is finished when the object is destroyed and it is reborn in the world, usually as a species of owl.

Commentary:

Because strange ghosts were greedy for material objects, they took their shape when they encountered material objects. **When the object is destroyed** means that the particular material object they were possessing wears out, and their karmic retribution has come to an end. The majority of the strange ghosts are then reborn as owls. That's what usually happens, but it's not a totally fixed principle. There's a line in the *Book of Poetry*: "The owl, the owl, the unfilial bird." Some owls can incubate a clod of dirt and hatch it. How do you explain this? Well, it's just the strange way that they are. When the owlets hatch, they eat the parent bird. A child that eats its parents is a manifestation of a weird being. This kind of bird is considered to be inauspicious. "Species" means that they are born as one kind of owl or another.

J2   Inauspicious category.

Sutra:

"The retribution of the drought ghost of the wind is finished when the wind subsides, and it is reborn in the world, usually as a species of weird creature which gives inauspicious prognostications.

Commentary:

Wherever drought ghosts happen to be, there will be no rain. Wherever they go, the land is arid. They were greedy for lustful experiences. Through lust they created karma, and eventually they became drought ghosts when they met with the wind. When they are finished with that retribution, they are reborn in the world, but they cannot become people. Instead they become weird beings that foretell evil. Why do they have to go through this? After creating the karma of lust, enduring the hells, and being reborn as drought ghosts, their residual habits are still not completely severed, and so they become such strange creatures as these. They may be reborn as birds that are extremely colorful, but have the habit of excessive lust, or they may be reborn as beasts that are fond of lust.

J3   Fox category.

Sutra:

"The retribution of the mei ghost of an animal is finished when the animal dies, and it is reborn in the world, usually as a species of fox.

Commentary:

For the most part, these *mei* ghosts are reborn as foxes after they have finished their karma as ghosts.

J4   Poisonous category.

Sutra:

"The retribution of the ku ghost in the form of worms is finished when the ku is exhausted, and it is reborn in the world, usually as a species of venomous creature.

Commentary:

A *ku* poison ghost takes its shape when it encounters worms. When the *ku* poison finally wears out and the ghost's retribution is ended, it is reborn in the world as a venomous creature – as a scorpion, cobra, or the like.

J5   Tapeworm category.

Sutra:

"The retribution of a pestilence ghost found in degeneration is finished when the degeneration is complete, and it is reborn in the world, usually as a species of tapeworm.

Commentary:

The retribution of a pestilence ghost found in degeneration is finished when the degeneration is complete. Whoever encounters this kind of ghost will waste away. These ghosts are really terrible; their demonic power is tremendous. When its retribution is ended, **it is reborn in the world, usually as a species of tapeworm.** These are the bugs in your intestines. I don't know if this kind of sickness exists in the West, but in China, these tapeworms can communicate; they can talk. They can talk to the person whose stomach they are occupying. There's no way to cure this kind of sickness with medicine, unless the person who has the sickness does not know that he is being given medicine. If the sick person knows it is medicine designed to eliminate the tapeworm, the tapeworm also knows. From this comes the expression, "You're not a tapeworm in my stomach, so how do you know what I'm thinking?"

Not only can tapeworms do this, but other kinds of weird beings can get into one's stomach and then carry on conversations. I've told you about the elder disciple I had in Hong Kong; she's probably more than eighty years old by now. She was about sixty when she took refuge with me. At that time she was deaf. Regardless of the fact that she couldn't hear, she came faithfully every time I gave a sutra lecture. She only understood Cantonese to begin with, and I was lecturing in Mandarin, and though there was a translator, she couldn't hear the translation. But she came anyway. It was more than three hundred steps up to the temple. I lectured from seven to nine at night, and she would come up and go down all those stairs. There was no light on the path. Despite her age, she was not afraid of falling. She was very sincere. One day she heard the recitation of "Homage to the Lotus Pool Assembly of Buddhas and Bodhisattvas," and thereafter her deafness was cured. She could hear again. That made her even more sincere, of course. Whenever I lectured and whatever sutra it was on, she would come to hear. Wind and rain did not keep her away.

But when you cultivate, if you are sincere, there will be demonic obstacles. As I've said before, if you want to cultivate well, your sins will catch up with you. Ties of resentment from your past lives will come to get you. If you want to become a Buddha, you have to endure the demons that come to test you. One night, then, this woman had a dream, or what seemed to be a dream and yet not to be one. In it she saw three plump children between the ages of two and three. After the dream she got sick. What was the nature of her illness? She had to eat all day long. She had to eat a meal every hour. She ate more than ten meals a day. Thinking it was a disease, she went to Western and Chinese doctors, but they told her she was not sick. This went on for two or three years. Finally one evening, on the seventh day of the second lunar month, the day before the celebration of Shakyamuni Buddha's accomplishment of the Way, when I'd come back from Ze Xing monastery on Da Yu mountain, she said to me, "Shih Fu, how is it that there's someone in my stomach talking to me?"

"What did it say?" I asked her.

She said, "Today I made some cakes with coarse rice. When I ate them, something in my stomach said to me, 'I don't like to eat that stuff.'"

"What did you say?" I asked.

She replied, "I said, 'You get full, that's good enough. If you don't eat that, what are you going to eat?'" She talked back to her stomach like that.

I said, "Don't worry, tonight I'll make you well. Go back home, and light a stick of incense at your altar at midnight and recite the Buddha's name."

She went back and did as I said. As she did it, she saw three children come out of her stomach. They were the three plump ones she had seen in the dream. Then she saw Wei Tuo Bodhisattva set down two bowls of noodles, and the three children fought over the food. When they finished eating, Wei Tuo Bodhisattva pinched the three of them by the ear and dragged them away. After they were gone, she felt that her stomach was totally empty. From then on her sickness of liking to eat was cured.

Tapeworms, too, can talk in a person's stomach. But what the old woman had were not tapeworms. They were three weird goblins; two were frogs, and one was a lizard. They were a kind of hungry ghost. Why did she have to endure this sickness? I looked into her causes and conditions, it became clear later that in a former life she was a Buddhist, and she knew someone who had this very same kind of sickness. He was already over the illness when she met him, but he told her about it. Her reaction was, "I don't believe that. Who ever heard of someone having a hungry ghost in their stomach, a hungry ghost that could talk to them?" Because she said she didn't believe it, she had to go through the personal experience in this life of having that same kind of illness. When she had it, there were a lot of people in Hong Kong who didn't believe it either. They said, "Whoever heard of such a thing? It's ridiculous." These were Chinese people who didn't believe – it's not just Westerners who have a hard time believing it. And I believe that the people in Hong Kong who expressed disbelief will also get this kind of illness in some future life. The cycle of cause and effect is fierce.

J6   Food category.

Sutra:

"The retribution of the ghost which takes shape in gases is finished when the gases are gone, and it is then reborn in the world, usually as a species of eating animal.

Commentary:

Since in the past it was greedy to be arrogant, it committed offenses. Now these offenses are paid for, and it can enter the world of people, but for the most part it gets reborn as an eating animal. There are two ways to explain "eating" here. First, the animal can't do anything but eat. That's all it's good for, like a pig or a sheep. Second, it is eaten by people. People eat the flesh of the pigs and sheep, and of cattle and chickens. This ghost, then, gets reborn as an animal which people consume. These kinds of animals are often domesticated so that they can be fattened up and then slaughtered and eaten.

J7   Clothing category.

Sutra:

"The retribution of the ghost of prolonged darkness is finished when the darkness ends, and it is then reborn in the world, usually as a species of animal used for clothing or service.

Commentary:

This is the paralysis ghost. When it takes rebirth, it is usually as an animal used for clothing or service. Animals used for clothing would include silkworms and animals whose fur or hide is used to make clothes. "Service" refers to dogs and cats which spend their lives in the households of humans, being obedient to them and of some service to them.

J8   Migratory category.

Sutra:

"The retribution of the ghost which unites with energy is finished when the union dissolves, and it is then reborn in the world, usually as a species of migratory creature.

Commentary:

The retribution of the ghost which unites with energy is finished when the union dissolves. These are the *wang liang* ghosts who take shape when they encounter essential energy. The text reads "when the union dissolves," but actually it should say "when the energy is dissolved." **It is then reborn in the world,**

usually as a species of migratory creature. These kinds of creatures have an instinct about time. They include the wild geese that, flying in formation, migrate north in the spring and south in the autumn. In the spring the swallows come and nest in the eaves. After they have reared their young they fly away again. They are another example of creatures that have an instinct for time and know when to migrate.

J9   Auspicious category.

Sutra:

"The retribution of the ghost of brightness and intellect is finished when the brightness disappears, and it is then reborn in the world, usually as a species of auspicious creature.

Commentary:

These are the servant ghosts. When they are reborn they become auspicious creatures like the unicorn, the phoenix, and such. They become animals and birds which are considered lucky.

J10   Domestic category.

Sutra:

"The retribution of the ghost that relies on a person is finished when the person dies, and it is then reborn in the world, usually as a species of domestic animal.

Commentary:

These kinds of animals are docile and obedient. Dogs, cats, horses, and the like are examples of this kind of rebirth.

I3   Probes the source and shows it to be non-existent.

Sutra:

"Ananda, all this is due to the burning out of his karmic fire in payment for his debts from past lives. The rebirth as an animal is also occasioned by his own false and empty karma. If he awakens to bodhi, then fundamentally none of these false conditions will exist at all.

Commentary:

Ananda, all the various kinds of rebirth just discussed are **due to the burning out of his karmic fire in payment for his debts from past lives. The rebirth as an animal is also occasioned by his own false and empty karma.** It's due to the karma he created in the past. **If he awakens to bodhi, then fundamentally none of these false conditions will exist at all.** If he awakens to the enlightened path, then all these false conditions will disappear. They are all empty.

---

14   Repeats answer to prior question.

Sutra:

"You mentioned Precious Lotus Fragrance, King Crystal, and bhikshu Good Stars. Evil karma such as theirs was created by them alone. It did not fall down out of the heavens or well up from the earth, nor did some person impose it upon them. Their own falseness brought it into being, and so they themselves have to undergo it. In the bodhi mind, it is empty and false – a cohesion of false thoughts.

Commentary:

You mentioned Precious Lotus Fragrance. You remember what kind of a bhikshuni she was? Do you remember how she acted? **King Crystal, and bhikshu Good Stars** were the others that you brought up. **Evil karma such as theirs was created by them alone.** They fell into the hells alive. But they brought it down on themselves. **It did not fall down out of the heavens or well up from the earth, nor did some person impose it upon them.** That is not how their evil karma came about. **Their own falseness brought it into being, and so they themselves have to undergo it. In the bodhi mind, it is empty and false.** In the bodhi mind, karma such as this is ephemeral and imaginary. It's not real; it is just **a cohesion of false thoughts.** The solidification of false thinking is what brings this karma into being.

Destiny of People

H4   Destiny of people.
I1   Traces prior teaching and the alarming result.
J1   The burden of debts must be repaid.

Sutra:

"Moreover, Ananda, if while repaying his past debts by undergoing rebirth as an animal, such a living being pays back more than he owed, he will then be reborn as a human to rectify the excess.

Commentary:

He lives out a life as an animal in order to pay back the debts he made in the past. If in the process he pays back more than he needed to, he then gets reborn as a person again to make up the difference.

Sutra:

"If he is a person with strength, blessings, and virtue, then once he is in the human realm, he will not have to lose his human rebirth after what is owed him is restored. But if he lacks blessings, then he will return to the animal realm to continue repaying his debts.

Commentary:

If he is a person with strength, blessings, and virtue, then once he is in the human realm, he will not have to lose his human rebirth. "Strength" means that he has the power of good karma. If on top of that he accumulates blessings and virtue, then he won't have to lose a human body **after what is owed him is restored** – after he's been paid back for the overpayment of debts he made while he was in the animal realm. **But if he lacks blessings** and virtue, **then he will return to the animal realm to continue repaying his debts.** He'll get reborn as an animal again to go on paying what he owes. There is no way to get off easy or cheat anyone out of anything. It must be just. Although there isn't any actual person controlling the whole process, the power of one's own karma is such that it does not allow any injustice. No one takes a loss unfairly.

J2   The burden of life: killing to eat is endless.

Sutra:

"**Ananda, you should know that once the debt is paid, whether with money, material goods, or manual labor, the process of repayment naturally comes to an end.**

Commentary:

Ananda, you should know that, while in the human realm, **once the debt is paid, whether with money, material goods, or manual labor, the process of repayment naturally comes to an end.** When the repayment is sufficient, the work naturally stops.

Sutra:

"**But if in the process he took the lives of other beings or ate their flesh, then he continues in the same way, passing through kalpas as many as motes of fine dust, taking turns devouring and being slaughtered in a cycle that sends him up and down endlessly.**

Commentary:

But if in the process, when he is tying up conditions with other beings, **he took the lives of other beings or ate their flesh, then he continues in the same way, passing through kalpas as many as motes of fine dust, taking turns devouring and being slaughtered in a cycle that sends him up and down endlessly.** He gets caught in a cycle that goes on for aeons and aeons, a cycle of eating and being eaten, killing and being killed. It goes on and on like the turning of a wheel – you eat me, and I eat you – one doesn't know how long it lasts. He goes up and down, depending on whether he ate more or was eaten more. But it never stops. It is ceaseless. It's extremely dangerous.

Sutra:

"There is no way to put a stop to it, except through shamatha or through a Buddha's coming to the world.

Commentary:

"Shamatha" is the Buddha's "still and illumining" samadhi; except through cultivating it and through upholding the durable Shurangama Samadhi, to obtain the great Shurangama Samadhi, there's no respite from this karmic obstacle, unless a Buddha comes into the world to release one from the appearance of these karmic offenses. Then both parties will know that they should not continue creating such karma. Only in that way can the cycle be stopped.

I2   A detailed listing of the ten categories.
J1   The category of corrupt and obstinate people.

Sutra:

"You should know that when owls and their kind have paid back their debts, they regain their original form and are born as people, but among those who are corrupt and obstinate.

Commentary:

"Their kind" refers to any other birds that are evil like owls are. Once they have undergone their karmic retribution, they return to their original form as human beings. But, although they are born again as people, they are corrupt and obstinate. When these creatures take birth again in the human realm, they become people who are totally perverse and hardheaded. They are stubborn and refuse to yield. They are totally unreasonable and unprincipled. Quite often they become robbers. They don't listen to reason. If you tried to explain some Buddhadharma to them, they would run away.

"Among those who are corrupt and obstinate" means that they get together with such people – people like themselves. So it is said:

> People join up with those who are like them,
> Creatures divide into their various species.
>
> The good get together,
> The bad form gangs,
> People find people who are of their own kind.

Students spend their time with other students. Workmen join together with other workmen. Gamblers get together with gamblers. Opium smokers mingle with other opium smokers. Hippies form communes with other hippies. It's all a manifestation of this principle – people find their own kind.

J2   The category of abnormal people.

Sutra:

"When creatures that are inauspicious have paid back their debts, they regain their original form and are born as people, but among those who are abnormal.

Commentary:

After they undergo their karmic retribution, they can be born in the human realm again, but as freaks. You see mention of this type of rebirth in the newspapers all the time. A woman gives birth to a child with two heads or a child that has two bodies but only one head. Or the infant's six sense organs will be out of place. Perhaps the eyes will be where the ears should be and the ears where the eyes belong. The nose may be where the mouth should be. The mouth may be where the nose should be. The sense organs exchange places. For the six sense-organs to be irregular is what is meant by "abnormal." Often such people die as soon as they are born, but even so they are counted as freaks. In general, "abnormal" means that there is something not right about them.

J3   The category of simple people.

Sutra:

"When foxes have paid back their debts, they regain their original forms and are born as people, but among those who are simpletons.

Commentary:

The fox is extremely intelligent. But his intelligence is of a ghostly kind. That is, it is false, and so when he gets rebirth as a person again, he has to be a simpleton. He becomes a very dense kind of person. You can say something to him over and over and he still won't understand. If you leave him alone, he gets along all right, but as soon as you try to reason with him or explain something, it becomes obvious that he's completely out of it. He can't understand at all.

J4   The category of hateful people.

Sutra:

"When creatures of the venomous category have paid back their debts, they regain their original form and are born as people, but among those who are hateful.

Commentary:

When creatures of the venomous category – including things like poisonous snakes and vicious beasts – **have paid back their debts, they regain their original form and are born as people, but among those who are hateful.** When they finish out their retribution, they come back in the world as people, but although they manage to get reborn in the human realm, they still have not changed their bad habits. They are extremely cruel and fierce. They are obstinate and angry. If they say they are going to kill someone, they do just that. That's because they are still like poisonous snakes who take no heed of whether their actions are justifiable or not; if you get in their way, they will bite and kill you and talk about it later. As people, they continue along in that same kind of evil habit of killing people. They are terribly cruel and unreasonable. Their poisonous habits haven't changed since their lives as snakes.

The *Shurangama Sutra* discussion of human nature and the nature of all creatures is an extremely detailed one. If you investigate it carefully, you see that it is all minutely set forth.

J5   The category of lowly people.

Sutra:

"When tapeworms and their like have paid back their debts, they regain their original form and are born as people, but among those who are lowly.

Commentary:

When tapeworms and their like have paid back their debts, they regain their original form. Do you remember that tapeworms are able to talk? Pretty strange, wouldn't you say? When this kind of creature has paid back its debts from former lives, then it can become a person again. Although it becomes a person, it lives out that human life **among those who are lowly.** Very worthless people, they are, who must work for others and do menial tasks. They are inferior, unimportant, and insignificant people.

J6   The category of weak people.

Sutra:

"When the edible types of creatures have paid back their debts, they regain their original form and are reborn as people, but among those who are weak.

Commentary:

When the edible types of creatures, who have been reborn as animals that people like to eat, **have paid back their debts, they regain their original form and are reborn as people, but among those who are weak.** When their karmic obstacle dissolves, they go back to being people again, but they must be reborn among the weak, because they have not changed their bad habits from the past. They are very manipulable. They cannot manage on their own in the world. In all that they do they have to rely on others for support. They are cowardly and meek to a fault.

J7   The category of laborers.

Sutra:

"When creatures that are used for clothing or service have paid back their debts, they regain their original form and are reborn as people, but among those who do hard labor.

Commentary:

When creatures that are used for clothing or service have paid back their debts, they regain their original form and are reborn as people. Living beings whose bodies or by-products are used for people's apparel or who must live a life of obedience and service to a human being eventually pay back their debts and can be reborn as people. But when they get born in the human realm it is **among those who do hard labor.** That's their lot in life.

J8   The category of literate people.

Sutra:

"When creatures that migrate have paid back their debts, they regain their original form and are reborn as people among those who are literate.

Commentary:

When creatures that migrate – wild geese and ducks – migratory birds and beasts – **have paid back their debts, they regain their original form and are reborn as people among those who are literate.** But their literary skills are not great. They have a little ability, that's all. They appear to be cultured, but they don't have exceptional talent.

J9   The category of intelligent people.

Sutra:

"When auspicious creatures have paid back their debts, they regain their original form and are reborn as people among those who are intelligent.

Commentary:

Their intelligence is not profound, however; it is a worldly intelligence which is skilled in argument.

J10   The category of well-informed people.

Sutra:

"When domestic animals have paid back their debts, they regain their original form and are reborn as people among those who are well-informed.

Commentary:

When domestic animals that have served people **have paid back their debts, they regain their original form and are reborn as people among those who are well-informed.** People like this comprehend what's going on. They understand social graces. But they do not have a genuine and comprehensive understanding that penetrates the past and present. They are not that well-educated. They simply attain a superficial kind of success in dealing with the world.

I3   Concludes with an expression of pity.

Sutra:

"Ananda, these are all beings that have finished paying back former debts and are born again in the human realm. They are involved in a beginningless scheme of karma and being upside-down in which their lives are spent killing one another and being killed by one another. They do not get to meet the Thus Come One or hear the proper dharma. They just abide in the

wearisome dust, passing through a repetitive cycle. Such people can truly be called pitiful.

Commentary:

Ananda, these are all beings that have finished paying back former debts and are born again in the human realm. Eventually they finished repaying the karmic debts they had to pay, and they get to become people. But **they are involved in a beginningless scheme of karma and being upside-down in which their lives are spent killing one another and being killed by one another.** They keep creating the same kind of upside-down evil karma by killing and being killed. **They do not get to meet the Thus Come One** – they never encounter a Buddha – **or hear the proper dharma. They just abide in the wearisome dust, passing through a repetitive cycle.** They remain forever in the wearisome mundane world. The "repetitive cycle" means that it's exactly the same over and over again. That's just how it always is for them. **Such people can truly be called pitiful.** The Buddha says that beings like these are very pathetic.

Destiny of Immortals

Sutra:

"Furthermore, Ananda, there are people who do not rely on proper enlightenment to cultivate samadhi, but cultivate in some special way that is based on their false thinking. Holding to the idea of perpetuating their physical bodies, they roam in the mountains and forests in places people do not go and become ten kinds of immortals.

Commentary:

Furthermore, Ananda, there are people who do not rely on proper enlightenment to cultivate samadhi. They do not rely on the great enlightened way of bodhi. They do not rely on the great Shurangama Samadhi, and they do not cultivate the skill of turning back their hearing to hear the self-nature. What they cultivate is a deviant samadhi of the externalist paths. It is based on false thinking and on the urge to climb on conditions – to take advantage of situations. They think like this: "I'll cultivate now, and when I accomplish some karma in the Way I'll display my spiritual penetrations for everyone to see. I'll get them to believe in me, respect me, make obeisance to me, and make offerings to me." That's what's meant by taking advantage of situations. It's not for the sake of becoming a Buddha or for the sake of practicing and upholding the Buddhadharma and causing it to spread and grow that they cultivate. They develop their skill with the idea of getting offerings for themselves. They display both greed and stupidity in that way. So they **cultivate in some special way that is based on their false thinking.** What do they have in mind? **Holding to the idea of perpetuating their physical bodies, they roam in the mountains and forests in places people do not go and become ten kinds of immortals.** They have the false thought that they will make their bodies strong and enduring, that they will become as solid as rock – that their bodies will never go bad. They go deep into the mountains or perhaps find an isolated island.

I2   Lists the immortals.
J1   Earth-traveling immortals.

Sutra:

"**Ananda, some living beings with unflagging resolution make themselves strong with doses of medicine. When they have perfected this method of ingestion, they are known as earth-traveling immortals.**

Commentary:

Ananda, some living beings with unflagging resolution make themselves strong with doses of medicine. They take this medicine with one aim in mind – to become an immortal. "Unflagging resolution" means that they are consistent in their practice. All the people to be discussed in this section are extremely faithful when it comes to their practice. It's not that they do it today and neglect it tomorrow. Every day, day after day, they develop their particular kind of skill. In this case it's ingesting drugs. By this they hope to gain immortality so that they don't have to die. **When they have perfected this method of ingestion, they are known as earth-traveling immortals.** The result of their efforts is that they are very light when they walk. Their bodies are buoyant. They can run very swiftly over the ground. They get to higher speeds than the emu in Australia, which can run as much as forty miles an hour.

This immortal travels over the ground as if he were flying; that's how he gets his name.

J2   Flying immortals.

Sutra:

"Some of these beings with unflagging resolution make themselves strong through the use of grasses and herbs. When they have perfected this method of taking herbs, they are known as flying immortals.

Commentary:

Some of these beings with unflagging resolution make themselves strong through the use of grasses and herbs. They pursue this practice with firm determination. If someone were to tell them to discontinue it, they could not do it. Their minds are like rock or iron. They are tougher than nails when it comes to perfecting their method of practice. In this case it is the use of grasses and herbs. They concoct a pill out of certain herbs and trees. They eat it every single day without fail. And due to their determination and to their wish to succeed, the method eventually starts to work. **When they have perfected this method of taking herbs, they are known as flying immortals.** Their bodies are as light as a wisp of smoke, and they can mount the clouds and drive the fog.

J3   Roaming immortals.

Sutra:

"Some of these beings with unflagging resolution make themselves strong through the use of metal and stone. When they have perfected this method of transformation, they are known as roaming immortals.

Commentary:

Some of these beings with unflagging resolution make themselves strong through the use of metal and stone. Their minds are determined – extremely strong and steadfast. They make a stove for concocting pills. They mix mercury and lead together, heating and reheating it, smelting and re-smelting it. They may smelt it for forty-nine days or for twenty-one days. It depends on the prescription they are taught. They combine gold and silver and when these too are sufficiently smelted they put all the ingredients together and eat the result. They're called pills of immortality; it's wonderful medicine. If one takes a pill of immortality one can "cast off the womb and transform one's bones." This is just a brief mention of the secret prescriptions for forging immortality. If they are successful, **when they have perfected this method of trans-formation, they are known as roaming immortals.** "Method of transformation" refers to the changes that take place as a result of the pills they concoct. The pills have a special ability to create change. As roaming immortals, they can go wherever they want.

J4   Space-traveling immortals.

Sutra:

"Some of these beings with unflagging resolution make themselves strong through movement and cessation. When they have perfected their breath and essence, they are known as space-traveling immortals.

Commentary:

Some of these beings with unflagging resolution make themselves strong through movement and cessation. These beings work with determination on movement and cessation. "Movement" can refer to the time that they work on developing their skill. "Cessation," then, is when they stop working. "Movement" can also refer to exercise such as *tai ji chuan.* "Cessation," then, is when they cultivate stillness. That is, they sit there and smelt the essence until it transforms into energy, they smelt the energy until it transforms into spirit, and they smelt the spirit until it returns to emptiness. How do they smelt the essence into energy? They sit in meditation and do not allow their essence to escape. They don't go near women. When their essence doesn't escape, it reverts inward. In that way it turns into energy, into *prana.* This energy becomes fused throughout the body. They manage to do it by concentrating their thoughts on it, just the way a chicken hatches an egg. They think about how their essence is being transformed into energy, how the energy is pervading their body, and then how it is being transformed into spirit. Then they smelt the spirit until it returns to emptiness – until it becomes like emptiness itself. They then smelt the emptiness until it returns to nothing. They go to the point that there's nothing at all. At that point they feel very free and at ease. They can "go out esoterically and enter the mysterious." That's the way the Taoists phrase it. That means they can go out from the top of their heads. The Taoists in China practiced exactly the methods that Shakyamuni Buddha describes here. They have a book called *Wu Shang You Huang Xin Yin Miao Jing*. They consider this book a real treasure. It tells how to smelt the essence to transform it into energy, smelt the energy to transform it into spirit, smelt the spirit to transform it into emptiness, and smelt the emptiness to transform it into nothing. These immortals can walk around in space. They can go out from the top of their heads. There are a lot of strange and esoteric things in this world. There's another Taoist book for sale called *Wu Liu Xian Zong*. In it there are pictures of a man sending a small person out the top of his head, and that small person sending out another small person, and so forth until there are lots of small people. That's supposed to be "millions of transformation bodies." But I'll tell you, making millions of transformation bodies is not as much trouble as all that. These Taoist books are just totally involved in attachment to appearances. Making transformation bodies can be done at will. There's no fixed formula for creating them. **When they have perfected their breath and essence, they are known as space-traveling immortals.**

J5   Heaven-traveling immortals.

Sutra:

"Some beings with unflagging resolution make themselves strong by using the flow of saliva. When they have perfected the virtues of this moisture, they are known as heaven-traveling immortals.

Commentary:

The previous immortal could roam in space. This one can go up to the heavens. **Some beings with unflagging resolution make themselves strong by using the flow of saliva.** When the tongue is placed on the roof of the mouth, the saliva flows down from above. Adherents of externalist paths call this "sweet dew," "heavenly drinking water," and a lot of other names. The process is complete when the saliva flows down and is swallowed into the stomach. Taoists call this the elixir of immortality. They have a saying;

> If you want to live forever
>   and not grow old,
> You must return the essence
>   to nurture the brain.

They contemplate having their essence form a cluster on top of their heads; in this way they strengthen their brains.

These particular immortals continually swallow the saliva and internalize the breath in a regularly scheduled practice. **When they have perfected the virtues of this moisture, they are known as heaven-traveling immortals.** Eventually their faces take on a glow. Although they are very old, their faces are like children's. They are red cheeked and fresh like a young boy's. These are the heaven-traveling immortals.

J6   Immortals of penetrating conduct.

Sutra:

"Some beings with unflagging resolution make themselves strong with the essence of sun and moon. When they have perfected the inhalation of this purity, they are known as immortals of penetrating conduct.

Commentary:

Some beings with unflagging resolution make themselves strong with the essence of sun and moon. Their minds are firm and resolved. These immortals make a practice of breathing in the essence of the sun and the secretions of the moon. They convert the sunlight and moonlight. **When they have perfected the inhalation of this purity, they are known as immortals of penetrating conduct.** They can travel to the heavens or anywhere else they want to go. How do they go about this practice? For example, in the morning they face the sun and make three hundred and sixty inhalations. In the evening they face the moon and make three hundred and sixty inhalations. They put all their time into smelting their stinking skin bags. That's what our bodies are – stinking skin bags. The Venerable Master Hsu Yun wrote the *Song of a Skin Bag* in expression of this fact. But this type of immortal puts all his energy into developing this kind of skill. They don't know that they should put that effort into developing the self-nature. So the difference between Taoism and Buddhism is that the former uses effort on what is apparent and the latter uses effort on what is not apparent. So one has an attachment and the other doesn't. That's the difference. Actually, the way of the immortals and the Buddhist Way are similar. The point is that one is involved in attachments and the other is not. The kind of skill these immortals develop is basically all right, but they get attached to it. They become totally engrossed in appearances. Because of that they have a hindrance. They feel they have to do things in a certain way. Because they have this hang-up, they cannot get completely out of the cycle of rebirth. They don't gain ultimate understanding and release. These are called immortals with penetrating conduct.

The first five immortals described previously were said to have one sort of "travel" or another because they are basically bound to the earth and cannot roam in the higher realms. The latter five, now being described, are said to have one kind of "conduct" or another, because they are more advanced and can roam in the higher regions.

J7   Immortals with way-conduct.

Sutra:

"Some beings with unflagging resolution make themselves strong through mantras and prohibitions. When they have

perfected these spells and dharmas, they are known as immortals with Way-conduct.

Commentary:

These beings have a firm determination to recite mantras. The Tibetan Lamas are an example of this category, provided that they perfect their skills. **Some beings with unflagging resolution make themselves strong through mantras and prohibitions.** They recite mantras and always hold prohibitive precepts. **When they have perfected these spells and dharmas, they are known as immortals with Way-conduct.**

J8   Immortals with illumining conduct.

Sutra:

"Some beings with unflagging resolution make themselves strong through the use of thought-processes. When they have perfected thought and memory, they are known as immortals with illumining conduct.

Commentary:

Some beings with unflagging resolution make themselves strong through the use of thought-processes. They turn their determination to their thoughts – without resting, they develop total thought.

When they have perfected thought and memory, they are known as immortals with illumining conduct. When they perfect this practice, they have a bit of light. In their thoughts they imagine that they are transformed into golden light. When they cherish this thought for a long time, eventually it's just like the old mother hen on her eggs, or the cat stalking the mouse: there's some success. That's why they are called immortals with illumining conduct. They have some light.

J9   Immortals with essential conduct.

Sutra:

"Some beings with unflagging resolution make themselves strong through intercourse. When they have perfected the response, they are known as immortals with essential conduct.

Commentary:

Usually "intercourse" refers to the sexual act between men and women. But that is definitely not the meaning here. Rather, the intercourse takes place within oneself. The Taoists call this the "young boy and girl." Each individual is capable of it. It's not a matter of seeking outside oneself. Everyone has a young boy and girl in his or her own body. The young boy refers to the trigram *li* (離) and the young girl refers to the trigram *kan* (坎). This is an allusion to the trigrams. The trigram *li* is "empty in the middle." The trigram *kan* is "full in the middle." The eight trigrams are:

☰ qian 乾	☲ li 離
☷ kun 坤	☵ kan 坎
☳ zhen 震	☱ dui 兌
☶ gen 艮	☴ sun 巽

They begin with the trigram *qian* (乾), which consists of three unbroken lines. *Qian* represents the male element. *Kun* (坤) is three broken lines and represents the female element. At age thirty-six a man's *qian* trigram is at its peak. Thereafter it will decline, and it turns into the trigram *li*. The *li* trigram has two outer *yang* lines and an inner *yin* line. Where did the *yang* line from the middle of the *li* go? It went over to the *kun* trigram, which subsequently turns into *kan*, which consists of two *yin* outer lines with a middle *yang* line.

The *li* trigram belongs to the mind and the *kan* trigram belongs to the body. So the "intercourse" referred to in this passage is the intercourse of "body" and "mind" as described here. The "intercourse" is simply an analogy for a union of body and mind. The entire process takes place in one individual's body. The *li* trigram belongs to *yang*, but within the *yang* is *yin*. The *kan* trigram belongs to *yin*, but within the *yin* is *yang*.

> The infant boy and girl meet
> at the yellow courtyard.

What is the yellow courtyard? It's the mind – the sixth consciousness. And the mind belongs to the hexagram *pi*. It would get tremendously involved if we were to go into this doctrine in detail. Time simply does not permit me to explain it further. In any event, the Taoists cultivate the dharma-door of this kind of intercourse. When people with deviant knowledge and deviant views see this passage of the *Shurangama Sutra*, they surmise that it says it's all right for men and women to mess around together – that cultivators of the Way can get away with that. So they get all mixed up together and don't hold the precepts at all.

J10   Immortals of absolute conduct.

Sutra:

"Some beings with unflagging resolution make themselves strong through transformations and changes. When they have perfected their awakening, they are known as immortals of absolute conduct.

Commentary:

Some beings with unflagging resolution make themselves strong through transformations and changes. Here it says that with firm resolve a cultivator investigates various kinds of methods and devices. When he's succeeded in developing them, he has some ability to function by means of them. Then his skill of cultivation is perfected.

When they have perfected their awakening, they are known as immortals of absolute conduct. They understand the doctrine of creation. This kind of immortal can move mountains and turn over seas. It's possible for them to exchange the mountains in the north for the mountains in the south. They can move seas around in the same way, replacing the ocean in the west with the ocean in the east and vice versa. They have the power to change the seasons. For example, when it's cold in the winter so that things won't grow, they can make it so that the things they have planted will grow and won't freeze. They can make the hottest places cool and the coldest places warm. They can turn spring into winter and summer into winter at will: they can turn spring, when things should be blossoming, into autumn, when things are dying. How can they do it? They have fathomed the doctrine of creation of heaven and earth and they can function by means of that understanding. They become capable of creation itself. They're called immortals of absolute conduct.

---

13   Determines this is the same as the turning wheel.

Sutra:

"**Ananda, these are all people who smelt their minds but do not cultivate proper enlightenment. They obtain some special principle of life and can live for thousands or tens of thousands of years. They retire deep into the mountains or onto islands in the sea and cut themselves off from the human realm. However, they are still part of the turning wheel, because they flow and turn according to their false thinking and do not cultivate samadhi. When their reward is finished, they must still return and enter the various destinies.**

Commentary:

Ananda, these are all people who smelt their minds but do not cultivate proper enlightenment. When they were people, they smelted their bodies and minds. They did not cultivate the Shurangama Samadhi of the treasury of the Thus Come One, which is neither produced nor extinguished. They didn't cultivate proper enlightenment.

They obtain some special principle of life and can live for thousands or tens of thousands of years. The various dharma doors described above are all ways they found which could extend the measure of their lifespans. Their gods of the externalist paths transmitted to them these externalist methods that lengthen life. So they have very long lifespans.

They retire deep into the mountains or onto islands in the sea and cut themselves off from the human realm. They go to places where people cannot go. There is a Mount Sumeru in this world system, and surrounding it are seven golden mountains and seven seas of fragrant waters. Out beyond those mountains and seas there is a vast expanse of soft water. This water is such that if a bird's feather lands on the surface, it will sink to the bottom. The feather would float on ordinary water, but this water is so soft that it does not have the power to support anything on its surface. Obviously, if a bird's feather sinks, any other thing like a boat or raft would certainly sink, too. Only flying immortals can cross it. So these people who cultivate and become immortals fly over this water to isolated islands where people can never go.

However, they are still part of the turning wheel, because they flow and turn according to their false thinking and do not cultivate samadhi. Although they may live for thousands of years, they are still within the cycle of rebirth. They have not been able to end birth and death entirely. The reason they still must transmigrate is because they still have things they are attached to. Specifically, they want immortality – they want to live long and not grow old. That's their false thinking, and so they don't cultivate proper concentration power.

When their reward is finished, they must still return and enter the various destinies. When their lifespan finally ends, they will go to rebirth, and they might become people or asuras or gods, or they might end up in the hells or as hungry ghosts or animals. It's not for sure where they'll end up.

Destiny of Gods

Sutra:

"Ananda, there are many people in the world who do not seek what is eternal and who cannot yet renounce the kindness and love they feel for their wives.

Commentary:

Ananda, there are many people in the world who do not seek what is eternal. This can mean that they do not seek to eternally abide in the world, and it can also mean that they do not seek the eternally abiding nature of the true mind. They **cannot yet renounce the kindness and love they feel for their wives.**

Sutra:

"But they have no interest in deviant sexual activity and so develop a purity and produce light. When their life ends, they draw near the sun and moon and are among those born in the Heaven of the Four Kings.

Commentary:

But they have no interest in deviant sexual activity. Having sexual activity with someone other than one's spouse is called "deviant." That which occurs within the marriage is not considered to be lust and is not deviant. However, it is better to be sparing about such activity, even in marriage. It should not be excessive. When you cultivate the Way, no matter how much merit and virtue you may have, you must not engage in deviant lustful activity. If you cultivate, but cannot cut off such activity, then you won't be successful no matter how hard you work at cultivation.

These people being discussed in the text here are not interested in deviant lust, **and so** they **develop a purity and produce light.** If one does not pursue lustful activity, one will be pure, and out of that purity will come light – the natural light of virtue. So it is said:

> Of all the myriad evils, lust is the foremost.
> Don't go down that road to death!

If one does not engage in deviant lust, then one's essence, breath, and spirit will be full and complete. From that fullness comes the virtuous light. During one's life one will glow and radiate with light. **When their life ends, they draw near the sun and moon and are among those born in the Heaven of the Four Kings.** This kind of rebirth includes a lot of people. One knows not how many people fit this category.

The Heaven of the Four Kings is located halfway up Mount Sumeru. It is the heaven closest to our human realm. The gods in this heaven have a lifespan of five hundred years. One day and night in that heaven is equivalent to fifty years in the human realm. So their lifespan is nine million years if calculated according to our time.

L2 Trayastrimsha heaven.

Sutra:

"Those whose sexual love for their wives is slight, but who have not yet obtained the entire flavor of dwelling in purity,

transcend the light of sun and moon at the end of their lives, and reside at the summit of the human realm. They are among those born in the Trayastrimsha Heaven.

Commentary:

Those whose sexual love for their wives is slight, but who have not yet obtained the entire flavor of dwelling in purity, transcend the light of sun and moon at the end of their lives. Those born in the Heaven of the Four Kings did not engage in deviant sex, but had not managed to decrease their involvement with their own wives. However, they remained faithful to their wives and did not get involved with any other woman. The same holds true for women: they did not get involved with any man other than their own husbands. Beings born in the Heaven of the Four Kings did not have lovers when they were in the human realm.

Now the text discusses people who have decreased their sexual activity within the marriage. It can apply either to wives with regard to their husbands, or husbands with regard to their wives. "Slight" means that they very, very seldom engaged in this practice. They might not get involved with one another even once in a year, or they might go for several years getting involved only once. They do not look upon sexual activity as important.

Why do some people have such heavy sexual desire? It's because of the heaviness of their karmic obstacles. Someone with few karmic obstacles, however, will not have such thoughts. Heavy karmic obstacles pursue people and cause them to think of nothing else but sex from morning till night. Such thoughts never stop. But it's just in the midst of such heavy karmic obstacles that you should wake up and realize that you should decrease your karmic obstacles. If you simply go along with your karmic obstacles, then the farther you go, the further you fall. In the future it's for certain you will become a cow or horse, a pig or a dog. And this kind of rebirth will go on and on without cease. Why? Because your emotional desire is too heavy. It will certainly cause you to fall. It's very dangerous.

Although the people discussed in this passage of text have very little regard for sexual activity, they still have not obtained the entire flavor of dwelling in purity. They have not gained genuine purity and its advantages, because they don't know how to cultivate. At the end of their lives, then, they will transcend the light of sun and moon **and reside at the summit of the human realm.** Because they don't have much emotional desire, the light of their self-nature comes forth. Anyone who does not have emotional desire will have light and will be able to be reborn in the heavens.

These people are **among those born in the Trayastrimsha Heaven.** "Trayastrimsha" is Sanskrit and means "Heaven of the Thirty-three." The lord of the Heaven of the Thirty-three resides above our heads. There are eight heavens in the east, eight in the west, eight in the north, and eight in the south, making thirty-two; the thirty-third is located among the others in the center and is at the peak of Mt. Sumeru.

How did the lord of the Heaven of the Thirty-three get reborn there? Originally she was a poor woman who saw a stupa which was falling apart. She resolved to repair it and set about begging and working to make the money to do it. Meanwhile, she got together with thirty-two friends; they had a meeting and decided to repair the stupa with their combined efforts. After they died, the thirty-two became lords of the accompanying heavens and the woman became the lord of the thirty-third heaven.

The lifespan of the gods in the Heaven of the Thirty-three is a thousand years. A hundred years of human time makes up one day and night in that heaven. As we progress upwards, the inhabitants of each higher heaven have a lifespan double that of the heaven below. The heights of the gods also increase proportionately. But it's rather tedious to go into all that, and so if you want to know about it in detail, you can investigate it on your own.

L3   Suyama heaven.

Sutra:

"Those who become temporarily involved when they meet with desire but who forget about it when it is finished, and who, while in the human realm, are active less and quiet more, abide at the end of their lives in light and emptiness where the illumination of sun and moon does not reach. These beings have their own light, and they are among those born in the Suyama Heaven.

Commentary:

There is a certain category of people in the world **who become temporarily involved when they meet with desire but who forget about it when it is finished.** This refers to the activity of married couples. Although occasionally they engage in sexual intercourse, these people forget about it when it's gone by. They don't think about it afterwards. **While** they are **in the human realm,** they are **active less and quiet more.** That means they spend the greater part of their time practicing Chan samadhi. They will **abide at the end of their lives in light and emptiness where the illumination of sun and moon does not reach.** The light of the sun and moon do not shine where these people go. **These beings have their own light** when they reach that place in emptiness. Their own bodies emit an everlasting light, and so at that place there is no day and night. It's always light there. How then do they reckon the passage of time? They use the lotus flower. When the flower opens they know it is day; when the flower closes, it is night. These beings **are among those born in the Suyama Heaven.** Their average height is two hundred twenty-five feet. Their lifespan is two thousand of their years. "Suyama" means "well-divided time" because it's always light there, day and night.

L4   Tushita heaven.

Sutra:

"**Those who are quiet all the time, but who are not yet able to resist when stimulated by contact, ascend at the end of their lives to a subtle and ethereal place; they will not be drawn into the lower realms. The destruction of the realms of humans and gods and the obliteration of kalpas by the three disasters will not reach them, for they are among those born in the Tushita Heaven.**

Commentary:

In this heaven there is an inner and an outer court. In the outer court the common gods dwell, and in the inner court sages dwell. At present, Maitreya Bodhisattva dwells in the inner court of the Tushita Heaven. He is explaining about the samadhi of mind-consciousness only. **Those who are quiet all the time, but who are not yet able to resist when stimulated by contact, ascend at the end of their lives to a subtle and ethereal place; they will not be drawn into the lower realms.** At all times and in all situations they never move. They are very tranquil. However, when an occasion arises for sexual intercourse, it's not for certain that they will not get involved. But they don't really want to get involved. They may occasionally indulge in this activity, but very, very rarely. At death these people who have few desires and are content will ascend; their souls will go to a subtle and ethereal place and will not fall down.

The destruction of the realms of humans and gods and the obliteration of kalpas by the three disasters will not reach them, for they are among those born in the Tushita Heaven. The three disasters are,

   1)   the disaster of fire
   2)   the disaster of water
   3)   the disaster of wind

Fire burns through the first dhyana, water drowns the second dhyana, and wind devastates the third dhyana. But because bodhisattvas reside in this Tushita Heaven, the three disasters cannot reach it. "Tushita" means "having few desires and being content." They simply don't have any greed. They are devoid of sexual desire. So if you want to get reborn in the heavens, just have few desires and be content. To have strong emotions and to forever be thinking of that kind of thing, never being able to put it down for even an instant, though – that's very dangerous indeed. It is, in fact, the most perilous matter of all. It's the source of one's fall. If you don't fear the fall, then think about that kind of stuff as much as you want. If you are afraid of falling, then quickly stop those emotional thoughts. If you don't stop, there's no telling where you'll end up in the future.

L5   Heaven of bliss by transformation.

Sutra:

"**Those who are devoid of desire, but who will engage in it for the sake of their partner, even though the flavor of doing so is like the flavor of chewing wax, are born at the end of their lives in a place of transcending transformations. They are among those born in the Heaven of Bliss by Transformation.**

Commentary:

Those who are devoid of desire, but who will engage in it for the sake of their partner, even though the flavor of doing so is like the flavor of chewing wax, are born at the end of their lives in a place of transcending transformations. "I don't have any desire at all, but you persist. You insist we do this thing." That's what transpires between couples where one partner is devoid of sexual desire while the other isn't. The one with desire pursues the one without desire. Have you ever chewed wax? Well, you can chew forever but you'll never get any taste from it. That's the analogy used to indicate that this kind of person gets no pleasure out of sex. They just don't have any thoughts of lust. After hearing this principle, you should certainly take care to control yourself.

Don't be loose any more. Don't run headlong down the road to death!

The rebirth of the kinds of beings discussed here transcends those of the heavens discussed earlier. **They are among those born in the Heaven of Bliss by Transformation.** Everything in their environment is transformed. It is an extremely blissful place – unspeakably joyous. But the bliss referred to is not like that of ordinary sexual involvement. It is a natural bliss. However, it is not an ultimate place of rebirth. It is still within the six desire heavens.

The gods in this heaven are three thousand and seventy-five feet tall. One day and night in that heaven is equal to eight hundred years among people, and their lifespan is eight thousand of their years.

L6   Heaven of comfort from others' transformations.

Sutra:

"Those who have no kind of worldly thoughts while doing what worldly people do, who are lucid and beyond such activity while involved in it, are capable at the end of their lives of entirely transcending states where transformations may be present and may be lacking. They are among those born in the Heaven of Comfort from Others' Transformations.

Commentary:

Those who have no kind of worldly thoughts of sexual desire **while doing what worldly people do, who are lucid and beyond such activity while involved in it** – these are people who occasionally involve themselves in intercourse with their marriage partner. But for them, not only does it have the flavor of wax, it's as if nothing were happening at all. They **are capable at the end of their lives of entirely transcending states where transformations may be present and may be lacking.** They reach a state where they can go out of their bodies and transform as they please, endlessly. **They are among those born in the Heaven of Comfort from Others' Transformations.** Everything in the environment of the heaven those beings go to does not originate there, but is rather a transformation made as an offering by beings in other heavens. It's extremely comfortable there. The bliss is vast, and there's no work to be done. There aren't any servants in that heaven – people who work for a living would starve there – because everything happens naturally and spontaneously. The bliss is extreme. It's a lot better than the human realm, that's for sure. But even though it's such a fine place, the beings there will nevertheless fall one day. Once they use up their heavenly blessings, they will fall back to the human realm or even into the hells – there's nothing fixed about it. Those heavenly beings are an average of four thousand five hundred feet tall. One day and night in that heaven is equal to fifteen hundred years on earth, and their lifespan is sixteen thousand of their years.

Those, then, are the six desire heavens. All of the beings in those heavens still have sexual desire in varying degrees. A verse describes it:

> In the Heaven of the Four Kings and the Trayastrimsha,
>   Desire is carried out through embracing.
> In the Suyama Heaven, they hold hands,
>   In the Tushita, they smile.
> In the Bliss by Transformation, they gaze,
>   In the Comfort from Others', a glance will do.

In the six desire heavens, this is the bliss they take to be true. "In the Heaven of the Four Kings and the Trayastrimsha, desire is carried out through embracing." They conduct sexual affairs the same way people do. "In the Suyama Heaven they hold hands; in the Tushita they smile." The beings in the Suyama Heaven unite in mind, but not physically. All they have to do to fulfill their sexual longing is to hold hands. In the Tushita Heaven, they smile. There's no physical contact involved. "In the Bliss by Transformation, they gaze. In the Comfort from Others', a glance will do." Men and women in the Bliss by Transformation Heaven need only look at one another – they don't even have to smile. They stare at each other for maybe three minutes or five minutes; that's how their sexual intercourse is completed. In the next heaven a brief glance is sufficient. An instant is all it takes. The higher the heaven, the lighter the thoughts of sexual desire.

This is a true principle; you should understand it clearly. Once you do, you'll be able to genuinely understand the Buddhadharma, for you will know that sexual desire is tremendously harmful. Do you remember the earlier passage in the sutra that says bodhisattvas look upon sexual desire as they would a poisonous snake? They know they will be bitten to death. People's ordinary flesh eyes cannot see how fierce it is. That's why they spend all their time, day and night, thinking about this nasty thing. They can't put it down. If you really understood, I think you wouldn't be so confused and upside-down about it.

_____

K3   Determines these belong to the desire realm.

Sutra:

"**Ananda, thus it is that although they have transcended the physical in these six heavens, the traces of their minds still become involved. For that they will have to pay in person. These are called the Six Desire Heavens.**

Commentary:

Ananda, thus it is that although they have transcended the physical in these six heavens, the traces of their minds still become involved. Although they have transcended the physical plane, they still get hung up mentally. Their minds, natures, and bodies still act out thoughts of sexual desire. **For that they will have to pay in person. These are called the Six Desire Heavens.** These heavens, from the Heaven of the Four Kings to the Heaven of Comfort from Others' Transformations, are called the Six Desire Heavens. The heavens are still in the desire realm because the beings in them are not totally pure. They still have thoughts of sexual desire.

J2   The four dhyana heavens.
K1   Four divisions.
L1   First dhyana heavens.
M1   Explains three heavens with different characteristics.
N1   Heaven of the multitudes of brahma.

Sutra:

"**Ananda, all those in the world who cultivate their minds but do not avail themselves of dhyana and so have no wisdom, can only control their bodies so as to not engage in sexual desire. Whether walking or sitting, or in their thoughts, they are totally devoid of it. Since they do not give rise to defiling love, they do not remain in the realm of desire. These people can, in response to their thought, take on the bodies of Brahma beings. They are among those in the Heaven of the Multitudes of Brahma.**

Commentary:

Ananda, now we will talk about the form realm, the heavens of the four dhyanas. **All those in the world who cultivate their minds but do not avail themselves of dhyana and so have no wisdom, can only control their bodies so as to not engage in sexual desire.** They haven't become skilled in the practice of dhyana – of stilling their thoughts, and so they don't have any genuine wisdom. What they can do is control their own bodies and refrain from engaging in lust. **Whether walking or sitting, or in their thoughts, they are totally devoid of it.** Walking, standing, sitting, and lying down – even in their sleep – at all times and in all places **they do not give rise to defiling love.** No matter how beautiful an object of form they may see, they do not give rise to defiling thoughts of love, and so **they do not remain in the realm of desire. These people can, in response to their thought, take on the bodies of Brahma beings.** They join with other pure beings. None of them have any desire. **They are among those in the Heaven of the Multitudes of Brahma.** They become part of the pure beings who inhabit this heaven. Each is a part of that general heavenly multitude – one among many.

N2   Ministers of brahma heaven.

Sutra:

"In those whose hearts of desire have already been cast aside, the mind apart from desire manifests. They have a fond regard for the rules of discipline and delight in being in accord with them. These people can practice the Brahma virtue at all times, and they are among those in the Heaven of the Ministers of Brahma.

Commentary:

In those whose hearts of desire have already been cast aside, the mind apart from desire manifests. They have a fond regard for the rules of discipline and delight in being in accord with them. People by nature like food and sex. These habits are innate in them. But at this point, these beings have gotten rid of their habits of sexual desire. Since they don't have desire, the mind apart from desire appears. They cultivate the precepts and the rules of awesome deportment. They like the precepts and follow them in their cultivation. These people can practice the Brahma virtue at all times, and they are among those in the Heaven of the Ministers of Brahma. At all times and in all situations, they cultivate pure practices. Their conduct is virtuous and pure. "Brahma" means purity. These people are born in the second heaven of the first dhyana. As ministers, they aid the Great Brahma Heaven King.

N3   Great brahma heaven.

Sutra:

"Those whose bodies and minds are wonderfully perfect, and whose awesome deportment is not in the least deficient, are pure in the prohibitive precepts and have a thorough understanding of them as well. At all times these people can govern the Brahma multitudes as great Brahma lords, and they are among those in the Great Brahma Heaven.

Commentary:

Those whose bodies and minds are wonderfully perfect, in the matter of being without any thoughts of desire, **and whose awesome deportment is not in the least deficient, are pure in the prohibitive precepts and have a thorough understanding of them as well.** They are not lacking in any of the three thousand awesome deportments or the eighty thousand minor aspects of conduct. They are perfect in them all. They uphold and are pure in all the precepts spoken by the Buddha. Not only do they hold them purely, they have a comprehensive understanding of them as well. They have enlightened to the appearance, substance, and dharma of the precepts. **At all times these people can govern the Brahma multitudes as great Brahma lords, and they are among those in the Great Brahma Heaven.** When these people's lives end, they are born in the heavens and they are able to rule the multitude in the Brahma Heavens.

M2   Concludes they are apart from suffering and their outflows are subdued.

Sutra:

"Ananda, those who flow to these three superior levels will not be oppressed by any suffering or affliction. Although they have not developed proper samadhi, their minds are pure to the point that they are not moved by outflows. This is called the First Dhyana.

Commentary:

Ananda, those who flow to these three superior levels will not be oppressed by any suffering or affliction. The three superior levels are the Heaven of the Multitudes of Brahma, the Heaven of the Ministers of Brahma, and the Great Brahma Heaven. These are transcendent levels – the heavens of the first dhyana – in which suffering and affliction do not harass one. **Although they have not developed proper samadhi** – although they don't understand the Buddhadharma and are not cultivating the proper concentration power – **their minds are pure to the point that they are not moved by outflows.** They hold the precepts purely, and within the purity of their minds they are not moved by outflows. They don't give rise to faults. They don't get involved in the endless desires of the material world such as food, clothing, and all the objects of desire. Those are all outflows. The inhabitants of these heavens don't have any of these weaknesses, afflictions, habits, or faults. **This is called the First Dhyana.** In cultivating the Way, your pulse stops if you reach the first dhyana. If you want to know whether you have any skill, check out your pulse. That's a sign of this level, which is the first step in cultivation. It is not a lofty state.

L2   Second dhyana heavens.
M1   Explains three heavens with different characteristics.
N1   Lesser light heaven.

Sutra:

"**Ananda, those beyond the Brahma heavens gather in and govern the Brahma beings, for their Brahma conduct is perfect and fulfilled. Unmoving and with settled minds, they produce light in profound stillness, and they are among those in the Heaven of Lesser Light.**

Commentary:

Ananda, those beyond the Brahma heavens gather in and govern the Brahma beings, for their Brahma conduct is perfect and fulfilled. Those at the next level above the Heaven of the Multitudes of Brahma, the Heaven of the Ministers of Brahma, and the Great Brahma Heaven are capable of governing and gathering in the beings in these three heavens. That's because they have perfectly learned the pure – "Brahma" – practices. **Unmoving and with settled minds, they produce light in profound stillness.** Their minds are tranquil and calm – they are unmoving. When there is stillness and profound tranquility, a kind of light will eventually emerge. These heavenly beings are **among those in the Heaven of Lesser Light.**

N2   Limitless light heaven.

Sutra:

"Those whose lights illumine each other in an endless dazzling blaze shine throughout the realms of the ten directions so that everything becomes like crystal. They are among those in the Heaven of Limitless Light.

Commentary:

Those whose lights illumine each other in an endless dazzling blaze shine throughout the realms of the ten directions so that everything becomes like crystal. Their lights shine on one another. They illumine each other. Have you ever noticed how compatible lights are? There aren't any that won't unite. If you have light and someone else has light, the two lights will not contend. They will not fight with each other. Really! Lights don't fight. It's never the case that a big light will bully a smaller light. There's no fuss among lights. That's what's being described here by the phrase, the "lights illumine each other." The combined illumination of these lights is infinite. It reaches throughout the ten directions, and everything seems to turn into crystal. These heavenly beings **are among those in the Heaven of Limitless Light.**

N3   Light sound heaven.

Sutra:

"Those who take in and hold the light to perfection accomplish the substance of the teaching. Creating and transforming the purity into endless responses and functions, they are among those in the Light-Sound Heaven.

Commentary:

Those who take in and hold the light to perfection accomplish the substance of the teaching. Together they obtain and uphold these lights and in this way perfect the substance of the teaching. In the Light-Sound Heaven, the beings do not have to speak out loud to communicate with one another. They use light for their voices. They communicate by means of their lights. They don't speak with their mouths; they don't use language. Thus, light is the substance of teaching in that heaven. That's really a case of this:

The mind understands without a word being said.

When they shine on each other in that heaven, each knows what the other is communicating. Their ideas are transmitted by means of the light. **Creating and transforming the purity into endless responses and functions, they are among those in the Light-Sound Heaven.** The function of their light is infinite.

M2 Concludes they are apart from worries and their outflows are subdued.

Sutra:

"**Ananda, those who flow to these three superior levels will not be oppressed by worries or vexations. Although they have not developed proper samadhi, their minds are pure to the point that they have subdued their coarser outflows. This is called the Second Dhyana.**

Commentary:

Ananda, those who flow to these three superior levels will not be oppressed by worries or vexations. In the heavens of the first dhyana, they were not oppressed by suffering or affliction. However, they still were subject to worry. If something came up, they had a bit of a hard time putting it all down. They got hung up in things. But now, in the second dhyana heavens, there is no worry, and there aren't any hang-ups. "Not to be oppressed" means that they don't give rise to worry within. They don't even have any internal hang-ups. They are a far cry from ordinary people, who get hung up on everything that comes along and spend all day from morning to night worrying about something or other. "Hang-ups" are otherwise known as "impeding obstructions." **Although they have not developed proper samadhi, their minds are pure to the point that they have subdued their coarser outflows.** These heavenly beings have not been intent upon cultivating proper samadhi. But they do have a certain level of attainment when it comes to the purity of their minds. Their coarse outflows are under control. But they still haven't been able to deal with the subtler outflows. On the surface of things, then, the gods in the second dhyana heavens appear to be without any worry and hang-ups.

When people who cultivate the Way sit in meditation and enter the second dhyana, their breath will cease. In the first dhyana, the pulse stops. In the second, the breath stops. Now although it is said that they cease, do you remember what I just told you about the young boy and girl? The skill which the Taoists develop and that which Buddhists develop have certain basic similarities. They are largely the same, with minor differences. If someone's pulse stops, doesn't that just means he or she is dead? No, not in this case, because, although the external evidence of a pulse is gone, the pulse of the self-nature within is active. The same applies to the breath. The true breath and pulse of the self-nature awaken and take over, so the coarse, physical pulse can stop.

In the same way, when the external evidence of breath ceases in the second dhyana, it does not mean that the cultivator has died. He's entered the samadhi of the second dhyana and has obtained a certain purity and bliss. Still, it's only his coarser outflows which are under control. It's not the case that all outflows are extinguished at this level. **This is called the Second Dhyana.**

L3   Third dhyana heavens.
M1   Explains three heavens.
N1   Lesser purity heaven.

Sutra:

"Ananda, heavenly beings for whom the perfection of light has become sound and who further open out the sound to disclose its wonder discover a subtler level of practice. They penetrate to the bliss of still extinction and are among those in the Heaven of Lesser Purity.

Commentary:

Ananda, heavenly beings for whom the perfection of light has become sound and who further open out the sound to disclose its wonder discover a subtler level of practice. For them, perfect light has become sound, and when they distinguish this sound more clearly, it reveals a subtle and wonderful level of practice. **They penetrate to the bliss of still extinction** by means of this subtle and wonderful practice. Still extinction is the absence of thought. Their minds and natures are in still extinction, **and** they **are among those in the Heaven of Lesser Purity.** These gods are in the Heaven of Lesser Purity. They have obtained a small amount of genuine purity. It's not total purity.

N2   Limitless purity heaven.

Sutra:

"Those in whom the emptiness of purity manifests are led to discover its boundlessness. Their bodies and minds experience light ease, and they accomplish the bliss of still extinction. They are among those in the Heaven of Limitless Purity.

Commentary:

Those in whom the emptiness of purity manifests are led to discover its boundlessness. They obtain genuine purity and afterward can discover the principle of emptiness. Knowing about emptiness, they are led to discover the boundlessness of purity. The purity has no end. **Their bodies and minds experience light ease, and they accomplish the bliss of still extinction.** At that time they are truly free; they have self-mastery. They have truly arrived at the wonderful existence within true emptiness and the true emptiness within wonderful existence. Something takes place then that most people do not know can happen. Most people are greedy for external forms, and so they flow out.

> Their nature flows out into emotion;
> Their emotions flow out into desires.

The thought of sexual desire is produced. They become fixed in the notion that they must find a partner. Then they let the fire of their desire catch hold and become spent in external seeking. That's sex. But is it really necessary for there to be an external form in order to have this experience? No. Within true emptiness there is true form. If you understand, then true form is just true emptiness. You can perceive true emptiness and wonderful existence right within this. The *Heart Sutra* says:

> Form does not differ from emptiness; emptiness does not differ from form. Form is just emptiness; emptiness is just form.

The bliss of still extinction – the principle of emptiness – is tens of millions of times more intense than the bliss derived from seeking external forms. If you want that experience, though, you must first stop your involvement with external forms. If you don't stop your involvement with external forms, the true emptiness within you cannot manifest.

Here, these heavenly beings have been led to discover the endlessness of purity – and their bodies and minds experience light ease. This is to reach the level where,

> Form does not differ from emptiness; emptiness does not differ from form. Form is just emptiness; emptiness is just form.

You cannot fake this. You can't say you've reached this level if you haven't. It can't be experienced through mere words; it only counts if you are really there, just as only the person who drinks a glass of water knows if the water is cold or warm. These beings who have accomplished the bliss of still extinction are **among those in the Heaven of Limitless Purity.**

N3   Pervasive purity heaven.

Sutra:

"**Those for whom the world, the body, and the mind are all perfectly pure have accomplished the virtue of purity, and a superior level emerges. They return to the bliss of still extinction, and they are among those in the Heaven of Pervasive Purity.**

Commentary:

Those for whom the world, the body, and the mind are all perfectly pure have accomplished the virtue of purity. In the heaven discussed previously, only the body and mind experienced total purity. The beings in the heaven now discussed have accomplished their skill to the point that they can change the world itself. This world is basically impure, but they can transform it into a pure one. The principle here is the same one expressed in the saying:

> The mind is itself the Pure Land;
> The self-nature is Amitabha Buddha.

If your mind is pure, the Buddhalands are pure. If your mind is not pure, you do not perceive the purity of the Buddhalands, either. If you're in the Land of Ultimate Bliss itself but do nothing but cry all day long, then there's no bliss. If you're in the Saha world and you are happy from morning to night, then you're like the bodhisattvas of the ground of happiness. The principle here is that "everything is made from the mind alone." It just remains to be seen if you can see through it all and put it down. If you can, you obtain comfort – self-mastery. If you can't see through everything and put it down, you won't experience comfort.

When these gods reach the point that they can purify the world, their bodies, and their minds, the purity and light of the virtuous nature is brought to perfection. Then **a superior level emerges.** How is this superior level to be described? This is something experienced in the mind. **They return to the bliss of still**

extinction, and they are among those in the Heaven of Pervasive Purity. There isn't any place that isn't true. They can purify everything in the entire dharma realm.

M2   Concludes they are tranquil and happy.

Sutra:

"**Ananda, those who flow to these three superior levels will be replete with great compliance. Their bodies and minds are at peace, and they obtain limitless bliss. Although they have not obtained proper samadhi, the joy within the tranquility of their minds is total. This is called the Third Dhyana.**"

Commentary:

Ananda, those who flow to these three superior levels will be replete with great compliance. That means they can comply with the minds of living beings. They can make living beings happy. **Their bodies and minds are at peace, and they obtain limitless bliss.** They do not have any false thoughts in their minds, and so they do not act out false thoughts with their bodies. They experience no unrest in either body or mind. Those in the first two dhyana heavens got rid of their sufferings and afflictions, their worries and hang-ups. The beings in these heavens have no such experiences. Their bodies and minds are quiet and peaceful.

They are also dependable. How are they dependable? They have no thoughts of desire. They don't have to go through trying to find someone of the opposite sex in every thought they have and in every move they make, the way ordinary people do. When your body and mind are not at peace, then a new thought arises as soon as the last one ceases. "Ah, that person is beautiful." Or, "So-and-so is really handsome." All day long you think about that kind of stuff. But if one's body and mind are at peace – the kind of peace described in this passage – then those kinds of thoughts simply do not arise any more. It all boils down to this one problem. I keep talking and talking, but in the last analysis, what leads you to create offenses is just this one problem. It's that first thought of ignorance that stirs up so many calamities as a consequence. Emotional love and desire come from that ignorance. So the first thing mentioned in the twelve links of conditioned causation is ignorance. From ignorance comes activity, and from activity comes consciousness. Once there is consciousness, there is name and form. It all starts right there.

Although the beings described here have not broken through ignorance, nonetheless they obtain limitless bliss. **Although they have not obtained proper samadhi, the joy within the tranquility of their minds is total.** They don't have genuine concentration, but in the peace and quiet of their minds there is a kind of joy. **This is called the Third Dhyana.** When you reach the third dhyana, your thoughts do not arise. You obtain the genuine bliss of still extinction. It is said:

> When no thought arises,
> The entire substance appears.
> When the six sense organs suddenly move,
> One is covered as if by clouds.

That moment without any thought arising is the original substance of the Buddha; thus it says that "the entire substance appears." Your eyes taking a look and your ears listening is the movement by which you are obscured. You're in the clouds. You cover your self-nature over.

Before the stage now being discussed, one's thoughts were still active. For instance, when one's pulse stopped one would think, "How is it my pulse has stopped?" and with that one thought the pulse would begin to pump again. When one's breath stopped one thought, "I'm not breathing!" and as soon as one had that thought the breath started up again. That's what happened before the thoughts stopped. Now, in the third dhyana, there isn't any of that. If the pulse stops or the breath ceases – no matter what happens – one pays no attention. Such thoughts do not arise any more. One has no thoughts at all. They can't be found. That's what's meant by the lines, "When no thought arises, the entire substance appears." These lines describe the state of the third dhyana.

Sutra:

"**Moreover, Ananda, heavenly beings whose bodies and minds are not oppressed put an end to the cause of suffering and realize that bliss is not permanent – that sooner or later it will come to an end. Suddenly they simultaneously renounce both thoughts of suffering and thoughts of bliss. Their coarse and heavy thoughts are extinguished, and they give rise to the nature of purity and blessings. They are among those in the Heaven of the Birth of Blessings.**

Commentary:

Moreover, Ananda, heavenly beings whose bodies and minds are not oppressed put an end to the cause of suffering and realize that bliss is not permanent – that sooner or later it will come to an end. At this point, suffering, difficulty, worry, and hang-ups no longer oppress these beings physically or mentally. They don't plant the causes for suffering, but they can't count on the bliss being eternal. Eventually it will go bad. **Suddenly they simultaneously renounce both thoughts of suffering and thoughts of bliss.** If they reach the Heaven of Pervasive Purity and become attached to the bliss they're experiencing there, they've made a mistake. They should put both bliss and suffering down, so there is neither a perception of suffering nor a perception of bliss. If they do that, they will have genuine bliss. **Their coarse and heavy thoughts are extinguished, and they give rise to the nature of purity and blessings.** The pure nature of blessings and virtue arises. This purity of blessings is just the absence of thoughts of suffering and bliss. They have a pure reward of blessings. These beings **are among those in the Heaven of the Birth of Blessings.**

O2   Blessed love heaven.

Sutra:

"Those whose renunciation of these thoughts is in perfect fusion gain a purity of superior understanding. Within these unimpeded blessings they obtain a wonderful compliance that extends to the bounds of the future. They are among those in the Blessed Love Heaven.

Commentary:

Those whose renunciation of these thoughts of suffering and bliss **is in perfect fusion gain a purity of superior understanding.** When they renounce the two kinds of thoughts mentioned above, the purity of blessings arises. Now they gain a superior understanding of this purity, that is, their wisdom has greatly increased. They gain the purity of wisdom. **Within these unimpeded blessings they obtain a wonderful compliance that extends to the bounds of the future.** There is nothing that can hinder this reward of blessings; its magnitude is too great. Out of these blessings arises the ability to constantly accord with living beings. This kind of compliance is such that,

> If channeled to the east, it flows east,
> If channeled to the west, it flows west,

just like a river. There is a total ease in all that one does. Everything one does is correct. One does not make any mistakes.

> Everything is in accord with one's intent.
> Everything one does is totally in accord
>   with the wishes of others.

However one goes about doing something, it is appropriate. There are no problems that arise. No matter what one does, no trouble comes from it. All the problems are resolved. That's what's meant by obtaining "a wonderful compliance that extends to the bounds of the future." This continues forever to the ends of the bounds of the future. What are the bounds of the future? They are just that: the bounds of the future. What else is there to say? These heavenly beings **are among those in the Blessed Love Heaven.**

O3   Abundant fruit heaven.

Sutra:

"Ananda, from that heaven there are two ways to go. Those who extend the previous thought into limitless pure light, and who perfect and clarify their blessings and virtue, cultivate and are certified to one of these dwellings. They are among those in the Abundant Fruit Heaven.

Commentary:

Ananda, from that heaven – that is, from the second heaven of the fourth dhyana, the Blessed Love Heaven – **there are two ways to go**. One way leads to the Heaven of Abundant Results and the other way leads to the No-thought Heaven. There's a fork in the road at this point. **Those who extend the previous thought** – the state of the Blessed Love Heaven – **into limitless pure light, and who perfect and clarify their blessings and virtue, cultivate and are certified to one of these dwellings.** That is, **they are among those in the Abundant Fruit Heaven.** Their virtuous nature is abundant and vast and their fruition is large, so they can dwell in this heaven.

O4   No thought heaven.

Sutra:

"Those who extend the previous thought into a dislike of both suffering and bliss, so that the intensity of their thought to renounce them continues without cease, will end up by totally renouncing the Way. Their bodies and minds will become extinct; their thoughts will become like dead ashes. For five hundred aeons these beings will perpetuate the cause for production and extinction, being unable to discover the nature which is neither produced nor extinguished. During the first half of these aeons they will undergo extinction; during the

second half they will experience production. They are among those in the Heaven of No Thought.

Commentary:

Those who extend the previous thought into a dislike of both suffering and bliss, so that the intensity of their thought to renounce them continues without cease, will end up totally renouncing the Way. If heavenly beings in the Blessed Love Heaven previously described develop a distaste for both suffering and bliss, they will do away with them both. Their investigation of the extinction of these two – suffering and bliss – continues on and on until they **end up by totally renouncing the Way. Their bodies and minds will become extinct; their thoughts will become like dead ashes.** At this point they are cultivating the samadhi of no-thought. **For five hundred aeons these beings will perpetuate the cause for production and extinction, being unable to discover the nature which is neither produced nor extinguished.** They have a lifespan of five hundred aeons, but the cause they are creating is based on production and extinction. **During the first half of these aeons they will undergo extinction.** This refers to their renunciation of both suffering and bliss. When they realize the perfection of that renunciation, such thoughts do not arise. But after two hundred and fifty aeons, they once again give rise to false thinking. **During the second half they will experience production.** The reward of their samadhi of no-thought is coming to an end. When the extinction ceases, they have a thought that slanders the Triple Jewel. When the production begins, marking the decline of their lifespan, when their samadhi is destroyed, they slander the Triple Jewel. What do they say? "The Buddha said that a fourth-stage arhat has ended birth and death and will not undergo any further becoming. Now, I've already been certified to the fourth fruition, so why am I on my way to undergoing birth and death again? The Buddha must have told a lie." That's how they slander the Triple Jewel. Actually, the fourth dhyana heaven they are in is certainly not the fourth fruition of arhatship. It's not even at the level of the first fruition. They make the mistake of thinking that they have become fourth-stage arhats. They get to the fourth dhyana and think it's the fourth stage of arhatship. But they are wrong. The unlearned bhikshu made this mistake. Those who go this road **are among those in the Heaven of No Thought.**

N2   Concludes they are unmoving and have pure heat.

Sutra:

"**Ananda, those who flow to these four superior levels will not be moved by any suffering or bliss in any world. Although this is not the unconditioned or the true ground of non-moving, because they still have the thought of obtaining something, their functioning is nonetheless quite advanced. This is called the Fourth Dhyana.**

Commentary:

Ananda, those who flow to these four superior levels will not be moved by any suffering or bliss in any world. Whether they experience suffering or bliss, their minds do not move. **Although this is not the** genuine **unconditioned** and is not **the true ground of non-moving,** they are still able to control their minds and keep them from moving. But it's a forced control; they have not been certified to the higher level. That is **because they still have the thought of obtaining something.** In the fourth dhyana they still harbor the thought of having gained something. For instance the unlearned bhikshu thought he had reached the fourth fruition of arhatship. **Their functioning is nonetheless quite advanced.** They have reached the maximum in their application of effort, given the level they are on. **This is called the Fourth Dhyana.** These are the heavens of the fourth dhyana.

M2   The five heavens of no return.
N1   Reveals the dwelling in the sagely fruit.

Sutra:

"**Beyond these, Ananda, are the Five Heavens of No Return. For those who have completely cut off the nine categories of habits in the lower realms, neither suffering nor bliss exist, and**

there is no regression to the lower levels. All whose minds have achieved this renunciation dwell in these heavens together.

Commentary:

Beyond these, Ananda, are the Five Heavens of No Return. These upper five heavens are sometimes considered to be among the heavens of the fourth dhyana. However, these five are the dwelling places of sages, and thus differ from the heavens of the first, second, third, and fourth dhyanas. Beings who have been certified to the fruition of arhatship reside in the five heavens of no return. **For those who have completely cut off the nine categories of habits in the lower realms, neither suffering nor bliss exist, and there is no regression to the lower levels.** The "nine categories of habits" refer to the first nine categories of the eighty-one categories of delusion of thoughts. We will not go into them in detail here. These beings do not have to return anywhere at this point. They will not regress to the lower levels. **All whose minds have achieved this renunciation dwell in these heavens together.** A multitude of beings reach this level of renunciation and dwell together in emptiness on a cloud that shelters the earth. Those who dwell there are sages who have reached the level of the five heavens of no return.

N2   The particular characteristics of the five heavens.
O1   The no affliction heaven.

Sutra:

"Ananda, those who have put an end to suffering and bliss and who do not get involved in the contention between such thoughts are among those in the Heaven of No Affliction.

Commentary:

They do not have thoughts of suffering and they do not have thoughts of bliss, and so there is no involvement in the struggle between the two. Those who don't experience this battle between suffering and bliss **are among those in the Heaven of No Affliction.** The beings in this heaven don't have any afflictions at all.

O2   The no heat heaven.

Sutra:

"Those who isolate their practice, whether in movement or in restraint, investigating the baselessness of that involvement, are among those in the Heaven of No Heat.

Commentary:

Those who isolate their practice, whether in movement or in restraint, investigating the baselessness of that involvement, are beings from the previous heaven who have progressed in their cultivation. In the first of the five heavens of no return, they did not get involved in contention between thoughts of suffering and bliss. This means that they were basically devoid of such thoughts, although occasionally a little of that kind of thinking might arise. They might still get a little bit involved sometimes. But at this level, in the Heaven of No Heat, they look into the fact that such involvement lacks any foundation whatsoever, until they reach the point where they simply cannot give rise to that kind of thought or have it in mind. For those beings, such thoughts never arise. They **are among those in the Heaven of No Heat.** They are cool and refreshed at all times.

O3   The good view heaven.

Sutra:

"Those whose vision is wonderfully perfect and clear, view the realms of the ten directions as free of defiling appearances and devoid of all dirt and filth. They are among those in the Heaven of Good View.

Commentary:

Those whose vision is wonderfully perfect and clear, view the realms of the ten directions as free of defiling appearances and devoid of all dirt and filth. Their vision is subtle and wonderful as well as being absolutely clear – not turbid or confused. Their view contains no defiling opinions. Their vision is said to be perfect and clear because it contains no defilement. All defiling things are extinguished. Ignorance and delusions as many as dust and sand have been cleared away. These heavenly beings **are among those in the Heaven of Good View.**

O4   The good manifestation heaven.

Sutra:

"Those whose subtle vision manifests as all their obstructions are refined away are among those in the Heaven of Good Manifestation.

Commentary:

Everything the beings in the previous heaven see is good. Now, with the manifestation of this subtle vision, everything they see is far superior to anything they have ever seen before. This heaven is a lot purer than the heavens already described. The word "refined" refers to the process of smelting, molding, and fashioning. It's like the firing done in a kiln or the shaping done on an anvil. What is refined here is the mind and nature of a sage so that it becomes unobstructed and comfortable in every way. These are the beings who dwell in the Heaven of Good Manifestation.

O5   The ultimate form heaven.

Sutra:

"Those who reach the ultimately subtle level come to the end of the nature of form and emptiness and enter into a boundless realm. They are among those in the Heaven of Ultimate Form.

Commentary:

Those who reach the ultimately subtle level come to the end of the nature of form and emptiness. "Ultimate" has the meaning of epitome or perfection. The "subtle level" refers to the detachment from desires. They reach the end of the nature of emptiness and the nature of form **and enter into a boundless realm. They are among those in the Heaven of Ultimate Form.** They reach the ultimate extreme of the nature of form.

Sutra:

"Ananda, those in the four dhyanas, and even the rulers of the gods at those four levels, can only pay their respects through having heard of the beings in the heavens of no return; they cannot know them or see them, just as the coarse people of the world cannot see the places where the arhats abide in holy Way-places deep in the wild and mountainous areas.

Commentary:

Ananda, those in the four dhyanas, and even the rulers of the gods at those four levels, can only pay their respects through having heard of the beings in the heavens of no return. The leaders of the gods in the heavens of the four dhyanas know about the sages dwelling in the five heavens of no return only through having heard about them. **They cannot know them or see them** themselves. In the same way **the coarse people of the world cannot see the places where the arhats abide in holy Way-places deep in the wild and mountainous areas.** The bodhimandas of the sages are in places where people do not go. Those who dwell in such places are great arhats and great bodhisattvas. Their presence is a supporting influence on the areas where they dwell. Ordinary people never see these holy beings. Although they all live in the same world, people cannot see the sages. So the text likens the five heavens of no return to the sages in the remote Way-places. The gods in the heavens of the four dhyanas don't know where the sages reside.

Sutra:

"Ananda, in these eighteen heavens are those who practice only non-involvement, and have not yet gotten rid of their shapes, as well as those who have reached the level of no return. This is called the Form Realm.

Commentary:

Ananda, in these eighteen heavens are those who practice only non-involvement, and have not yet gotten rid of their shapes. The eighteen heavens are the three each of the first, second, and third dhyanas; the four of the fourth dhyana; and the five heavens of no return. Together they comprise the heavens of the form realm. As to the "practice of non-involvement," the beings in each of these heavens have their own particular causes and effects regarding cultivation. They have eliminated the coarser desires and transcended that realm, but they still have their own forms. The form realm also includes **those who have reached the level of no return.** However, because these heavens are inhabited by sages, they are really in a class by themselves. The text likens them to arhats whose dwellings in the wilds are unknown to the average person. **This is called the Form Realm.**

J3   The four places of emptiness.
K1   The fork that is other than sagehood.

Sutra:

"Furthermore, Ananda, from this summit of the form realm there are also two roads. Those who are intent upon renunciation discover wisdom. The light of their wisdom becomes perfect and penetrating, so that they can transcend the defiling realms, accomplish arhatship, and enter the bodhisattva vehicle. They are among those called great arhats who have turned their minds around.

Commentary:

Furthermore, Ananda, from this summit of the form realm there are also two roads. At this point there is another fork in the road. **Those who are intent upon renunciation discover wisdom.** Once they practice renunciation they can uncover their wisdom. **The light of their wisdom becomes perfect and penetrating,** so that there are no more obstructions. Then **they can transcend the defiling realms.** They can leave the triple realm by taking this fork in the road and **accomplish arhatship**. They attain the fruition of arhatship **and enter the bodhisattva vehicle**. These kinds of living beings **are among those called great arhats who have turned their minds around.** That means they have turned from the small and come around to the great. They have turned from the lesser vehicle, and they tend toward the great vehicle.

K2   Listing the four heavens.
L1   Heaven of the station of boundless emptiness.

Sutra:

"**Those who dwell in the thought of renunciation and who succeed in renunciation and rejection, realize that their bodies are an obstacle. If they thereupon obliterate the obstacle and enter into emptiness, they are among those at the Station of Emptiness.**

Commentary:

We have finished the discussion of the four dhyanas and now begin the explanation of the four stations of emptiness. **Those who dwell in the thought of renunciation and who succeed in renunciation and rejection, realize that their bodies are an obstacle.** These gods accomplish renunciation of bliss and rejection of suffering. They know that physical bodies are an obstruction, and so, **if they thereupon obliterate the obstacle and enter into emptiness, they are among those at the Station of Emptiness.** They don't want to be hindered by anything and so they contemplate their bodies as being just like empty space. In this way they wipe out that obstacle. These beings then take the other road at the fork and enter the Heaven of the Station of Boundless Emptiness.

L2   Heaven of the station of boundless consciousness.

Sutra:

"**For those who have eradicated all obstacles, there is neither obstruction nor extinction. Then there remains only the alaya consciousness and half of the subtle functions of the**

. **manas. These beings are among those at the Station of Boundless Consciousness.**

Commentary:

For those who have eradicated all obstacles, there is neither obstruction nor extinction. At the summit of the four dhyana heavens, those who wished to progress upward felt that the body was an obstacle. So they obliterated the obstacle and entered emptiness. Now that they have advanced to the formless realm, there is no more hindrance of physical form. There's no obstacle, and so there is nothing to extinguish either.

Then there remains only the alaya consciousness and half of the subtle functions of the manas. At this point there is no body, only a consciousness. That consciousness is the *alaya*, or eighth, consciousness, also known as the storehouse consciousness. The "storehouse" is actually the treasury of the Thus Come One, but at this point it has not yet completely returned to the nature of the treasury of the Thus Come One, and so it is still called a consciousness. Every move you make, every word you speak, everything you do and encounter in the course of every day is stored in this consciousness. For these beings, the alaya consciousness remains, along with "half of the subtle functions of the *manas*." The manas is the seventh consciousness, also known as the defiling consciousness. Transformations take place in this consciousness. It is true that we say ignorance arises in the eighth consciousness, but here it is extremely close to becoming the nature of the treasury of the Thus Come One and to being free of defilement. It is only when the information stored in the eighth consciousness passes to the seventh consciousness that it becomes defiling. Now, however, even the manas is functioning only at half its capacity and so the defilement that remains is extremely subtle.

These beings are among those at the Station of Boundless Consciousness. They are born into the Heaven of the Station of Boundless Consciousness.

L3   Heaven of the station of nothing whatsoever.

Sutra:

"Those who have already done away with emptiness and form eradicate the conscious mind as well. In the extensive tranquility of the ten directions there is nowhere at all to go. These beings are among those at the Station of Nothing Whatsoever.

Commentary:

When they reach this level there isn't anything at all. This is really a case of:

> The house is destroyed,
> People are gone.
> It's hard to find words to express it.

Everything is gone. **Those who have already done away with emptiness and form** now **eradicate the conscious mind as well.** The house is destroyed, the people are gone. In the station prior to this there still was consciousness, but now consciousness is gone as well. It's hard to find words to express it. If you don't even have a consciousness, how are you going to talk? There's basically nothing that can be said, anyway. **In the extensive tranquility of the ten directions there is nowhere at all to go.** All the worlds of the ten directions throughout the entire dharma realm have disappeared. A stillness pervades. There's nowhere to go. Nor is there anywhere to come to. There's no coming and no going. **These beings are among those at the Station of Nothing Whatsoever.** Although there's nothing whatsoever, nonetheless the nature of these beings still remains. Their nature is the same as emptiness. Therefore, the gods at the Station of Nothing Whatsoever still have a lifespan. How long is it? Sixty thousand great aeons. Since the gods' lifespan and physical height increases to such vast proportions in the realms of form and formlessness, I haven't mentioned the figures, they are too huge. I decided to wait till the end and impress you with one gigantic number. If you want to know all the numbers between, you can look them up.

This, then, is the second-to-last heaven, and the lifespan of the gods is sixty thousand great kalpas. We call it a lifespan, but actually these gods are in samadhi for that long. At the end of that time their samadhi is destroyed, and then they once again transmigrate into the other realms of existence. It's not for sure what path of rebirth they will wind up in. These are the beings in the Heaven of the Station of Nothing Whatsoever.

L4   Heaven of the station of neither thought nor non-thought.

Sutra:

"When the nature of their consciousness does not move, within extinction they exhaustively investigate. Within the endless they discern the end of the nature. It is as if it were there and yet not there, as if it were ended and yet not ended. They are among those at the Station of Neither Thought nor Non-Thought.

Commentary:

This is the Heaven of Neither Thought Nor Non-thought, the highest of the heavens. The lifespan of these heavenly beings is eighty thousand great aeons. However, after enjoying that long period of heavenly blessings, they too fall back into rebirth. In the Heaven of the Station of Boundless Consciousness, the consciousness still functions occasionally, but now it doesn't move at all. **When the nature of their consciousness does not move, within extinction they exhaustively investigate.** Ultimately even investigation and all other forms of pursuing knowledge come to an end. **Within the endless they discern the end of the nature.** "The endless" refers to the absence of anything, as just described. Within it they discern the end of the nature which is endless. When they discern this nature, however, **it is as if it were there and yet not there, as if it were ended and yet not ended.** It seems to be gone but it isn't. **They are among those at the Station of Neither Thought nor Non-Thought.** There is a bit of thought left, but at this station it does not function. They remain in samadhi for eighty thousand great aeons. They are the gods with the longest lifespan.

People who cultivate the Way should not give rise to thoughts. Once your mind is set in motion and thoughts arise, you will be stuck with the retribution in the future. You'll have to work it off. For example, there was an old cultivator in the past who cultivated the samadhi of neither thought nor non-thought, and he could probably have entered the heaven of the station of neither thought nor non-thought. One day, as he was cultivating by the seashore and was just on the verge of entering samadhi, a fish in the water disturbed him. In the Chan hall, people who are incessant talkers are dubbed "machine guns." They are always able to think up reasons to interrupt others with questions and discussions which disturb the hall. To create disturbances is to be a pest who gives other people trouble. In this case, it was a fish that created the disturbance. It flipped out of the water with a "plunk," and that little feat of acrobatics prevented the cultivator from entering samadhi. Unable to enter samadhi, the cultivator got angry, and he thought, "What a nuisance that fish is! I want to enter samadhi, and he comes to trouble me. I don't have any spiritual penetrations yet, but when I get them, I'm going to come back as a kingfisher and eat his species up. That's what he'll get for obstructing my practice!" Of course, since he was so angry the fish didn't dare play around with him anymore. It was scared away. Left undisturbed, the cultivator accomplished his cultivation and was born in the heaven of the station of neither thought nor non-thought. However, after he enjoyed eighty thousand great aeons of residence in that heaven, guess what happened. The retribution came ripe from that one thought of anger he'd had by the seashore that day. He fell into the animal realm and was reborn as a kingfisher. His entire existence consisted of eating fish from the sea. This continued until Shakyamuni Buddha came into the world and came to where he was to speak the dharma for him. Only then was he able to relinquish the body of a kingfisher and become a person. He once again left the home life and cultivated the Way, and this time he was certified to the fruition of arhatship.

Whatever you do in cultivation of the Way, then, don't get angry. Whether people are good to you or not, you should maintain thoughts of loving kindness for them, thoughts of compassion and protection. Don't feel hatred toward anyone, don't be upset by them. It won't be a problem if you perfect your cultivation and transcend the triple world. But if you remain in the triple world, you will have to undergo retribution for your hatred. There's a saying that's appropriate here:

> You can move the waters of a thousand rivers,
> But you can't disturb the mind of a cultivator of the Way.

To disturb a cultivator and cause him to get angry is a serious matter, and the cause and effect will ripen in the future.

K3   The rise and fall of sages and ordinary people.

Sutra:

"These beings who delve exhaustively into emptiness, but never fathom the principle of emptiness, go from the Heaven of No Return down this road which is a dead end to sagehood. They are among those known as dull arhats who do not turn their minds around. Just like those in the Heaven of No Thought and the heavens of externalists who become engrossed in emptiness and do not want to come back, these beings are confused, prone to outflows, and ignorant. They will accordingly enter the cycle of rebirth again.

Commentary:

These beings who delve exhaustively into emptiness, but never fathom the principle of emptiness, go from the Heaven of No Return down this road which is a dead end to sagehood. You'll remember that at the summit of the form realm the road is forked. One path leads to the great arhats who turn their minds around. Now we've come to the end of the road which the other fork leads to – to the arhats who do not turn their minds around. They never fathom the principle of emptiness entirely. They have cultivated, but they don't really understand; they don't have any genuine wisdom. **They are among those known as dull arhats who do not turn their minds around.** They don't have the wisdom of sages. They don't turn from the small and go toward the great. "Dull" means stupid and dull-witted. **Just like those in the Heaven of No Thought and the heavens of externalists who become engrossed in emptiness and do not want to come back, these beings are confused, prone to outflows, and ignorant.** The beings in those heavens and the ones who pass through the four stations of emptiness and wind up at this dead end all become attached to emptiness and don't know how to return to cultivate the way to bodhi. They end up confused and stupid. **They will accordingly enter the cycle of rebirth again.** In cultivation you must keep yourself in line and not go down the wrong road.

K4   Understanding the difference between ordinary people and sages.

Sutra:

"Ananda, each and every being in all these heavens is ordinary. They are still answerable for their karmic retribution. When they have answered for their debts, they must once again enter rebirth. The lords of these heavens, however, are all bodhisattvas who roam in samadhi. They gradually progress in their practice and make transferences to the Way cultivated by all sages.

Commentary:

Ananda, each and every being in all these heavens is ordinary. You shouldn't think that they have succeeded in their cultivation. They are all still ordinary beings. They have not been certified to the fruition of sagehood. **They are still answerable for their karmic retribution.** Despite their long lifespans, they still must go off to repay their debts when their karma catches up with them. **When they have answered for their debts, they must once again enter rebirth.**

The lords of these heavens, however, are all bodhisattvas. They are transformation-body bodhisattvas, **who roam in samadhi. They gradually progress in their practice and make transferences to the Way cultivated by all sages.** They make transference to bodhi, the enlightened way. They are certified to the fruition and join the family of sages. The Way they cultivate is the same that is cultivated by all the sages.

K5   Conclusion of those belonging to the formless realm.

Sutra:

"**Ananda, these are the Four Heavens of Emptiness, where the bodies and minds of the inhabitants are extinguished. The nature of concentration emerges, and they are free of the karmic retribution of form. This final group is called the Formless Realm.**

Commentary:

Ananda, these are the Four Heavens of Emptiness. They are:

1. The Heaven of the Station of Boundless Emptiness,
2. The Heaven of the Station of Boundless Consciousness,
3. The Heaven of the Station of Nothing Whatsoever,
4. The Heaven of Neither Thought Nor Non-thought.

This is **where the bodies and minds of the inhabitants are extinguished. The nature of concentration emerges, and they are free of the karmic retribution of form.** They don't have physical bodies, and they have no minds other than a consciousness which does not move. The nature of their samadhi power becomes evident. "They are free of the karmic retribution of form." They don't have to go through that in these heavens. **This final group is called the Formless Realm.** This is the end of life in the three realms. The four stations of emptiness are the heavens of the formless realm. They are the last of the heavens.

I2   Reiterates and generally concludes.

Sutra:

"The beings in all of them have not understood the wonderful enlightenment of the bright mind. Their accumulation of falseness brings into being false existence in the three realms. Within them they falsely follow along and become submerged in the seven destinies. As pudgalas, they gather together with their own species or kind.

Commentary:

The beings throughout the three realms just described **have not understood the wonderful enlightenment of the bright mind.** They don't have the wisdom to understand and become enlightened. **Their accumulation of falseness brings into being false existence in the three realms.** From the one truth, falseness arises. Ignorance is produced in the nature of wonderful true suchness. The three realms are created by living beings themselves. Once **within them they falsely follow along and become submerged in the seven destinies.** We usually speak of the cycle of rebirth in the six paths, but here the text mentions seven. That's because the path of the immortals is included here, having been discussed earlier in the sutra. The seven are:

1. gods,
2. asuras,
3. immortals,
4. people,
5. animals,
6. hungry ghosts,
7. hell dwellers.

They bob up and down, suddenly getting reborn in the heavens and then falling again into the hells. They go from being people to being hungry ghosts. That's what's meant by "submerged." **As pudgalas, they gather together with their own species or kind.** "Pudgala" is a Sanskrit word that means sentient beings. "Gathering together with their own kind" means that they undergo retribution for whatever kind of karma they have created. If they are immortals, they gather together with that kind. If their reward is the heavens, then they gather together with other gods. If they are destined to be asuras, they get together with other asuras. The same applies to the other destinies.

Destiny of Asuras

Sutra:

"Furthermore, Ananda, there are four categories of asuras in the triple realm.

Commentary:

Furthermore, Ananda, there are four categories of asuras. "Asura" is also a Sanskrit word. Sometimes it's translated as "non-gods." That's because some asuras have the blessings of the heavens but not the virtue of the gods. Another translation is "not upright in appearance"; however, only the male asuras are that way. The asura women are extremely beautiful. Asuras are found among beings of the four kinds of birth: womb-born, egg-born, moisture-born, and born by transformation. Each of these will now be discussed.

Sutra:

"Those in the path of ghosts who use their strength to protect the dharma and who can ride their spiritual penetrations to enter into emptiness are asuras born from eggs; they belong to the destiny of ghosts.

Commentary:

Those in the path of ghosts who use their strength to protect the dharma and who can ride their spiritual penetrations to enter into emptiness are asuras born from eggs. Some ghosts are good and act as dharma protectors. Guan Di Gong is an example. He is a great and powerful ghost. These kinds of ghosts protect and support the Triple Jewel. They can use their spiritual powers to go into emptiness. These asuras **belong to the destiny of ghosts.**

J2   Womb-born people.

Sutra:

"Those who have fallen in virtue and have been dismissed from the heavens dwell in places near the sun and moon. They are asuras born from wombs and belong to the destiny of humans.

Commentary:

Those who have fallen in virtue and have been dismissed from the heavens dwell in places near the sun and moon. They started out in the heavens, but they didn't have the virtue to remain there. They fell and were thrown out into empty space. They take up residence in places close to the sun and moon. **They are asuras born from wombs and belong to the destiny of humans.**

J3   Transformation-born gods.

Sutra:

"There are asura kings who uphold the world with a penetrating power and fearlessness. They fight for position with the Brahma lord, the god Shakra, and the four heavenly kings. These asuras come into being by transformation and belong to the destiny of gods.

Commentary:

There is another category of asuras: **kings who uphold the world with a penetrating power and fearlessness.** Their strength is enormous. They can shake the entire world system. If they grasp the peak of Mt. Sumeru with their hand and push, they can topple the mountain right down. That's the kind of strength they have. With such great spiritual powers, they think they'd like to be the Great Brahma King or the lord Shakra. So they fight for power and ·authority. **They fight for position with the Brahma lord, the god Shakra, and the four heavenly kings. These asuras come into being by transformation and belong to the destiny of gods.** They use their spiritual powers to undergo this transformation.

The lord of the asuras had a beautiful daughter who became the reason why he went to war with the god Shakra. She was an exquisite young goddess, and when Shakra laid eyes on her he went to the lord of the asuras to ask for her hand. The asura father consented. It turned out, however, that the asura woman was extremely jealous and selfish. The lord Shakra liked to listen to the Buddhadharma and would go regularly to hear the dharma masters lecture on the sutras. The asura woman noticed his absence and became jealous. She thought, "Now that he's married me, he doesn't love me anymore. I bet he's going out and having an affair." Possessed by such jealous thoughts as this, she secretly followed the lord Shakra one day to find out where he went. When the lord entered the dharma assembly and took his place, his wife observed that there were a lot of women in the gathering. This fired her jealousy even more, and with that she became visible. When Shakra saw her he asked, "What are you doing here?"

"You come here to get friendly with women and don't invite me along!" she replied in a jealous fit.

Shakra slapped her face, and she began to cry and ran home to the asura king to tell her tale. "The god Shakra is breaking the rules and always going out to find women," she reported. "When I followed him, he hit me."

Of course, when the asura king heard that, he was outraged. "We're going to war! We'll overthrow him and usurp the throne!" He sent out the entire company of asura soldiers and generals to join battle against Shakra. Well, guess what; the combined military might of Shakra, Brahma, and the four heavenly kings could not overcome the asura troops. It was a stalemate. Finally Shakra had to go to the Buddha to ask for help. "What's to be done?" he said. "I can't beat these asuras."

Shakyamuni Buddha replied, "Go back and tell all your officers and enlisted men to recite the phrase 'Mahaprajnaparamita,' and I guarantee that everything will turn out all right."

Shakra did as he was told, and the asuras gave up without further fight. That's how Shakra finally won. But these kinds of asuras are always fighting for position and authority.

J4   Moisture-born animals.

Sutra:

"Ananda, there is another, baser category of asuras. They have thoughts of the great seas and live submerged in underwater caves. During the day they roam in emptiness; at night they return to their watery realm. These asuras come into being because of moisture and belong to the destiny of animals.

Commentary:

Ananda, there is another, baser category of asuras. They have thoughts of the great seas and live submerged in underwater caves. These asuras belong to the animal realm. Dragons and the like are examples. Since they think so much about the sea, they end up living in it. **During the day they roam in emptiness; at night they return to their watery realm.** They go back to their underwater caves in the evening. **These asuras come into being because of moisture and belong to the destiny of animals.**

F3   Concludes they are false and exhorts him to be apart from them.
G1   Brings up the medicine and the sickness.
H1   Generally mentions the false sickness.

Sutra:

"Ananda, so it is that when the seven destinies of hell-dwellers, hungry ghosts, animals, people, spiritual immortals, gods, and asuras are investigated in detail, they are all found to

be murky and embroiled in conditioned existence. **Their births come from false thoughts. Their subsequent karma comes from false thoughts.** Within the wonderful perfection of the fundamental mind that is without any doing, they are like strange flowers in space, for there is basically nothing to be attached to; they are entirely vain and false, and they have no source or beginning.

Commentary:

Ananda, so it is that when the seven destinies of hell-dwellers, hungry ghosts, animals, people, spiritual immortals, gods, and asuras are investigated in detail, they are all found to be murky and embroiled in conditioned existence. They all still have some form of appearance. **Their births come from false thoughts. Their subsequent karma comes from false thoughts,** and it leads them into their next rebirth. **Within the wonderful perfection of the fundamental mind that is without any doing, they are like strange flowers in space, for there is basically nothing to be attached to.** The seven destinies are like illusory flowers in emptiness; they are nothing to cling to. **They are entirely vain and false, and they have no source or beginning.**

H2 Points out the deep root of the illness.

Sutra:

"Ananda, these living beings, who do not recognize the fundamental mind, all undergo rebirth for limitless kalpas. They do not attain true purity, because they keep getting involved in killing, stealing, and lust, or because they counter them and are born according to their not killing, not stealing, and lack of lust. If these three karmas are present in them, they are born among the troops of ghosts. If they are free of these three karmas, they are born in the destiny of gods. The incessant fluctuation between the presence and absence of these karmas gives rise to the cycle of rebirth.

Commentary:

Ananda, these living beings in the seven destinies, **who do not recognize the fundamental mind, all undergo rebirth for limitless kalpas.** They don't know of the wonderful perfection of the fundamental mind which is without any doing, and so they keep having to undergo birth in the six paths. They are born and then die; they die and then are reborn. In this life they're a cow, and in the next life they're a horse, and maybe in the life following that they become a person. It's a continuing cycle. How long does it go on? There's no way to calculate how many aeons one passes through in this way. **They do not attain true purity.** They never uncover their inherent pure substance. Why? **Because they keep getting involved in killing, stealing, and lust.** They get all hung up in them and can't stop their involvement. **Or it is because they counter** the three karmas of killing, stealing, and lust **and are born according to their not killing, not stealing, and lack of lust. If these three karmas are present in them, they are born among the troops of ghosts.** If they commit acts of killing, stealing, and lust, they go to the realm of ghosts where all their friends and relatives are also ghosts. **If they are free of these three karmas, they are born in the destiny of gods. The incessant fluctuation between the presence and absence of these karmas gives rise to the cycle of rebirth.** The continuous battle between creating those karmas and not creating them goes on and on. Sometimes they create them, sometimes they don't. That's the nature of rebirth.

H3   Decides on a medicine that can get rid of it.

Sutra:

"For those who make the wonderful discovery of samadhi, neither the presence nor the absence of these karmas exists in that magnificent, eternal stillness; even their non-existence is done away with. Since the lack of killing, stealing, and lust is non-existent, how could there be actual involvement in deeds of killing, stealing, and lust?

Commentary:

For those who make the wonderful discovery of samadhi, neither the presence nor the absence of these karmas exists in that magnificent, eternal stillness. Some beings in the seven destinies can attain wonderful and genuine samadhi power. That refers to the great Shurangama Samadhi. They return the hearing to hear the self-nature, and the nature accomplishes the Unsurpassed Way. They cultivate the perfect penetration of the organ of the ear and attain true and proper samadhi power. If the three karmas are present, one goes into the three evil destinies of hell dwellers, hungry ghosts, and animals. If they are absent, one can attain rebirth among humans, immortals, gods, or asuras. But in this samadhi, those karmas are neither present nor absent; **even their non-existence is done away with.** The absence of divisions into the three evil destinies and the four good paths is dispensed with as well. **Since the lack of killing, stealing, and lust is non-existent, how could there be actual involvement in deeds of killing, stealing, and lust?** If they fundamentally don't exist, how could there be involvement in those acts of karma? How could such karma actually be created? It isn't.

G2   Collective and individual karma are both false.

Sutra:

"Ananda, those who do not cut off the three karmas each have their own private share. Because each has a private share, private shares come to be accumulated, making collective portions. Their location is not arbitrary, yet they themselves are falsely produced. Since they are produced from falseness, they are basically without a cause, and thus they cannot be traced precisely.

Commentary:

Ananda, those who do not cut off the three karmas each have their own private share. Every creature that does not sever the three karmas of killing, stealing, and lust creates its own individual share of karma. **Because each has a private share,**

private shares come to be accumulated, making collective portions. Their location is not arbitrary. When beings create similar kinds of individual karma, they will undergo similar retributions; this is called the collective portion. It's not a random coincidence; it's not an arbitrary circumstance. However, though it seems to be precise, that precision is itself a result of falseness. Its source is false to begin with, and so the text says: **yet they themselves** – the individual shares and collective portions – **are falsely produced. Since they are produced from falseness, they are basically without a cause.** The falseness is insubstantial. Falseness has no seed. It is vain and empty and not actual. **Thus they cannot be traced precisely.** You can search but you cannot find the root. They arise falsely and just as falsely cease to be. You may be determined to find their source, but it doesn't exist. They are like a person's shadow. It's only a shadow, and you won't succeed in finding its source. You may say that its source is the body, but the appearance of the shadow is not the body itself. The shadow is merely an illusion.

G3   Likeness and difference both false.

Sutra:

"**You should warn cultivators that they must get rid of these three delusions if they want to cultivate bodhi. If they do not put an end to these three delusions, then even the spiritual penetrations they may attain are merely a worldly, conditioned function. If they do not extinguish these habits, they will fall into the path of demons.**

Commentary:

Shakyamuni Buddha calls to Ananda: **You should warn cultivators that they must get rid of these three delusions if they want to cultivate bodhi.** The "three delusions" here are the three karmas of killing, stealing, and lust. They are called "delusions" here because the karma arises from delusion. If one were not confused and deluded, the karma would not be created. **If they do not put an end to these three delusions** – that is, if there is even the tiniest bit of any of these three delusions in your makeup – a hair's breadth of killing, stealing, or lust that you don't get rid of – **then even the spiritual penetrations they may attain are merely a worldly, conditioned function.** Perhaps they may get a bit of spiritual power or a small amount of wisdom, but even that cannot be considered to be unconditioned spiritual penetration. It resides in form and appearance and depends upon an intent in order to function. It is spiritual penetration which is attached to appearances. **If they do not extinguish these habits, they will fall into the path of demons.** If the habits of killing, stealing, and lust are not brought to a stop, you will sink into the demonic paths in the future.

Now you see why I say that such-and-such a cultivator is a demon king. He does not observe precepts regarding killing, stealing, or lust. If one is like that, how can one obtain genuine wisdom? It's impossible.

Sutra:

"Although they wish to cast out the false, they become doubly deceptive instead. The Thus Come One says that such beings are pitiful. You have created this falseness yourself; it is not the fault of bodhi.

Commentary:

Although they wish to cast out the false, they become doubly deceptive instead. They add falseness to falseness, falsehood to falsehood. They start out by telling a lie, by speaking incorrectly. But afterwards they say that they didn't lie, and that's another lie. If you tell a lie, there's no use in arguing. Admit it and then it's just one lie. But someone who denies the lie he told ends up by telling two. In this way he increases his offenses. **The Thus Come One says that such beings are pitiful.** People who never do things properly are really pathetic. **You have created this falseness yourself; it is not the fault of bodhi.** All this false delusion and karma is something that you brought into being. There's no fault on the part of bodhi. Therefore, you can't say, "If we were all Buddhas how come we gave rise to falseness?" You make a mistake if you talk like that.

F4   Decides the deviant and proper.

Sutra:

"An explanation such as this is proper speech. Any other explanation is the speech of demon kings."

Commentary:

An explanation such as this is proper speech. If you talk in this way, you are in accord with the Buddhadharma. **Any other explanation is the speech of demon kings.** If the explanation is not along these lines, you can know it's a demon king talking. You should make the distinction clearly. The theories spoken by demon kings are based on falseness. For instance, he knows about a particular situation but says he doesn't know. That's lying. Cultivators should know that the straight mind is the bodhimanda. Be straightforward in all situations. Don't be deceptive.

General Index

Master's Address to Ajahn Sumedho

and the Sangha at Amaravati Buddhist Centre

England, 6 October 1990

Wherever I go, I feel as much as home as if I were at the City of Ten Thousand Buddhas. That way in my view, we are of the same substance as the Dharma Realm, the universe. So today for our delegation from America to have this once-in-a-lifetime opportunity and these rare affinities to come to England as your guests makes me very happy indeed.

In Buddhism, we should unite the Southern and Northern traditions. From now on, we won't refer to Mahayana or Theravada. Mahayana is the "Northern Tradition," and Theravada is the "Southern Tradition." Theravada, the Southern tradition, shouldn't run so far towards the South. Mahayana, the Northern Tradition, shouldn't run off to the North. Both traditions should move back towards the center, instead. Both the Southern and the Northern Traditions' members are disciples of the Buddha, we are the Buddhas' descendants. As such, we should do what Buddhists ought to do. To mutually accuse each other of not being true, or of not being real Buddhists, is simply to not recognize Buddhism.

All dharmas the Buddha spoke were meant to tally with the various potentials of living beings. No matter the Southern or the Northern Tradition, both share the common purpose of helping living beings bring forth the Bodhi-mind, to put an end birth and death, and to leave suffering and attain bliss.

For we who followed the Buddha to establish sects and schisms and to accuse others of being false Buddhists does harm to Buddhism as a whole. We should not be at each other's throats. We should not hold the attitude that others are not true Buddhists, and that we alone hold the authentic, orthodox lineage. Such an attitude brings no benefits to the Dharma at all.

I have always hoped that the Southern Tradition will stop travelling so far South, and the Northern Tradition will turn back from its Northern course. I hope we will both move towards the center and reunite there, so that we can evolve a better mutual understanding. This will be useful to Buddhism. Otherwise, if you go your way, and I go mine, then our only choice will be to fall into sectarianism and divisions, and the strength of Buddhism will scatter and dissipate. We should get to know each other here in the middle, where we belong. The alternative holds no advantages for anyone.

From the time I first left home to the present, I felt it strange that such a perfect teaching as Buddhism, with its inclusive principles, should be understood by so few people in the world. Why is it so? I concluded that Buddhism had not become a universal teaching because few people, at least in the Northern tradition that I was familiar with, had as yet translated the Sutras into the world's languages.

I felt it was simply a shame for a religion to remain unknown by so many people, a religion that benefits humanity so thoroughly, a religion that people should always have access to. Yet the fact remains that few people in the world understand the Dharma, all because so few Sutras existed in their own mother tongue. For example, we know that Catholicism and Protestantism has traveled so far in the world and become international religions because the Bible was translated into many languages. Anyone could understand it in his or her own tongue. But Buddhadharma, with few exceptions, was only rarely translated.

So I made a vow when I was a young cultivator to see the Buddhadharma translated into the world's many languages. Although I made this vow after leaving home over fifty years ago, I have not yet achieved my goal. I'm still looking forward to the completion of the vow, towards success in the future. I myself don't speak English. Nonetheless, if there are people who share my wish, and who walk the same road, then let us work together, and pool our efforts to translate the Buddha's Sutras.

In Burlingame, south of San Francisco, we have now established the International Translation Institute (ITI) for the translation of Buddhist texts, and I hope that cultivators from both the Southern and the Northern Tradition will come forth to put our Sutras into the worlds' languages. This work is extremely important.

To simply stand to the side and engage in back-biting and insults, labeling each other false, or petty, only squanders time and energy. In the end we gain nothing, the time has passed in vain, and we have wasted our lives.

We should recall that when the Buddha first spoke the Dharma, it took forty-nine years and he presided over 300 assemblies. Many of the disciples he converted were former leaders of religions outside Buddhism, who came to believe in the Dharma. Look at Mahamaudgalyayana, Venerable Shariputra, the Patriarch Mahakasyapa, they were all leaders of the various indigenous sects in India, who came to believe in the Dharma. Why don't we within Buddhism encourage each other on, help and support each other, so that we all can go forward together? Mutual criticism and fault-finding simply amounts to self-harm; its just like biting your own flesh.

Now you might conclude that since I myself don't speak English, it takes a lot of gall to make a bold vow to translate the Sutras into the worlds' languages. And you'd be right! But I feel certain, nonetheless, that the Buddha would be pleased by this idea. Even though I speak only Chinese, I feel that you who speak a variety of foreign tongues should resolve to accomplish this goal, and bring the work to success. It is most important!

So I hereby invite all Buddhists of the world to come together, to unite our strength and our wills for the task of translating Sutras! Let's realize this goal in our lifetime. I now lay this request before all of you, hoping we will bring this vow to completion.

A Chinese proverb says,

> *"Every citizen has a responsibility for the rising or falling of his country."*

In similar fashion, the flourishing or failing of Buddhism is also the personal responsibility of every Buddhist disciple. Each Buddhist should view the future success of the Dharma as his or her own individual duty. It should be our responsibility to propagate Buddhadharma in every tiny atom of every continent, and in every human heart, so that it pervades the Dharma Realm and the universe, filling up all places. When Buddhism pervades everywhere, we can expect the entire Dharma Realm to blaze forth with a brilliant light! I hope none of you Bhikshus or Bhikshunis will fall behind in this work. That's the reason I am still traveling everywhere with my cane in my hand.

In Taiwan, until just recently, an elderly Upasaka named Li Bing-nan, at 90 years, regularly lectured on the Dharma, even after he became an invalid, and was unable to walk. He was unable to walk, but his mind was very clear. He insisted on lecturing even though his legs refused to cooperate. How? Two men would pick him up bodily, and carry him up on to the platform. When the talk was over, they would carry him back down. That's how vigorous and committed he was, even into his nineties. He made lecturing on Sutras his own personal responsibility until the end of his life.

For a lay-person to be so vigorous is remarkable. How much the more should we left-home people be constant in our vigor, and go straight ahead to do what we ought to do! I'm not playing chess with you all as I say these things, nor have you been checkmated. After you have heard my message, those of you who choose to follow my suggestions can do so, if you choose. Those who disagree with me won't be forced to comply. Compliance or opposition are entirely up to you. Whenever one uses force or coercion to compel accord, one will be sure to fail. People should do what they like to do. Action must come from your volition.

For example, what I told you about my vows comes from my wishes. I want to do those things, of my own free will. I feel they must be done. By the same token, I consider myself a disciple of the Buddha, regardless of whether or not I am qualified to be one. I feel I should go ahead and do the Buddha's work regardless. I've been working for the Buddhadharma all my life, simply because I feel it must be done. Even if the Buddha were to refuse to accept me as a disciple I would still feel this work had to be done. That's simply the kind of person I am.

I hope the Southern and the Northern Buddhist traditions can wake up from their confused dreams and get on with what they're supposed to do.

Whether my words to you are right or wrong is up to you to decide.

> *"If it's the Path, advance along it.*
> *If it's not the Path, retreat from it."*

The Dharma Realm Buddhist Association

Mission

The Dharma Realm Buddhist Association (formerly the Sino-American Buddhist Association) was founded by the Venerable Master Hsuan Hua in the United States of America in 1959. Taking the Dharma Realm as its scope, the Association aims to disseminate the genuine teachings of the Buddha throughout the world. The Association is dedicated to translating the Buddhist canon, propagating the Orthodox Dharma, promoting ethical education, and bringing benefit and happiness to all beings. Its hope is that individuals, families, the society, the nation, and the entire world will, under the transforming influence of the Buddhadharma, gradually reach the state of ultimate truth and goodness.

The Founder

The Venerable Master, whose names were An Tse and To Lun, received the Dharma name Hsuan Hua and the transmission of Dharma from Venerable Master Hsu Yun in the lineage of the Wei Yang Sect. He was born in Manchuria, China, at the beginning of the century. At nineteen, he entered the monastic order and dwelt in a hut by his mother's grave to practice filial piety. He meditated, studied the teachings, ate only one meal a day, and slept sitting up. In 1948 he went to Hong Kong, where he established the Buddhist Lecture Hall and other Way-places. In 1962 he brought the Proper Dharma to the West, lecturing on several dozen Mahayana Sutras in the United States. Over the years, the Master established more than twenty monasteries of Proper Dharma under the auspices of the Dharma Realm Buddhist Association and the City of Ten Thousand Buddhas. He also founded centers for the translation of the Buddhist canon and for education to spread the influence of the Dharma in the East and West. The Master manifested the stillness in the United States in 1995. Through his lifelong, selfless dedication to teaching living beings with wisdom and compassion, he influenced countless people to change their faults and to walk upon the pure, bright path to enlightenment.

Dharma Propagation, Buddhist Text Translation, and Education

The Venerable Master Hua's three great vows after leaving the home-life were (1) to propagate the Dharma, (2) to translate the Buddhist Canon, and (3) to promote education. In order to make these vows a reality, the Venerable Master based himself on the Three Principles and the Six Guidelines. Courageously facing every hardship, he founded monasteries, schools, and centers in the West, drawing in living beings and teaching them on a vast scale. Over the years, he founded the following institutions:

The City of Ten Thousand Buddhas and Its Branches

In propagating the Proper Dharma, the Venerable Master not only trained people but also founded Way-places where the Dharma wheel could turn and living beings could be saved. He wanted to provide cultivators with pure places to practice in accord with the Buddha's regulations. Over the years, he founded many Way-places of Proper Dharma. In the United States and Canada, these include the City of Ten Thousand Buddhas; Gold Mountain Monastery; Gold Sage Monastery; Gold Wheel Monastery; Gold Summit Monastery; Gold Buddha Monastery; Avatamsaka Monastery; Long Beach Monastery; the City of the Dharma Realm; Berkeley Buddhist Monastery; Avatamsaka Hermitage; and Blessings, Prosperity, and Longevity Monastery. In Taiwan, there are the Dharma Realm Buddhist Books Distribution Association, Dharma Realm Monastery, and Amitabha Monastery. In Malaysia, there are the Prajna Guanyin Sagely Monastery (formerly Tze Yun Tung Temple), Deng Bi An Monastery, and Lotus Vihara. In Hong Kong, there are the Buddhist Lecture Hall and Cixing Monastery.

Purchased in 1974, the City of Ten Thousand Buddhas is the hub of the Dharma Realm Buddhist Association. The City is located in Talmage, Mendocino County, California, 110 miles north of San Francisco. Eighty of the 488 acres of land are in active use. The remaining acreage consists of meadows, orchards, and woods. With over seventy large buildings containing over 2,000 rooms, blessed with serenity and fresh, clean air, it is the first large Buddhist monastic community in the United States. It is also an international center for the Proper Dharma.

Although the Venerable Master Hua was the Ninth Patriarch in the Wei Yang Sect of the Chan School, the monasteries he founded emphasize all of the five main practices of Mahayana Buddhism (Chan meditation, Pure Land, esoteric, Vinaya (moral discipline), and doctrinal studies). This accords with the Buddha's words: "The Dharma is level and equal, with no high or low." At the City of Ten Thousand Buddhas, the rules of purity are rigorously observed. Residents of the City strive to regulate their own conduct and to cultivate with vigor. Taking refuge in the Proper Dharma, they lead pure and selfless lives, and attain peace in body and mind. The Sutras are expounded and the Dharma wheel is turned daily. Residents dedicate themselves wholeheartedly to making Buddhism flourish. Monks and nuns in all the monasteries take one meal a day, always wear their precept sash, and follow the Three Principles:

> *Freezing, we do not scheme.*
> *Starving, we do not beg.*
> *Dying of poverty, we ask for nothing.*
> *According with conditions, we do not change.*
> *Not changing, we accord with conditions.*
> *We adhere firmly to our three great principles.*
> *We renounce our lives to do the Buddha's work.*
> *We take the responsibility to mold our own destinies.*
> *We rectify our lives to fulfill the Sanghan's role.*
> *Encountering specific matters,*
>   *we understand the principles.*
> *Understanding the principles,*
>   *we apply them in specific matters.*
> *We carry on the single pulse of*
>   *the Patriarchs' mind-transmission.*

The monasteries also follow the Six Guidelines: not contending, not being greedy, not seeking, not being selfish, not pursuing personal advantage, and not lying.

International Translation Institute

The Venerable Master vowed to translate the Buddhist Canon (Tripitaka) into Western languages so that it would be widely accessible throughout the world. In 1973, he founded the International Translation Institute on Washington Street in San Francisco for the purpose of translating Buddhist scriptures into English and other languages. In 1977, the Institute was merged into Dharma Realm Buddhist University as the Institute for the Translation of Buddhist Texts. In 1991, the Venerable Master purchased a large building in Burlingame (south of San Francisco) and established the International Translation Institute there for the purpose of translating and publishing Buddhist texts. To date, in addition to publishing over one hundred volumes of Buddhist texts in Chinese, the Association has published more than one hundred volumes of English, French, Spanish, Vietnamese, and Japanese translations of Buddhist texts, as well as bilingual (Chinese and English) editions. Audio and video tapes also continue to be produced. The monthly journal Vajra Bodhi Sea, which has been in circulation for nearly thirty years, has been published in bilingual (Chinese and English) format in recent years.

In the past, the difficult and vast mission of translating the Buddhist canon in China was sponsored and supported by the emperors and kings themselves. In our time, the Venerable Master encouraged his disciples to cooperatively shoulder this heavy responsibility, producing books and audio tapes and using the medium of language to turn the wheel of Proper Dharma and do the great work of the Buddha. All those who aspire to devote themselves to this work of sages should uphold the Eight Guidelines of the International Translation Institute:

1. One must free oneself from the motives of personal fame and profit.
2. One must cultivate a respectful and sincere attitude free from arrogance and conceit.
3. One must refrain from aggrandizing one's work and denigrating that of others.
4. One must not establish oneself as the standard of correctness and suppress the work of others with one's fault-finding.
5. One must take the Buddha-mind as one's own mind.
6. One must use the wisdom of Dharma-Selecting Vision to determine true principles.
7. One must request Virtuous Elders of the ten directions to certify one's translations.
8. One must endeavor to propagate the teachings by printing Sutras, Shastra texts, and Vinaya texts when the translations are certified as being correct.

These are the Venerable Master's vows, and participants in the work of translation should strive to realize them.

Instilling Goodness Elementary School, Developing Virtue Secondary School, Dharma Realm Buddhist University

"Education is the best national defense." The Venerable Master Hua saw clearly that in order to save the world, it is essential to promote good education. If we want to save the world, we have to bring about a complete change in people's minds and guide them to cast out unwholesomeness and to pursue goodness. To this end the Master founded Instilling Goodness Elementary School in 1974, and Developing Virtue Secondary School and Dharma Realm Buddhist University in 1976.

In an education embodying the spirit of Buddhism, the elementary school teaches students to be filial to parents, the secondary school teaches students to be good citizens, and the university teaches such virtues as humaneness and righteousness. Instilling Goodness Elementary School and Developing Virtue Secondary School combine the best of contemporary and traditional methods and of Western and Eastern cultures. They emphasize moral virtue and spiritual development, and aim to guide students to become good and capable citizens who will benefit humankind. The schools offer a bilingual (Chinese/English) program where boys and girls study separately. In addition to standard academic courses, the curriculum includes ethics, meditation, Buddhist studies, and so on, giving students a foundation in virtue and guiding them to understand themselves and explore the truths of the universe. Branches of the schools (Sunday schools) have been established at branch monasteries with the aim of propagating filial piety and ethical education.

Dharma Realm Buddhist University, whose curriculum focuses on the Proper Dharma, does not merely transmit academic knowledge. It emphasizes a foundation in virtue, which expands into the study of how to help all living beings discover their inherent nature. Thus, Dharma Realm Buddhist University advocates a spirit of shared inquiry and free exchange of ideas, encouraging students to study various canonical texts and use different experiences and learning styles to tap their inherent wisdom and fathom the meanings of those texts. Students are encouraged to practice the principles they have understood and apply the Buddhadharma in their lives, thereby nurturing their wisdom and virtue. The University aims to produce outstanding individuals of high moral character who will be able to bring benefit to all sentient beings.

Sangha and Laity Training Programs

In the Dharma-ending Age, in both Eastern and Western societies there are very few monasteries that actually practice the Buddha's regulations and strictly uphold the precepts. Teachers with genuine wisdom and understanding, capable of guiding those who aspire to pursue careers in Buddhism, are very rare. The Venerable Master founded the Sangha and Laity Training Programs in 1982 with the goals of raising the caliber of the Sangha, perpetuating the Proper Dharma, providing professional training for Buddhists around the world on both practical and theoretical levels, and transmitting the wisdom of the Buddha.

The Sangha Training Program gives monastics a solid foundation in Buddhist studies and practice, training them in the practical affairs of Buddhism and Sangha management. After graduation, students will be able to assume various responsibilities related to Buddhism in monasteries, institutions, and other settings. The program emphasizes a thorough knowledge of Buddhism, understanding of the scriptures, earnest cultivation, strict observance of precepts, and the development of a virtuous character, so that students will be able to propagate the Proper Dharma and perpetuate the Buddha's wisdom. The Laity Training Program offers courses to help laypeople develop correct views, study and practice the teachings, and understand monastic regulations and ceremonies, so that they will be able to contribute their abilities in Buddhist organizations.

Let Us Go Forward Together

In this Dharma-ending Age when the world is becoming increasingly dangerous and evil, the Dharma Realm Buddhist Association, in consonance with its guiding principles, opens the doors of its monasteries and centers to those of all religions and nationalities. Anyone who is devoted to humaneness, righteousness, virtue, and the pursuit of truth, and who wishes to understand him or herself and help humankind, is welcome to come study and practice with us. May we together bring benefit and happiness to all living beings.

Dharma Realm Buddhist Association Branches

The City of Ten Thousand Buddhas
P.O. Box 217, Talmage, CA 95481-0217 USA
Tel: (707) 462-0939   Fax: (707) 462-0949
Home Page: **http://www.drba.org**

Institute for World Religions (Berkeley Buddhist Monastery)
2304 McKinley Avenue, Berkeley, CA 94703 USA
Tel: (510) 848-3440

Dharma Realm Buddhist Books Distribution Society
11th Floor, 85 Chung-hsiao E. Road, Sec. 6, Taipei, Taiwan R.O.C.
Tel: (02) 2786-3022   Fax: (02) 2786-2674

The City of the Dharma Realm
1029 West Capitol Avenue, West Sacramento, CA 95691 USA
Tel: (916) 374-8268

Gold Mountain Monastery
800 Sacramento Street, San Francisco, CA 94108 USA
Tel: (415) 421-6117   Fax: (415) 788-6001

Gold Wheel Monastery
235 North Avenue 58, Los Angeles, CA 90042 USA
Tel: (323) 258-6668

Gold Buddha Monastery
248 East 11th Avenue, Vancouver, B.C. V5T 2C3 Canada
Tel: (604) 709-0248   Fax: (604) 684-3754

Gold Summit Monastery
233 1st Avenue, West Seattle, WA 98119 USA
Tel: (206) 284-6690   Fax: (206) 284-6918

Gold Sage Monastery
11455 Clayton Road, San Jose, CA 95127 USA
Tel: (408) 923-7243   Fax: (408) 923-1064

The International Translation Institute
1777 Murchison Drive, Burlingame, CA 94010-4504 USA
Tel: (650) 692-5912   Fax: (650) 692-5056

Long Beach Monastery
3361 East Ocean Boulevard, Long Beach, CA 90803 USA
Tel: (562) 438-8902

Blessings, Prosperity, & Longevity Monastery
4140 Long Beach Boulevard, Long Beach, CA 90807 USA
Tel: (562) 595-4966

Avatamsaka Hermitage
11721 Beall Mountain Road, Potomac, MD 20854-1128 USA
Tel: (301) 299-3693

Avatamsaka Monastery
1009 4th Avenue, S.W. Calgary, AB T2P OK8 Canada
Tel: (403) 234-0644

Kun Yam Thong Temple
161, Jalan Ampang, 50450 Kuala Lumpur, Malaysia
Tel: (03) 2164-8055 Fax: (03) 2163-7118

Prajna Guanyin Sagely Monastery (formerly Tze Yun Tung)
Batu 5½, Jalan Sungai Besi,
Salak Selatan, 57100 Kuala Lumpur, Malaysia
Tel: (03) 7982-6560 Fax: (03) 7980-1272

Lotus Vihara
136, Jalan Sekolah, 45600 Batang Berjuntai,
Selangor Darul Ehsan, Malaysia
Tel: (03) 3271-9439

Buddhist Lecture Hall
31 Wong Nei Chong Road, Top Floor, Happy Valley, Hong Kong, China
Tel: (02) 2572-7644

Dharma Realm Sagely Monastery
20, Tong-hsi Shan-chuang, Hsing-lung Village, Liu-kuei
Kaohsiung County, Taiwan, R.O.C.
Tel: (07) 689-3717 Fax: (07) 689-3870

Amitabha Monastery
7, Su-chien-hui, Chih-nan Village, Shou-feng,
Hualien County, Taiwan, R.O.C.
Tel: (07) 865-1956 Fax: (07) 865-3426

Verse of Transference

May the merit and virtue accrued from this work,
Adorn the Buddhas' Pure Lands,
Repaying four kinds of kindness above,
And aiding those suffering in the paths below.

May those who see and hear of this,
All bring forth the resolve for Bodhi,
And when this retribution body is over,
Be born together in the Land of Ultimate Bliss.

Dharma Protector Wei Tuo Bodhisattva